building the American-European market
. . . planning for the 1970's

building the American-European market

...planning for the 1970's

THE ATLANTIC COUNCIL OF THE UNITED STATES

EDITORIAL CHAIRMEN:
Theodore C. Achilles
Richard J. Wallace

EDITOR: Gene E. Bradley

ASSOCIATE EDITOR: James R. Roberts

Design by Charles J. Hepburn

EDITORIAL ADVISORY BOARD:
W. Randolph Burgess   Livingston T. Merchant
Attilio Cattani   Christopher H. Phillips
Jay H. Cerf
Walter Dowling   Otto Schoeppler
Werner P. Gullander   Samuel C. Waugh

Publishers
DOW JONES-IRWIN, INC. · *Homewood, Illinois*

Printed in the United States of America

Library of Congress Catalog Card No. 67–15796

THE ATLANTIC COUNCIL OF THE UNITED STATES

1616 H Street, N.W., Washington, D.C.   20006

The Atlantic Council of the United States believes that great benefit can result from encouraging an Atlantic dialogue among executives of the government-business community spanning the two continents. In these pages will be found many viewpoints—thoughtful, creative and sometimes controversial—on how Atlantic cooperation and business growth can best be stimulated for the benefit of all. It should be clearly stated, however, that the opinions of the guest authors and those interviewed are strictly their own and do not necessarily represent the views of the Atlantic Council, its Board of Directors, or the individuals who comprise the editorial board for this publication.

Preface

Gene E. Bradley has served with the Atlantic Council of the United States in developing its study of business expansion and allied unity. An executive of the General Electric Company, and headquartered in Washington, D.C., he has corporate responsibility for international government relations. Active in national security and international affairs for 25 years, his assignments have included Special Assistant to R. Sargent Shriver, then Director of the Peace Corps, in establishing the Peace Corps School-to-School Program for which he received the Freedoms Foundation Freedom Leadership Award. He is a consultant to and director of the Atlantic Council; Washington Vice President of the National Strategy Information Center; and serves on various international committees including that of the National Association of Manufacturers, the American Chamber of Commerce in France, the U.S. Council of the International Chamber of Commerce, and the National Foreign Trade Council.

Photo by
Fabian Bachrach

This book will raise more questions than it answers. Indeed, it would take a "six-foot shelf" to answer all the questions it raises—assuming that all the answers were available (which most certainly is not the case).

Even a cursory look at the Atlantic Community, now and a decade hence, can be useful. It can be more than useful. It is essential, *if* we are even to approach the high goals set forth by Eric Wyndham White, Director General of the General Agreement on Tariffs and Trade:

First, to cash in on all the possibilities of expansion and growth among the industrialized nations, beginning with the Atlantic Community; and

Second, to work toward uniting their efforts in dealing with the staggering problems of "the third world."

So great an advance will not occur by happenstance. The world of the 1970's and 1980's will have to be charted with an enthusiasm, dedication, and intelligence somewhat akin to our efforts in charting our course toward the moon and outer space. Both voyages are part and parcel of the age of the technological revolution. Both require professional business management and a "systems approach" superior to the other great national and corporate adventures of the past.

But here the parallel ends. In exploring space, the prime responsibility belongs to the governments with, of course, essential backup support from the private sector. In charting a more dynamic business community capable of meeting the world's growing (and often desperate) human needs, it is the private sector which must take the lead—with, of course, indispensable cooperation from the several governments. Such progress cannot come through governmental edict; it must flow from literally thousands of decentralized decisions by corporate executives in several score countries; and the decisions must be ratified and financed by hundreds of millions of private citizens who are the shareowners and who constitute the consuming public.

The growing importance of the private sector is reported by the Atlantic Council in its business-climate survey:

The U.S. corporate executive has a critical role to play in the creation of a true Atlantic Community—an alliance built more on common interest than upon the fear of a common enemy. Whether or not the private businessman wants to become an element and force in national policy is now beside the point. Like it or not, what he does—or fails to do—tangibly affects the economic growth, technological progress, and cultural and social solidarity of the two great continents.

Therefore, again and again we return to the role, the opportunity— if you will, the obligation—of the private businessman to match his experience and wisdom against one of the paramount challenges of history. If he fails to do so, it is entirely conceivable that the forward thrust of economic growth and international interdependence will receive some jarring jolts. Already, on both sides of the Atlantic, there are disturbing signs that divisive nationalism could result in a retreat from present positions with unfortunate results all the way around. Once set in motion, restrictionism can escalate into a growing series of reprisals; and these in turn could trigger recessions and depressions which, until now, the Communist world has hoped for in vain. The free world can ill afford an inward-looking American Great Society, a glorious France, an isolated England, or a resurgent and ultranationalist Germany, each "protected" from the other by unnatural trade barriers and investment restrictions.

Hence the need for better understanding and positive planning for the issues involved. This book is directed toward that need; it reports on the individual judgments of several hundred policy officials—from both business and government—in North America and Western Europe. It is these men to whom this book is dedicated, men such as General Lauris Norstad who headed up SHAPE (Supreme Headquarters Allied Powers Europe), Eric Wyndham White of GATT (General Agreement on Tariffs and Trade), Secretary Henry H. Fowler of the U.S. Treasury, Belgium's Paul-Henri Spaak, France's Jean Monnet, Germany's Hermann Abs, Italy's Attilio Cattani, and England's Reginald Maulding, to mention only a few of the pioneer statesmen in Atlantic Community political-economic affairs. This book reflects their efforts and judgments. In balance, most of our colleagues and respondents have represented positions of leadership in business and industry.

In this book, we shall endeavor to:

1. Describe the present state of affairs in Atlantic Community relations, including the issues and the seeming dilemmas.
2. Shake down and sort out priorities in terms of what can be *done* about the issues, by individuals, by companies, by governments, by international organizations and by regional groups.
3. Identify a few tangible goals which our associates believe are politically, socially, and economically attainable—*provided* adequate thought and action are put behind them.

This book can report findings and proposals; it cannot capture in print the enthusiasm with which such conclusions were presented—either in the individual interviews or in the often heated policy conferences at Paris, Fontainebleau, Crotonville (N.Y.), and Geneva. And that, perhaps, is the most essential ingredient of all, when "hard-nosed" businessmen and "tough" political negotiators report a vision greater than themselves, greater than their organizations, greater than any superstructures in the world to date. These are not illusive visionaries but very practical executives who believe that the world's first two experiences in trying to build major "common markets"—first in the U.S.A. and more recently in Europe—are just the beginnings of what can be achieved, and in our time.

There is neither time nor space to give full credit to those who deserve credit and appreciation for their efforts which resulted in this book. To mention just a few:

George J. Pantos of the Chamber of Commerce of the United States who spearheaded our first business-climate survey in Europe, and whose work was remarkably effective thanks to the response of the European "Am Chams;"

C. Stewart Baeder, then with the National Association of Manufacturers, who organized and helped conduct our final series of European visitations;

Association chief executives whose counsel and support have been invaluable, including Arch N. Booth and Jay Cerf of the Chamber of Commerce of the United States, Werner P. Gullander and Daniel Parker of the National Association of Manufacturers, Christopher H. Phillips of the U.S. Council of the International Chamber of Commerce, Dr. Alfred C. Neal of the Committee for Economic Development, Dr. Clifford Nelson of the American Assembly, Leo Cherne of the Research Institute of America, and counterpart chief executives in European countries;

W. Randolph Burgess, Chairman of the Executive Committee of the Atlantic Council, and the other Council Directors whose insights and counsel were indispensable;

U.S. government officials in the White House, State, Treasury, and Commerce Departments, U.S. Information Agency, and overseas embassies, a list literally too long to enumerate; and

On the reportorial-editorial side, Roland Sawyer (now with the General Accounting Office) who edited the report on the Atlantic Community business climate; *The Harvard Business Review* which published the first article based upon the Atlantic Council studies; James R. Roberts of The General Electric *Forum* who on his own time served as the book's associate editor; artist Charles J. Hepburn who created and contributed the book's design; and Sharon H. Eichler and Betty Lou Stroh who have been not just secretaries but full-fledged time-and-a-half partners for the past two years.

To these, the Atlantic Council gives its deep appreciation.

On a personal note, I wish to acknowledge the three men associated with the Atlantic Council who have been the prime force behind the movement which this book reflects: namely, Ambassador Theodore C. Achilles, The Honorable Samuel C. Waugh, and Council Director

General Richard J. Wallace. Two of these gentlemen—Messrs. Achilles and Waugh—are officially "retired" from public life. Yet during this so-called retirement, both have poured into the Atlantic Community experiment a measure of time, of talent, of personal resources, of dedication, and of inspiration which I have never seen surpassed in public affairs; and because of this, both have literally become an inspiration to me and set an example of what can be accomplished by men of goodwill in international diplomacy. With "national assets" such as these on hand and in motion, there is great hope for what can be accomplished as we buckle down to the tough tasks suggested in the title of this book: *Planning for the 1970's.*

Washington, D.C.   GENE E. BRADLEY
   August, 1967

Foreword

by General Lauris Norstad

General Lauris Norstad was Supreme Allied Commander, Europe, and Commander-in-Chief, U.S. European Forces, for six critical years from 1956 through 1962. A graduate of the U.S. Military Academy in 1930, he held a number of staff and command positions in Washington and the African and European theaters and became a four-star general in 1952. Since his military retirement in 1963 he has become President of the Owens-Corning Fiberglas Corporation and Chairman of the Atlantic Council of the United States.

Photo by Conway Studios

On the two shores of the North Atlantic the seed of Western civilization was planted, and here it has flowered. Here are the deepest roots of faith in the dignity and worth of the individual, the rule of law, and the successful practice of democratic government. Here lies the great reservoir of moral and material resources, of intellect, science, and of the political, economic, social, industrial, and cultural development necessary to accelerate the progress of the less developed nations. And here rests a main challenge of this seventh decade of the 20th century.

xiii

What must be done? In broad terms, we need the development of a common politico-military strategy and an agreed policy with respect to the use of nuclear and other weapons. We need economic growth, rising standards of living, and financial stability. We need expansion of trade on the widest possible basis. We need the most efficient use of resources. We need coordinated and equitably contributed material and technical assistance for the development of less developed countries. We need exchange equilibrium and common financial institutions to deal with matters of common concern.

The pressing requirement is to define the total opportunity and to devise ways of meeting it. How do we shape the machinery for getting from the world of 1967 to the world of a decade hence?

The Businessman's Challenge

This hands the challenge to the private businessman. He has an especially critical role to play, for it is in the economic arena that we find today's greatest opportunity to strengthen the bonds between our peoples and to construct the economic and technological foundations upon which our societies must be built.

Already the bonds developed through normal business relations are more in tune with the realities of this age than are differences at the political level. It is proper, therefore, that as businessmen and citizens, corporate executives undertake to discourage restrictive nationalism, with all its dire international and domestic consequences. They must take as their position the development of the positive potential of multinational economic growth.

In early 1965, the Atlantic Council of the United States became convinced that both national and corporate interests could benefit greatly by stimulating government and industry to focus more deliberately on the economic problems—and opportunities—of the fast-growing Atlantic business community.

Therefore, the Council initiated a survey and a communications program geared to the problems and the opportunities of the expanding Atlantic business community. Phase one of the program—the survey—involved personal discussion with several hundred policy leaders of industry, finance, government, and business associations in the United States and Western Europe.

The second phase saw the beginning of a continuing dialogue among such policy leaders. Four conferences, as described later in this book, were held in cooperation with the Atlantic Institute—at Paris and Fontainebleau in France, at Crotonville, New York, and Geneva, Switzerland. The discussions were frank and direct, with a spirit of understanding. The approach was to talk out the issues, to separate those not of substance and to help determine actions favorable to all.

These discussions were only the beginning of a long-range program to bring Americans and Europeans together where their interests are so obviously intertwined. What we have learned already, as outlined in the chapters that follow, points to the strong consensus that exists across the Atlantic, behind the headlines.

Facing up to Common Problems

At the Fontainebleau Conference, Eric Wyndham White suggested as the first priority that we "face up to the problems which are really *common* problems." He felt that simply in the process of discussing and clarifying the issues, people will clear their own minds as to where their common interests lie.

Second, as Ambassador Attilio Cattani advised at Fontainebleau and develops more fully in this book, perhaps we need to look at and modernize the rules in governing Atlantic business relations. The point is not to hamper expansion but to find new ways to harmonize business laws and customs, with strong incentives for all businesses to compete and meet the needs of the customer.

Despite all that the private businessman does, however, solutions to such problems of fundamental importance and scope can only be found if the principal Atlantic governments have the will to seek common goals. The political framework within which the economic forces must operate is of paramount importance, as the distinguished Belgian statesman, Paul-Henri Spaak, points out in the following pages.

What political form the Atlantic Community will eventually take, no one can yet say. It will not be based on the Treaty of Rome, nor on the Constitution of the United States, nor on any other single instrument. It will be something new designed by practical men and responsible men to meet the political, military, and economic challenges of this era.

President Kennedy put it this way:

Acting on our own by ourselves, we cannot establish justice throughout the world. We cannot insure its domestic tranquillity, or provide for its common defense, or promote its general welfare, or secure the blessings of liberty to ourselves and our posterity. But joined with other free nations, we can do all this and more. We can assist the developing nations to throw off the yoke of poverty. We can balance our worldwide trade and payments at the highest possible level of growth. We can mount a deterrent powerful enough to deter any aggression, and ultimately we can help build a world of law and free choice, banishing the world of war and coercion.

The Atlantic Community will come. The forces that tend to divide us, strong as they may seem at times, are as nothing compared with the forces bringing us together, impelling us inevitably toward greater unity. It will not be a new superstate, but it will be a magnetic nucleus—the heart and core of an eventual world order of peace, freedom, and opportunity.

Foreword

by Paul-Henri Spaak

 One of the principal architects of NATO and the Common Market, Paul-Henri Spaak is widely known as "Mr. Europe." First elected to the Belgian Parliament in 1932, he received a Cabinet post three years later at the age of 36. He became Foreign Minister for the first time in 1936 and was Premier two years later, still not yet 40. In all, he served his country six times as Foreign Minister, and twice as Premier, before retiring in 1966. From 1957 to 1962 he also served as Secretary-General of NATO. Recently, **the New York Times** commented: "His turbulent 34-year career exemplifies the belief that it frequently requires more talent, political creativity, foresight, and courage to govern a small country in a world of big powers than to manage a big power. Great powers can afford risks and mistakes; small ones cannot."

Photo by Henri Dauman

It is a fact that we are not now in a period of "normal" political relations within the Atlantic World. We are living instead in a moment of political crisis. We know what the Atlantic Organization has been for nearly 18 years, but we do not know what it will be like tomorrow.

This basic political reality must be recognized as we search for new initiatives to take advantage of Atlantic economic opportunities. We shall advance along the road to prosperity only if peoples and governments can be confident that their partners share their feelings and are ready to make the same sacrifices.

If confidence does not prevail, nothing grand, bold, or effective can be accomplished among the countries of the Atlantic Alliance.

Thus, all of our excellent designs in the economic field—whether a successful implementation of the Kennedy Round, more American investments in Europe and more European investment in the United States, acceleration of development in the underdeveloped countries —these can all be reduced to nothing in the context of a continuing political crisis. Our economic goals can lead to practical results only if the political structure of the Atlantic Organization and the development of the Common Market remain the bases on which to build.

Economic Revolution Just a Beginning

It is clear that the Common Market is, on the whole, a great success. In any case, public opinion in the six countries does not dispute this. And I believe that all the relevant statistics prove that the progress accomplished in the Common Market these last years has been more spectacular than that in any other region of the world (with the one exception of Japan, whose progress has also been phenomenal).

The problem of the future, therefore, is whether it is possible to continue economic integration if political integration stalls or falls back. We were fully aware in 1957 that the Common Market represented an economic revolution. Yet this economic revolution was not considered as an end, but as a beginning.

The economic revolution could only be accomplished and endure if it were accompanied by a political revolution which would allow us actually to create a united Europe. While economic integration has progressed beyond all our hopes, political organization not only has not budged; it has receded.

Is it possible to imagine a world in which the economic interests of the Six are steadily integrating more completely—including taxation, a common currency, and similar matters—if all this is not finally capped by a political organization? Or if this economic integration is coupled with a political world in which the policies of the governments would be opposed or contradictory?

This is why the problems of the Common Market are so intimately linked with those of NATO.

The Crisis in NATO

There has often been talk of a crisis in NATO, but this time it is more serious. It is the principles of the Organization as we have conceived it which are involved. What we have done in NATO since World War II has been truly bold, and has required from each individual country sacrifices and changes in traditions and customs. It was an adventurous policy.

We created the Atlantic Alliance in 1949 for two essential reasons:

(1) to place a barrier in Europe, and to the extent necessary in North America, against the Communist imperialism of the time; and (2) to succeed in creating a balance of power which would avoid war. Against all those who criticize NATO, to all those who say it must be altered, to all those who say it is necessary to withdraw from it, there is a decisive argument: *we have succeeded.* For 20 years communism has not made any progress in any of the countries who lived, or who live, under the banner of the Atlantic Alliance. We have established a balance of power which is such that, as far as we can now see into the future, a war which would necessarily be a world war cannot break out in Europe or as a result of a European problem.

Why change? Why destroy what exists when we have succeeded, as we had hoped, without using force, without recourse to war? To destroy something which is a success appears to me imprudent (not to use a stronger word). But to destroy it without offering any other coherent system is insane and irresponsible.

What Would Return to Nationalism Mean?   xix

What would it mean in Europe if each nation retired within itself? First, the Americans would return home. We in Europe have considered it an unprecedented success that the United States of America in recent years has taken positions on the great world problems, and particularly the problems of security, *before* a war erupted. How many times have we declared and repeated that if the aggressors had known in 1914 or in 1939 that the Americans had taken their position at the side of the free and democratic world, the history of the world would have been changed and the two wars would not have occurred! We were right. We achieved the immense success of knowing with certainty that this time there was no possible doubt about the attitude of the United States.

Second, if the Americans return home, the British will return home.

Third, for the little countries like mine to retire within themselves is an absurdity, an impossibility. In 1914 and in 1939 the little countries of Europe still had armies which resembled the armies of the great countries; they had the same arms, cannon, machine guns, airplanes, and tanks—less of them to be sure, but set up militarily on the same basis. Today if we retire within ourselves, if we do not form part of a great whole, there would remain only one thing to do—disarm and return to neutrality.

Finally, there remains Germany. Germany will not agree to disarm, but will seek an ally, and probably find one in the United States. And in time, Germany will be the first military power in Europe after the U.S.S.R.

After World War II, I was one of the first to preach reconciliation. But what we wanted was to integrate Germany into her place in Europe and the Atlantic Alliance. We never thought that the world it was necessary to build was a world in which Germany would be given a military place that would make her by far the strongest of all the countries of the continent.

The inevitable conclusions, should each of the partners of the Atlantic Alliance retire within itself, are inadmissible and impossible. Such retirement would be not only a threat to the Atlantic World but also, I believe, a threat to the world of the East. For the world of the East has every interest in preserving the military balance which has been established for 20 years. It finds much more security in this balance than it would in a Europe or in an Atlantic World moving towards disorder.

Such a policy would be the end of all hope for a United Europe. Is it conceivable that one day we could have a Europe completely integrated from the economic point of view but in which defense and foreign policies were completely different? What would remain of the ideal of a United Europe if some countries of this Europe were the allies of the Americans, if others were to take a position favorable to the U.S.S.R., and if others were neutral? Even the ideal of European unity would disappear and collapse.

It is truly unfair to allege that the Europe we have desired would make the European countries satellites of American policy. What we have sought for 20 years is to unite Europe so that she could become a valid partner of the United States, able to debate with the United States as an equal and to play her role in the Alliance without ever having the feeling of acting against our will.

These are some of the considerations of a political nature which bear directly on the search for solutions to our economic problems.

In its own fields, private industry and finance are taking the lead, and so much the better. It is necessary for the experts, the technicians, and those who specialize in economic problems to study them and stimulate the will of the politicians. But they cannot do so without an understanding of practical political realities.

Where from Here?

In present circumstances there is but one thing for NATO and the European Community to do: hold fast. We must be faithful to the rules laid down for NATO in 1948 and for the Common Market in 1957. We must persevere and not give way.

Within NATO, this means basically that in the political field we must consult together more and more closely on a widening range of problems, with a view to evolving a joint Atlantic policy. It means that from the military standpoint, after establishing a set of principles and determining the eventuality for which we must prepare, we must integrate conventional and nuclear means of defense to the highest possible degree. That will be the best reply to those who doubt the indivisibility of defense.

Within the European Community we must continue the work auspiciously begun. If possible, we must accelerate tariff abolition; advance rapidly toward a common policy in trade, transport, and social affairs; tackle the great monetary problem; complete our agricultural policy; and, by avoiding autarchy and protectionism, demonstrate that the European Community is an open organization.

These ideas are still held today by the overwhelming majority of European statesmen. They are also shared by the overwhelming majority of European peoples. Let us not, then, be dismayed. The dissident element constituted by current French policy may be a cause of delay, but it cannot prevent the ultimate success of the great undertakings to which Europe and the United States have set their hands.

Naturally, I would like to see things move faster. But I believe that for the present we can hang onto the Common Market and its accomplishments. In the political crisis through which we are passing, it is a solid rock of which we can be proud.

And I believe that if we continue to progress in the economic field at the rate of recent years, if we succeed in forming a single community by forming a single Commission to cover the three Communities, then we can rally to another idea, of which I am not too fond but which nevertheless has a certain force. That is the idea of fatalism, of historic inertia. If we interrelate the economic interests of our various countries, the absolute necessity of a political authority will eventually enforce itself upon them.

This method is not the best one and it is undoubtedly the slowest. But if the clear, direct, and rapid method of political progress is today impossible, then we must certainly accept the other.

Table of Contents

building the American-European market
. . . planning for the 1970's

1 The Challenge

Dr. Aurelio Peccei, managing director of the Olivetti Company from 1964 to 1967, is currently vice chairman of the company. He began his business career in 1930 with the Fiat Automotive Company and is presently a member of its Executive Committee. Since 1957 he has headed Italconsult, a leading international consulting and engineering firm, based in Italy, which specializes in development projects in Africa, Asia, and Latin America. Dr. Peccei is a well-known student and writer on economic-industrial development and a dynamic contributor to international discussions on these subjects.

Photo by Conway Studios Corp.

When the sun sets on Monday, December 31, 1979, on the eve of a new decade, those of us and our sons who are then alive will perhaps pause a while before looking ahead, to sum up in retrospect the momentous seventies. Which judgment will then be passed on the human deeds of the dying decade? We do not know. At this moment we can only speculate.

If we are bound by pessimism, we may envisage for that distant date a world in such a shambles as to make Cassino, Dresden, Stalingrad, and Hiroshima—do we still care to remember them now?—look like inept, amateurish jobs. This is a tragic view.

Yet in earnest we cannot discard from our speculation a horizon of endless destruction, only interspersed by traces and remnants of human life, stunned and debased, since this could well be the result and the retribution of our own efforts.

On the other hand, if we are inspired by optimism, we may see all over the spectrum a picture so bright as could never have been dreamt at any time in the past. Indeed, we can envisage for the close of the seventies the existence of a really great society, whose expanding boundaries and bounties, starting from the initial stronghold in the United States, would reach people heretofore condemned to meager existence, influencing ways and standards of living in the farthest corners of the world.

This is not a dreamlike hypothesis. It is a possibility within our reach: its rationale is perfectly sound. Dramatic educational developments, taking place practically everywhere, would further insure that our civilization will safely continue to expand and prosper.

I have used these two extreme assumptions of the outcome of the seventies, not only because both lie within the realm of the feasible, but because their life and death dichotomy, in my opinion, clearly expresses the challenge before us.

A Breathtaking Decade

The next decade will be breathtaking and crucial. Its importance is unique, not just because it will "happen" to us, but because never before in human history have the waves of the future been so gigantic and fast-moving and the alternatives so global, overwhelming, and really extreme. We must, therefore, exert an all-out effort of research and imagination to influence the future, planning and preparing for it.

Looking at the challenge in its broadest perspective, it is clear that it must be faced on a worldwide basis. Yet it is the Western nations that hold all options in their hands. By this I mean they have the time to set the desired objectives for the coming decade, with a fair chance of fulfilling them.

At this point, one may ask a few questions: Whose challenge is it really? Where can we find the ability to meet it? By which machinery can study and action plans be set in motion? And finally, who will shoulder the greatest part of the burden necessary to enact such plans?

By and large, the answers to these and to a host of similar questions in the general area of planning for the seventies are all centered in and around the advanced nations of Western civilization. In the accelerated flow of history, this is their lot and privilege. If they shirk it and let it slip by, or if, in their action, they do not live up to the required standards of leadership, it seems most unlikely to me that they may have another chance in the 1980's or 1990's.

The singling out of the Atlantic nations as leaders in the great tasks ahead calls for some qualifications. First of all, with regard to their internal relations, it is obvious that a much higher degree of integration, political as well as economic, is imperative among them. And it should begin already in these late sixties, if they are to take up their role effectively.

This is the scope of the Atlantic Council and of the Atlantic Institute. Our efforts toward implementing this scope must be drastically stepped up. We cannot be satisfied until the notion is deeply ingrained in Europe and in America that neither can hope to control its own destiny in today's world; and neither can hope to stir and help the rest of the world towards new goals of development and progress if it is not united with the other. This task is urgent, particularly with regard to the amalgamation of the less developed member of the Atlantic Community—Europe—and its overcoming the technical gap that separates it from America.

However, we would fool ourselves if we thought of this as anything but a minimum prerequisite to set the stage for the seventies. In terms of the coming decade the very concept of the Atlantic Community must be broadened to match its responsibilities. To start with, the idea of an Atlantic world should be expanded to include partners which now seem peripheral, such as Australia, New Zealand, and Japan. Technological progress will undoubtedly wipe out the differences in outlook and interests created by relative distance.

Opportunities for East–West Cooperation

Then there is the question of the Soviet Union and Eastern Europe, which is essential. Look at it this way: if the Western nations are set to forge forward in the seventies, these Eastern nations will be moved to engage in a similar course, because for them it will also be the only choice in the long run. The two blocs will be brought closer. Modern technology, which is already dismantling the ideologies of the past, will provide them with ever new opportunities for cooperation. Their thinking and planning will run parallel. Docking could be feasible sometime in the future.

On the other hand, we must realize that simple coexistence, the achievement of our decade, cannot hold out as a pattern for the seventies. Should the West and the Soviets be unable to generate enough ingenuity and determination to escalate their fragile coexistence into a reasonably solid cooperation—and fast at that—both will be losers. The Soviet efforts to grow the mass consumption economy coveted by its people will be crippled for many years to come, to nobody's benefit. And the West will probably miss its chance to move the world toward an era of unprecedented material and intellectual advance.

Anchoring Latin America to the West

Another necessary associate in the group of nations which will set the pace of the world in the seventies is Latin America. Because of Latin America's geographical position, its historical and cultural heritage, and the progress it has already realized so far in terms of economic development and integration, what happens in Latin America in the next decade will, to a considerable degree, influence the direction of developing nations throughout the world. It is, therefore, of the utmost importance that our plans include the anchoring of Latin America to the Western Atlantic nations.

We are considering here the greatest adventure ever undertaken by mankind: to save itself from overall self-destruction, caused by its own irrationality and intolerance, and to exert an all-out, comprehensive effort to master the forces and the resources it has created.

The engineers of this plan can only be the group of advanced nations I mentioned. Nowhere else are the know-how and the resources available for such a gigantic effort. However, as the scheme belongs to a universal conception, it must also have the support and the understanding of other people who will benefit and participate in it, either directly or indirectly. To this end it is essential that the group of Atlantic nations be outward-looking, open-minded, generous, and progressive. These are the attributes of leadership necessary to shape the world of tomorrow. If we were to try to build an inward-looking, narrow-minded community, inspired only by the aim of maximizing the benefits already accruing to it from its privileged position, we would have no chance of success in the long run. For the increasing interdependence which characterizes world relations is not compatible with continued imbalance in the levels of economic life and growth among nations.

One cannot overstate the importance—for the United States and Europe—of what will happen in the less developed nations. This is simply because it is not possible, in the long run, to disentangle our future from theirs. It is not possible to conceive of a world permanently divided into a minority of prosperous nations, bent on enjoying and safeguarding their ever-increasing affluence, and, on the other side, the majority of mankind, including the people of Africa, Asia, and Latin America, all well aware of how poor is their lot and obviously restless about it.

The Roots of the Challenge

I, for one, am only too aware of the job's staggering complexity and hazards, matched only by that of the challenge itself. Thus, I will venture just to put forth a few ideas in the hope that they may lead us in the right direction.

Planning for the next decade obviously must be based on the assumption that no catastrophic event will derail civilization. On the other hand, planning in itself could be an efficient instrument to prevent such an occurrence.

The first and preliminary step is to promote the political will and decision conducive to planning. It is not up to me, in this context, to suggest how this can be done or who, among countries or international organizations, should be called on to participate. One point, however, I would stress: the approach must be universal.

The second step would consist of carrying out studies and surveys aimed at bringing the future, with all its open avenues, within sight, thus permitting a global view and the formulation of a general plan. Because of the magnitude and urgency of this project I recommend that it be handled in the boldest and most imaginative way. What is needed is an overall, expert, and objective assessment. It must be based on all available data, experience, and knowledge of the probable trends concerning the major determinants of the world society in the next decade.

Regional Planning Needed

One could start by separately considering fairly homogeneous geographic regions and subregions, later combining the information concerning each of them into a global picture. Such a procedure will permit us to take into account the fact that the same determinants do not carry the same weight in different areas. For instance, population growth may have more serious consequences in crowded developing countries than in the advanced ones. Aid will be a major factor in the recipient countries, yet hardly a drag for the dispensing West. Agricultural development may be the deciding factor in some populous, less advanced regions.

On the other side, automation will probably be a major factor in the West, where it will permit heretofore unimaginable productivity levels, and likely produce social tensions and educational and leisure problems. But it will barely affect the developing countries. Educational improvements will increasingly have paramount importance practically everywhere, although they will mean different things in different places.

Objectives for the Seventies

Only after we have such an overall expert assessment of the situation can we proceed a step further and, taking into account all alternatives and variables, map out sets of coherent objectives for the seventies. Thus, a frame of reference will be provided for concrete, long-term policy decisions. Finally, we will be able to take options, define ways, mobilize means, and carry out concrete action. And the march toward the future will take an intelligently charted course rather than be guided by chance and gamble. What should be new in our thinking is the realization that a fresh look at the world in its entirety and a new, overall planning are necessary within the next few years, before this late hour becomes too late.

As I belong to the optimists, I will conclude on a positive note. I have no doubt that the countries of the West will rise to the task and meet the challenge, carrying in their stride most of the other nations. I am convinced that if only *half* of the brain power of the existing "think factories," wherever they may be, and half of the purposefulness dedicated during so many years to the cold war, by one and all, should be directed to the task of preparing for the seventies, these cannot fail to result in a glorious decade.

1 PART 2 *Atlantic Council Report*

After 20 years of unparalleled progress in Atlantic unity and economic growth there are today serious threats to continued advancement—especially in the realm of politics, diplomacy, and defense.

True, there is much for which to be grateful. Economic growth and integration have been phenomenal within countries and internationally. The clouds of war, at least in Europe, have been pushed back. America's astonishing surge forward in business, technology, and industry is a matter of record. And Europe's full economic recovery from the disorganization and destruction of war—converted into new achievements in high standards of living—is certainly beyond the expectations of even the most optimistic.

This surge forward has been largely due to the hard, intelligent efforts of individual free men. But it has also been furthered by new collective efforts, fostered by such organizations as the Organization for Economic Cooperation and Development (OECD), NATO, the European Common Market, the European Free Trade Association, General Agreement on Tariffs and Trade (GATT), the International Monetary Fund, and the International Bank for Reconstruction and Development (World Bank).

Yet, there is today faltering and hesitation in this forward movement. NATO unity and strength are threatened. Great hopes for continued swift progress in the Common Market have dimmed as nationalism has reasserted itself. Political disputes have weakened the ability of many governments to act together effectively. Indeed, the very success of Atlantic Community cooperation has encouraged, at least in some sectors, an unhealthy euphoria and a feeling that perhaps a close cooperation is no longer needed.

In a world of conflicting forces and pressures—a movement toward further integration on one hand, and pressures toward splintering on the other—the corporate executive finds himself in a uniquely favorable position to further the basic interests of his own nation, the cause of Atlantic unity, and the market and financial position of his own corporation. For it is within his power and prerogative to build solid economic ties at the very time when political ties seem to be weakening. He can forge close relationships in the private sector, transcending national boundaries, which, in turn, can help to establish a better political rapport.

In short, drawing on business and financial interdependence can serve both the national and the corporate interest. Dr. Aurelio Peccei, in introducing this chapter, has described the nature of the challenge in terms of human needs and, indeed, human survival. In his closing remarks at a Geneva conference, June 1, 1966, he urged that practical businessmen, in partnership with government officials, educators, and other international professionals, convert thought into action.

Dr. Peccei summarized:

> We must devise new instruments, institutions, and philosophies to cope with what is in store during the next decade. We must make a deeper search into our souls, exercise a far greater intellectual effort, and reach a more universal understanding of the entire world as it is and its other human societies which are so different from ours and with which we might be at loggerheads. If we look to the future in this perspective, it does not matter very much if this conference and summary report have some shortcomings because we should consider them just a stepping-stone for better achievements.

The Size of the Challenge

Businessmen, above all, have to be practical in building "stepping-stones." The stepping-stones must lead to something that will justify corporate action in terms of, first, contributing needed products or services, and second, providing a fair return to shareowners. What, then, is the nature of the challenge that Dr. Peccei defined in terms of products and services?

One measurement is in the size of the demand for new investment capital. During the next decade, for the United States alone, private industry must invest some $600 billion in capital expansion and modernization projects in order to achieve a satisfactory growth rate. This is the estimate of Gerald L. Phillippe, chairman of the board of The General Electric Company. He also estimates that Western Europe's needs should about equal those of the United States. (See Chapter 2.)

The total need for new investment in the Atlantic Community during the next 10 years is, therefore, more than $1 trillion. While we can only guess at the needs of the remainder of the free world, another $1 trillion would appear reasonable. All told, the 10-year expansion program with which the United States and Western Europe must be intimately concerned amounts to about $2 trillion.

In retrospect, this estimate may even seem conservative as we view our global task of building stronger societies, raising living standards, improving cities and agriculture, stimulating world trade, providing international security, and strengthening the peace. For example, the following questions hint at some of the new markets to be developed if modern international management can devise the appropriate ways and means:

1. In the face of the population explosion, where the human race will double in the next 35 years, what new business initiatives are needed to double the supply of food in order to prevent mass starvation, and to head off rampant disease and indescribable human misery?

2. In the face of an urbanization explosion, what creative corporate planning is required if our great nations are to prevent urban stagnation and deterioration many times worse than that already occurring today in the United States?

3. In a more subtle but no less dynamic area of human life, are today's corporations in all of the industrialized nations gearing up to meet the challenges and problems that arise with the advent of a consumer economy in an affluent society—the effective use of leisure time . . . enriched cultural leisure and recreational activities . . . the expansion of services and the curbing of crime?

4. In terms of manpower utilization, what plans have we made to mobilize our research and development resources to achieve the world society that is now technologically feasible? It is a fact that there are simply not enough engineers, scientists, and business managers to go around.

5. How can businessmen—in cooperation with their governments—design, produce, and put into place a worldwide communication system, enhanced by a universal satellite and relay system? How can we best transmit information automatically to peoples in the most remote corners of the earth? This segment of the challenge alone should run into multibillions of dollars.

6. High on the priority list must be such questions as controlling thermonuclear reaction, preventing its proliferation, and creating virtually unlimited sources of new energy at prices economically acceptable.

7. Most certainly, businessmen will want to aid and abet the "revolution" already under way, which may prove to be the most fundamental of all: namely, universal education. What is needed in corporate research and development to devise new approaches, new hardware, software, and systems to wipe out ignorance, disease, poverty, and the tragic prejudices that lead to violence and war?

But none of the above anticipates some of the more "exotic" programs which advanced corporate planners have demonstrated they are eager to get under way, from probing the planets to mining the oceans, converting salt water into fresh, and making the deserts ripe for harvest.

Even more precisely, it is interesting and useful to review the remarkable business expansion forecasts for the next decade. Specific business indicators from one reliable forecast relating to the U.S. market, during the next decade, include the following yearly estimates:

Autos and Parts—to go from $29.7 billion to $48.4 billion.
Plant and Equipment—from $56.1 billion to $98.3 billion.
Housing (residential nonfarm)—from $25.6 billion to $44.6 billion.
Federal expenditures (nondefense)—from $16.8 billion to $32.7 billion.
State and local government expenditures—from $66.7 billion to $120.0 billion.

In truth, the real challenge for all companies and countries is not in analyzing how to "divide up the pie," but rather how to create a much larger pie than now projected—for the benefit and profit of all.

Climate for Progress

So much for the size and the scope of the challenge. What is the climate for meeting it?

Within the Atlantic Community, the rate of growth is matched only by the speed of change. And change is fomenting dynamic upheavals in Europe's status quo. Hence, both opportunities and hazards are substantially greater today than they were just a few years ago, and problems are coming to the surface which previously were latent or even nonexistent.

On the European side of the Atlantic, the political-economic climate for U.S. investments is sensitive. Across the continent, fear is voiced over American "domination." Illustrating this is the following warning from *La Nouvelle Republique:* "To withstand the terrible pressure from the powerful American companies, we must create European enterprises." Even in the more sympathetic markets there is growing fear of "indigestion." Areas loaded to peak economic capacity simply are not capable of absorbing sudden new inflows of investment dollars, from Americans or any other nationality.

On this side, U.S. balance of payments deficits are forcing swift and dramatic changes by U.S. business managers. Despite the temporary "voluntary restraints," U.S. companies feel obligated to pursue expansion projects already planned or in progress, but in ways that support rather than derail the President's program. Even more to the point, American businessmen are not unaware of the political ferment epitomized by troubles within NATO and the Common Market. As a result, they are having second thoughts as to the wisdom of expanding in an environment where the American presence may seem less than welcome.

Hence there is concern in Europe and in America that the two continents could be approaching a "parting of the ways," a setback that would be tragic.

Is Unity Losing Ground?

Note the logic in the following private letter from a thoughtful European international businessman—and a strong friend of the United States:

Until not so long ago, there was a close community of purpose and an identity of structure which, alas, have lost ground rapidly.

Europe has gone through postwar reconstruction and has achieved the so-called miracle in a surprisingly short time. The main contributing factors to the miracle were: the ingenuity of the Europeans, American aid, and, above all, the availability of unhoped-for technological means. Having reached a satisfactory level of political and economic viability, Europe flattered herself to compare favorably even with the United States, and became complacent if not cocky.

In the meantime, however, the United States ran away with the new technological revolution, outdistancing Europe in many respects. This has created a technological gap which, in my view, Europe cannot fill with her own resources and ingenuity alone. An ever closer cooperation between the United States and Europe is, therefore, imperative.

In consequence, the threat becomes apparent that another gap could develop between the United States and Europe: a sociological gap. The world has become too small to allow for such further division to happen. It would be impossible for the Western world to counteract effectively the political pressure of the Communist world. Even more, it would be impossible for the industrialized world to act effectively in assisting the developing world and in steering its path in the right direction.

Yet despite the differences, a **single** **im**pressive conclusion has evolved out of two years' solid research, policy conferences on both sides of the Atlantic, and private discussions with several hundred policy officials from government, industry, finance, and the professions in a dozen leading nations: *The desire for cooperation far exceeds the differences which have dominated the headlines of most newspapers.*

Officially, in the eyes of one seasoned observer, relationships are at the lowest ebb since World War II.

But on a person-to-person basis, many of the relationships have never been better. At the corporate executive level, the desire is for closer cooperation with Americans in order to help close the gap. At the individual consumer level, the desire is to partake of the fruits of the technological revolution, regardless of whether the products are American or European. This cordial climate for business expansion is best found in the field of U.S.–French trade, where Roger Ricklefs observed in *The Wall Street Journal* of August 10, 1966: "Franco-American relations may be chilly enough these days for U.S. diplomats, but they're heating up noticeably for Yankee businessmen."*

The Case of Trade

Significantly, the above-quoted article was brought to our attention through a special mailing by the Press and Information Service of the French Embassy. This would seem to imply that perhaps "official" French-American relations may not be as "chilly" as news reports would indicate, at least in the sphere of commercial relationships.

The article then proceeds to document how attitudes toward the United States, as reflected by French consumers, have never been better:

In the first six months of 1966, French imports from the United States climbed to $604.4 million from $559 million a year earlier, according to the American Embassy in Paris.

---

* Roger Ricklefs, "U.S. Firms' Export to France Booming . . . ," *The Wall Street Journal*, August 10, 1966.

French imports from the United States for 1965 topped $1 billion, more than double the annual average during the 1950's.

Though steadily rising French exports to the United States topped half a billion dollars the previous year, this was still nearly a half billion dollars less than French imports from the United States.

Even these statistics do not tell the whole story, since the total volume of American sales is still higher based upon products produced in Europe by U.S. companies operating abroad. "Our sales are running higher than last year's level so far," Francis G. Gaudier, president of Colgate-Palmolive, told *The Wall Street Journal* reporter Roger Ricklefs. "Political differences have had absolutely no effect on volume."

The report continues:

The sale of "Barbie dolls" (and her friends) were running 50 percent ahead of a year ago, with more than 300,000 sold since 1963.

Coca-Cola French sales soared an average of 24 percent annually in the last five years.

Levi Strauss & Co. reported that its jeans sales were rising 20 percent a year in France.

American movies, always popular in France, were drawing about 30 percent of the nation's movie attendance.

And even Early American furniture, rare in France until a few years ago, was in style, with a large Paris furniture company ordering well over $100,000 worth of colonial furniture from New England.

A Friendly Market for U.S. Exports

Thomas E. Drumm, Jr., commercial counselor at the American Embassy in Paris, urged the Atlantic Council to stress the extremely favorable and cordial relations which exist between France and the United States. France is not a hostile market for American exports, he emphasized, but extremely friendly and becoming more so.

From the consumer viewpoint, transatlantic cordiality would seem to be a two-way street, or in Dirk Stikker's words, "a highway that unites." The display windows and shelves of America's department stores, supermarkets, and specialty shops testify that, at the purchasing level, there is little resistance to foreign products. American businessmen would say that this is merely one more demonstration of the commercial fact of life: "The customer is King."

The extent to which the customer can be king in the future, in a world trade community, will be based not just upon consumer preferences, but upon the laws and agreements worked out among the trading partners at the national and multinational level—hence, the stress on the issues introduced by Eric Wyndham White, director general of the GATT (General Agreement on Tariffs and Trade), in his appraisal opening Chapter 11 on "Stimulating Worldwide Trade."

Efforts to Broaden Understanding

Again and again, in our many discussions, the word "gap" has arisen—the technological gap, the management gap, the education gap, the gross national product gap, and so on. But as one of our colleagues stated at the Atlantic Institute's Geneva conference, the fundamental gap which underlies all the rest—and at the same time the most superficial—is the "cultural gap," or the gap in understanding.

The most encouraging development—through the series of conferences jointly sponsored by the Atlantic Council and the Atlantic Institute—was not in the concrete findings or finite proposals, but rather in the spirit of cooperation which helped to narrow the cultural or understanding gap.

For example, at an international conference at Fontainebleau in the fall of 1965, where the Europeans made up the majority of the conferees, the prevailing mood was at first quite negative to American business; but after two days of give-and-take discussion, it was the European leadership, not the American, which proposed a major rewrite of the final communiqué to reflect the "positive need for cooperation rather than the negative concern of American domination."

At the next conference, at Crotonville, New York, held six weeks later, the Americans constituted the majority. The first draft of the conference report dismissed European fears as "groundless" or "exaggerated to a large extent;" but it was the Americans who drafted the rewrite to acknowledge European concerns and to suggest areas where a business-cultural rapprochement was in order.

The following spring saw the Americans and Europeans coming together in Geneva in approximately equal proportion to write a communiqué proposing an Atlantic Action Program, where representatives from all nations would work systematically among themselves

and with their respective governments to plan "next steps" in five
fundamental areas of mutual concern:

1. Trade expansion, including the Kennedy Round and beyond.
2. North American investments in Europe.
3. European investments in North America.
4. Relations with the developing world.
5. East-West business relations.

Understanding the Cultural Differences

In parallel with efforts to smooth out differences in the economic
area, there is also emerging a better understanding of the cultural
differences. Jean Monnet, the genius and driving force behind the
European Economic Community, put these differences in enlightened
perspective in a statement appearing in a recent issue of the *Atlantic
Community Quarterly*.

For many Europeans, he states, the New World is a different world.
The United States is seen as a country without a history, without
subtlety, endowed with immense resources but enslaved by the same
material wealth. He notes, "Many Frenchmen feel ill at ease to see the
force and violence which explode in racial conflicts, the ever-growing
power of this vast country which they do not understand." In contrast, M. Monnet observes that Americans "tend to see in us a deeply
rooted but declining civilization, adapting itself with difficulty to the
modern world. They see marked social inequality, small-scale industry, agriculture made up of small family holdings, national sentiment which finds expression more often in nationalism than in constructive action."

He added, "America's strength does not lie only in machinery and
goods. She devotes much of her resources to material ends. She also
puts a substantial proportion to the service of liberty and civilization."
Many Europeans, M. Monnet continues, often fail to realize the active
interest in the arts in the United States. "Her museums, some of which
possess collections as rich as those of the Louvre or the Vatican, are
crowded with people eager to look and learn. The capital of modern
painting is now no longer Paris, but New York."

M. Monnet then compares the high standards in music, literature, education, and in cultural and civic activities, concluding that "the American way of life is typified not simply by the great cities, but also by those small communities where there are no walls between the gardens and where good-neighborliness is the guiding spirit."

Irritations Can Heat Up

Yet, these emerging bonds of sympathetic cultural interest are not yet adequately projected on the international scene, and the hypersensitivity at the political level means that any irritation can heat up the scene. To illustrate, let us note a few business cases symptomatic of what happens in Europe when there is a lack of cultural understanding or sensitivity on the part of Americans:

In one case, a sudden reduction in the number of plant personnel, because of a business slump, resulted in a sit-in strike; the handling of the strike was masterminded by an absentee manager.

In another case, when an operation began to fail, the American staff totally disappeared, and the remaining employees were instructed to abandon the operation.

Use of English-language handouts, without translation, has been made by some companies to announce major events to the press.

Not recognizing that many Europeans prefer to buy products made in Europe, some Americans have insisted that their products bear an American label—even when they are actually produced by a European corporate subsidiary.

Unhappy experiences are a small minority. They probably represent less than one percent of the total U.S. corporate story in Europe. On the other hand, countless successes could be reported to demonstrate growing sensitivity on the part of U.S. entrepreneurs.

The files are beginning to bulge with testimonials of "good conduct," where governments, industry associations, and consumers have paid tribute to American management and employee practices. And the best stories are those which never reach print, where a company has become so thoroughly internationalized that it is not even known as a "foreign operation." As one official in France phrased it, the real key to success is "to work yourselves into the landscape as quickly as possible." A seasoned binational executive in Spain termed it, "keeping a low silhouette." Case studies documenting how this is being done are presented in the concluding pages of Chapter 12.

In the Atlantic Council survey of industry and government leaders in eight Western European countries, it was learned that the vision of the "ugly American" has long since ceased to be created (if indeed it ever was) by the seasoned, long-established companies. They have become "part of the landscape." But many of the newer companies are credited—justly or unjustly—with stirring up antagonisms as a result of their executives' reluctance to learn the local language, plan ahead well, hire local managers, and so forth.

Important and interesting as such reactions may be, however, they are not our concern here. More important, our focus must be upon what U.S. businessmen can do about the issues of substance. The central question is not, "Is there too much or too little U.S. invest-ment?" It is more fundamental; and in the judgment of most Euro-peans, it is the determining question to their whole economic future—namely: "Can Europe keep pace with America in new technological developments and economic growth?"

In this light, being bypassed by American companies is as bad as (or worse than) being "swallowed up." The central question then breaks down into three subquestions:

1. The question of technology.
2. The question of size and power.
3. The question of management attitudes and practices.

Each of these questions will be the subject of a future chapter in this book. First, however, is the subject of the corporate executive, himself, and the need for him to define his own role as he comes to terms with these questions. The corporate role will be analyzed in the next chapter.

2 Role of the Corporate Executive

PART 1 Introduction
by Gerald L. Phillippe

Thirty years after joining General Electric as a business trainee in 1933, Gerald L. Phillippe was elected chairman of the board. The fifth chairman since the company's inception in 1892, Mr. Phillippe has held a number of financial positions. He served for eight years as comptroller and chief financial officer, and in 1961 was named president. He is a member of the Committee for Economic Development, a trustee of the National Industrial Conference Board, and serves on a number of other business and economic task forces and committees.

Photo by General Electric Co.

As every schoolboy knows, the history of world trade is filled with great eras and events and undertakings: the Roman Empire, the travels of Marco Polo, the voyages of Columbus and Henry Hudson, the clipper ships, the great canals of Suez and Panama, the British Commonwealth of Nations.

But none of these eclipse in significance the era in international business that began 20 years ago. It may be fairly said that in the early postwar years, world trade largely depended on an artificial device, the Marshall Plan, which transported more than $18 billion in monetary aid and goods from the United States to a ruined and exhausted Europe in its first three years of operation.

The Marshall Plan was a brilliant economic initiative. It not only helped the nations of Europe to preserve their free societies, but it provided the impetus for what has now become a giant $200 billion-a-year world trading community, double in size from just eight years ago and growing faster than the economy of any single nation.

With this regeneration in trade, we also have witnessed the creation of a new generation of nations, a new generation of young people, and a new generation of technologically oriented multinational business enterprises, which must now consider political, economic, and sociological problems as part of their business environment. The common aim of this new, bustling international arena is a better way of life on this planet—a hope that is no longer a meaningless platitude. The free world has the means now for improving the lot of men in any part of the world, if the nations will but use these means.

This is the great problem facing the international business community. How shall we implement what we know how to do? How shall we build a world trading community that truly serves all the needs of the peoples of six continents?

Three Hopeful Signs

As we look this world over, it may seem to some that we are a long, long way from the kind of an international trading community in which goods and services flow easily, with minimum restrictions, among nations. There has been, in recent years, a resurgence of protectionism and nationalism. Industrial nations are almost universally concerned with their own balance of payments and the stability of their own currencies, with dwindling regard for the long-term flow of trade and investment. Developed nations are struggling to balance full employment and high industrial capacity utilization with stable prices. Many less developed nations have had trouble in establishing the orderly, favorable climate needed for investment and economic growth.

For all this, I think some hopeful signs have emerged in the past two years. First, there is the continued growth of world trade business. Consistently, this has been at a rate greater than the growth of the national economies. As a result, world trade represents an increasingly important part of our national economies. In the United States, export trade is now responsible for perhaps three million jobs in the labor force and is becoming an increasingly substantial factor in the continued expansion of our economy.

Second, is the growth of international business. Export sales of nonelectrical power generating equipment have risen 210 percent in the past five years; export sales of computers and related equipment have gone up 145 percent in the same period. Moreover, more than four fifths of the 200 largest U.S. companies are now considered multinational enterprises. And among companies based in other countries, two thirds of the top 200 can be classified as international in the scope of their operations. Increasingly, the multinational company is playing an important role in the expansion of world trade and investment, in the spread of technology, and in the healthy increase of competition in world markets.

The third hopeful sign in the current world business picture is a growing maturity in business' approach to its problems. I believe that U.S. companies, particularly, have learned some important things about international trade in the past few years. I would not say that we have achieved complete maturity in our approach to world trade problems, but I think we are moving in this direction in ways that are most heartening.

There are many evidences of this. The State Department and other governmental agencies overseas are more aware now of the importance of the private sector in international affairs. They are be-ginning to develop constructive approaches toward the establishment of better business-government relationships on both sides of the Atlantic.

The Department of Commerce is working overtime to keep American firms abreast of the opportunities and problems of international trade and investment. The Secretaries of Commerce and Treasury have led the way in bringing to the attention of the U.S. business community our balance of payments problems, and in promulgating the means by which the payments deficit can be reduced.

For its part, the U.S. business community has developed much greater understanding of the problems that the government is coping with. Businessmen have voluntarily cooperated in a program to try to reduce the serious deficits in the balance of payments. At the same time, U.S. businessmen are trying to maintain a balance in their long-term involvement in the economies of other nations that depend on the dollar as a reserve currency.

This response by the U.S. business community has produced dramatic results. There has been a notable improvement in the balance of payments problem—from a $2.8 billion deficit in 1964 to $1.4 billion in 1965. In 1966, though hopes for reducing the total payments deficit still further were washed out by higher military spending in Vietnam, U.S. com-

23

panies cut their flow of dollars abroad for direct investment in the first half of the year by even more than the government had requested. And business earnings from direct foreign investments more than offset overseas spending among the 722 companies participating in the voluntary payments program.

So, despite some disappointments, there have been real achievements. The U.S. business community, as well as the government, now see these international trade and investment problems realistically, and they know that their solutions will require patient understanding and long negotiations.

Progress toward international monetary reform, for example, has seemed painfully slow in recent months. But in discussing the apparatus of possible plans for new international monetary reserves, the Group of Ten has at least engaged the attention of the major nations involved. Five years ago, proposals for increased international liquidity may have been argued by academicians, but certainly they were not of immediate concern to fiscal policy makers. Today, they are the subject of working negotiations between the centers of international power.

In a similar way, the Kennedy Round of the GATT negotiations may not have had all the results that were hoped for. But the discussions and agreements helped to create not only a greater understanding of the formal restrictions, such as tariffs, but a greater appreciation of the nontariff barriers as well. While these may not be deliberately so designed, they have the effect of distorting free world trading conditions, more than the tariffs themselves.

The so-called technological gap seems to many of our friends in Western Europe to be widening. But here, again, this may be too narrow a view. Thoughtful leaders in the Atlantic Community are recognizing that the fastest, most effective way to deal with this problem is not by additional restrictions and restraints on the part of the nations involved. The means by which this gap will be narrowed, or eliminated altogether, is through the broadest possible movement of people, and of capital, and of products, with the *fewest* possible restrictions in any of these areas.

Needed: Determination

In our preoccupation with our own national problems, perhaps we have grown overly concerned with the pressures and the stresses between ourselves and our friends on the other side of the Atlantic and the Pacific. We might get a fresh viewpoint if we try to imagine what the Western world might have been like if these people had not had the desire and the determination, after World War II, to become once again great economic forces in the world, and if all of us had not had the vision to invest in their aspirations.

We can see just this kind of desire and determination now in many of the underdeveloped nations. Unquestionably, their progress has been too slow, too irregular, and too uncertain. Emotional nationalism has frequently placed unnecessary limits on economic progress. And this is a source of great frustration, because for the first time in history the developed nations have tools and capabilities and resources which can be made available to those peoples who really want to reverse the downward spiral, and begin the upward spiral to becoming self-sustaining economies.

Can large corporations, with their technological and human resources, help create the climate and conditions for the investments that are badly needed?

Fortunately, we are being met more than halfway by many of the countries of Southeast Asia, and other developing areas of the world, for as Paul Hoffman says, "You can't export know-how. It has to be imported." Many are asking for help in their planning, either through regional development organizations, or directly. At General Electric we are currently engaged in systems or planning studies for a number of countries. What we are looking for and want to support are "things that could happen," that will result in a more productive use of local or regional resources on however limited a scale, and will help to create an effective, indigenous management group.

There are a number of requirements for "things to happen." There must be a workable potential in human and natural resources, and a climate for the development of local enterprise. There must be a realistic attitude and acceptance of the steps that will lead to an upward spiral. There must be a national climate in which an industrial society will be a viable undertaking. And private enterprise and government have to work together.

Obviously this approach is not on the grand scale that is being suggested in some quarters. No nation —much less a corporate enterprise—can tackle these huge problems alone. But General Electric is attempting, in a limited way, to see how private enterprise might be used by these countries in setting their economies on an upward path.

To build up the economies of these underdeveloped lands to full consumer and industrial status is going to be a long and painstaking process—as long and as painstaking, undoubtedly, as the combined business and government efforts to tear down the barriers that are impeding the progress of international trade among the developed countries. But on both counts, we have begun. And not the least impelling aspect of this beginning is the mounting realization among business leaders in the international community that they will have important contributions to make in decisions affecting the future course of events.

Common International Business Duties

Indeed, the impact of business now on the structure of the free world is such that, in my judgment, no economic course can be charted without a contribution from responsible leaders of our international enterprises. In this regard, it seems to me that international businessmen have a number of duties in common.

First, we have a duty to help maintain the security of the free world against the forces of aggression and subversion which have the aim of destroying free governments and free institutions wherever they exist. It is profoundly important to maintain the concept of collective security among the free nations of the world, regardless of what forms the alliance may take.

Second, let us make clear that business thrives best when it helps the nations of the world to achieve their legitimate aspirations. Voices from the past still hurl the discredited charge that business, in order

to earn a profit, must exploit its customers or employees, or the nations where it operates. This is not only bad history; it is also bad business.

Modern business management, when it undertakes a business venture in another nation, takes on a responsibility to help build up the economy of that nation, so that it will be a better market for all business. In this respect, it is good to remember that we are all developing nations—not only the nations of Asia, Africa, and Latin America, but also the nations of Europe, North America, and Australia.

Third, let us try to assist in the development of the kind of climate in which all the people in a multinational business organization can rise to their full potential. We will need all of our resources to get the work done. It just would not make good business sense, for example, for a U.S. firm to try to conduct all its overseas operations with American technical and managerial talent. A successful international company must call upon and try to develop the full range of local skills and brainpower—in research, in marketing, in design, in technical knowledge and managerial ability.

Fourth, let us face up realistically to the enormous capital needs of the world, and eliminate the unnecessary barriers to international investment.

The serious question is not

whether there will be too much movement of capital between nations, but whether there will be enough. The creaking machinery of international trade and investment is straining under the demands of modern, worldwide economic activity.

Fifth, let us work with our governments to reduce the needless barriers to international trade. The GATT negotiations have concentrated primary attention on the tariff barriers, and these are significant; but in my opinion the more destructive barriers are the informal ones: the restrictive purchasing practices based on national interests; the informal embargoes and quotas on certain types of products; the licensing difficulties; arbitrary antidumping procedures; the border taxes and export subsidies that purport to equalize competitive advantages among nations, but actually put nations that rely on direct taxation at a considerable disadvantage.

I think the international business community is moving with increasing effectiveness in every one of these critical areas. We are standing up to our new responsibilities and we have all become attentive students in a new kind of learning. This is why I have so much confidence in the future of international trade.

The problems of this increasingly complex and crowded planet will not diminish appreciably unless we continue to face them candidly with greater knowledge and maturity this year than we possessed last year—and the hope that the year ahead will bring more progress. This is the only climate in which we can ever realize the promise of progress with peace, to which the continued expansion of world trade and investment can contribute so much.

---

2 PART 2 *Atlantic Council Report*

Since a group of indignant colonists disguised themselves as Indians and threw tea into Boston Harbor, American businessmen have been personally and deeply involved in international commerce and international affairs. And their actions have had tangible, measurable impact upon national policy and America's relationships in the family of nations.

In this century, World Wars I and II were won for the forces of freedom only when U.S. industry was called upon to marshal the full might of its resources for a victory against the totalitarian states.

Throughout the cold war, communism has been contained through superior weapon systems—researched, designed, produced, and maintained by American industry working in partnership with the military forces.

Particularly since the advent of the technological revolution, corporate officials have been in a position to support national policy—indeed, to make possible new policies which advance the national and the free world interest. For example, America's security and worldwide responsibilities rest to a large measure upon the network of computers and satellites, tracking stations and scanning systems, jet-age logistics with supersonic carriers—all determining factors in the kind of foreign policy which it is technologically feasible for this nation to conduct.

In some instances, government officials lead the way by identifying the national challenges requiring new corporate and scientific solutions; other times, business managers find themselves in the leadership role with innovations opening up fresh opportunities for national initiatives. But in nearly all instances, the end product cannot be credited exclusively either to government or to industry; it represents a joint endeavor.

Until the 1960's, "the American team"—meaning government, industry, and labor—was more often a slogan than a fact, except during war and other crisis periods of great challenge. But during the last few years, we have seen international affairs present America with the kind of continuing national challenge which should result in an ever closer relationship, and a wider view by Americans of their individual responsibilities. Successfully met, the challenge can bring better business, more solid employment, and closer harmony on the world scene.

Perhaps nowhere is the team concept better exemplified than in the "systems approach" of management, born out of the military research-development-production aspects of the cold war. This same systems approach is applicable in nondefense areas—in fighting the war on poverty, in attacking urban blight and polluted air, in devising revolutionary educational systems, in helping to build viable societies in the developing world, and especially in building a stronger and more prosperous Atlantic Community.

The most obvious way that the American businessman can serve the national and Atlantic Community cause is simply by doing what he is paid to do; namely, to be a good manager of a profitable business.

In truth, the corporation is the engine of economic growth. America's ability to meet its international commitments in defense and aid rests directly upon the ability of America's corporations to expand, prosper, and pay taxes. America as a nation will be competitive in the world market only as individual companies are competitive, creative, enterprising, and resourceful.

Our Atlantic Council survey has documented that both government and industry are increasingly aware of their growing interdependence. As phrased in its summary report, "The Climate for American Business in Europe," perhaps the most significant aspect of the U.S. survey is the disclosure of the extent of basic agreement and consensus already existing between government and industry spokesmen who operate near the center of international business operations.

Atlantic Council Study

The objective of the Atlantic Council study on "Atlantic Cooperation and Economic Growth" was not to duplicate the work of the many fine government and private organizations already in operation, but rather:

1. To survey programs already under way.
2. To serve as a catalyst for new ideas and programs, thereby implementing through existing groups.
3. To stimulate a dialogue between government and industry leaders, and between the leadership community on both sides of the Atlantic, in order to encourage understanding and cooperation on trade, investment, and government policies of mutual concern.

Cooperation was outstanding. Full support came from the White House; the Departments of State, Treasury, and Commerce; the Federal Reserve Board; and the USIA. There was active participation by international business organizations, including the Chamber of Commerce of the United States, the National Association of Manufacturers, the U.S. Council to the International Chamber, the National Foreign Trade Council, and the USA–Business and Industry Advisory Council to the Organization for Economic Cooperation and Development (USA–BIAC to the OECD). Executives of these organizations constituted the coordinating committee for the Atlantic Council conference held at the General Electric Institute, Crotonville, New York, December 12–15, 1965.

The European phase of the study and the dialogue would have been impossible without the fine support from the American Chambers of Commerce in Europe (where the U.S. ambassador often serves as honorary chairman in each country), from the American embassies, and from host-national government and trade organizations, as well as private companies. In both Europe and America, corporate managers were among the most outspoken in urging closer liaison and joint efforts.

There was no "government viewpoint" or "business viewpoint" per se. While most government officials stressed the need for closer working relations on the international business front, a number cautioned that the appearance of too close a front would increase the anxiety of Europeans already apprehensive of American policies.

U.S. Foreign Economic Policy

While most businessmen similarly welcomed closer collaboration, a number were concerned that closer ties would bind their freedom of movement. One area of out-and-out controversy was over the nature of America's "foreign economic policy." Sharp criticisms were heard that if such a policy existed, it was not made known to the business community. As one exporter complained, "The United States has no clear and definite foreign economic policy. This might be caused by the fact that while other countries have a centralized spot where foreign economic policy is made, foreign economic policy in the United States is a composite of the action of different departments. Coordination may sometimes solve contradictions, but it often results in a compromise rather than in a sense of direction."

Business was not alone in this conclusion. As one retired ambassador indicated: "I agree with the prevailing comment that there is no present foreign economic policy. There is a real need for leadership on the national level in this area."

The principal complaint from businessmen, however, was that the U.S. government furnishes less support for American companies than is provided by European governments for their firms. This, in turn, was said to have placed American companies in disadvantageous competitive trading positions vis-à-vis their overseas counterparts. The British Board of Trade, the French and German "Plans," were cited as being more understanding and more effective than the rapport now existing within "the team" in the United States.

But this complaint was sharply refuted, both by government officials and by many knowledgeable businessmen. In balance, it does not appear to be an entirely fair complaint. It is largely a holdover from earlier decades when business and government held each other at arm's length and often viewed each other's policies from opposite sides of the fence. Based upon the evidence, a U.S. ambassador in Western Europe was well justified in his rebuttal:

> I do not believe the views expressed in your section on government-industry relations are typical. I certainly do not consider it applicable to the reactions of American businessmen doing business in this country. I say this because this Embassy always has its doors open to any American businessman and I know of no one who feels that he has not received all the help that could be given.

Businessmen "closest to the action," for the most part, vigorously agreed with the ambassador. A U.S. corporation president operating in Spain concluded: "If any U.S. businessman doesn't get cooperation out of the U.S. government, it's his own damn fault!"

There still exists some corporate misgiving over the caliber of U.S. commercial attaches in overseas embassies, but criticisms have been fading as more and more attention—through the last several administrations—has been directed toward securing the best people available. As we approach the 1970's, the international business fact of life is that there are many more government services available to businessmen to help them expand profitably overseas than businessmen are currently utilizing.

Case Example: Balance of Payments

Few issues have captured business page headlines and government office discussions as has the U.S. balance of payments problem.

The record shows that American businessmen have made serious efforts to support the U.S. balance of payments program through export-expansion efforts and through restricting dollar outflows for overseas investments—for the short run. But Atlantic Council transcripts also indicate that businessmen fear serious economic consequences if the government asks restraints for the long haul.

Also on the record are statements by the Secretaries of Treasury and Commerce indicating their appreciation that, over the long haul, U.S. investments abroad provide a healthy return to the United States in improving America's balance of payments picture. The question then boils down to how government-corporate liaison can improve the short-term picture without damaging American business ability to expand in the future for the benefit of both the nation and private companies.

The dialogue on this issue provides convincing evidence that knowledgeable business leaders who are still antigovernment, or government leaders still antibusiness, are indeed rare. Both sides work overtime to understand each other's problems, priorities, and positions. There are sharp differences of opinion over how to reach common objectives, but strong agreement on the objectives themselves:

1. Need for solvency in international payments.
2. Necessity for profitable overseas business operations.
3. More sophisticated approaches by American business abroad to other governments, other peoples, other customs.
4. Developing new businesses, new investments, and new export markets for the United States.

One businessman believes that the long-term solution to the balance of payments problem may well be to encourage direct investments rather than discourage them, and above all, to try to get many more companies involved in trade and investment than are involved today. He noted, "Five hundred companies with significant direct investments is a very small number considering the number of successful companies in this country. We would be on much safer ground if our investments abroad were spread through a wider range of companies, products, and industries, and then our exports would also be so much better spread."

In turn, government leaders have been searching for fresh solutions over and beyond the conventional approaches of stimulating exports and encouraging local borrowing by Americans in Europe. One such program is developed in detail in Chapter 7, "Stimulating European Investments in the United States."

Corporate Programs at All-Time High

Part of the Atlantic Council program was a survey by the Research Institute of America (RIA) on U.S. companies doing business abroad, based upon the attitudes and experiences of 1,000 RIA members.

The results here were surprising, even to the RIA executive staff. As RIA executive director Leo Cherne reported at the Crotonville conference, U.S. business involvement in foreign markets is at an all-time high. Three out of five respondents to the survey reported that they are engaged in exporting or selling goods for export. One out of five derives some income from foreign licensing of patents, trade names, or copyrights. And nearly as many receive income from owned or affiliated corporations abroad. Two significant aspects of these findings are:

1. A very substantial part of the increase in U.S. operations abroad represents the entry of medium and smaller businesses into the foreign market—during the past five to eight years particularly.
2. Companies operating successfully in foreign markets gain a competitive edge at home.

The RIA survey also dealt with the balance of payments problem, noting that American business as such does not have a deficit in international business. On the contrary, the profit it earns has helped to hold down the national payments deficit. Nearly four out of five companies engaged in foreign business expected their individual foreign "balance of payments" to improve in the following year.

No subsidies or direct financing were wanted by American exporters, despite the widely felt need for more effective indirect government assistance. The most important service the government could undertake in this area, according to the respondents, would be "negotiating reduced foreign restriction on U.S. products." Again, this is a challenge to government and industry as a team, as will be brought out in Chapter 11 on "Stimulating Worldwide Trade."

A second service requested by businessmen was making available information and advice. Here the RIA observed—as indicated earlier—that the Department of Commerce now provides a great deal of information on products and countries, practices and problems, but simply does not have the money available to promote and distribute fully the information it has.

Significantly, foreign investment is no longer confined to the pace-setting industry giants. A significant and growing number of middle-sized and small companies are actively involved today. Nearly 40 percent of those active in international business in any way said that they directly owned at least a 10 percent interest in a foreign subsidiary or affiliate. As could be anticipated, Western Europe is the most important area for investment (as for export trade) among the companies in the RIA survey. In fact, more money is invested in Western Europe than in all the rest of the world (except Canada) combined.

This phenomenon—the internationalization of U.S. business—is consistent with conclusions voiced by Mr. Cherne in an earlier survey carried out in cooperation with *The General Electric FORUM*, in which he said:

There is hardly a trace of the traditional economic or political isolationism in the American businessman. He is not fearful of foreign competition at home or in world markets. The truth seems to be that the businessman is reflecting all of the main streams of American political life—all the contradictions, all the separate and differing views.

There is, in short, no one such narrow thing as the typical businessman, where America's national goals and purposes are concerned. His attitudes on questions of national policy substantially contradict those who say he is motivated by nothing more than greed and profit. Altogether to the contrary, our probe reveals views on national policy which show a motivation going far beyond the narrow economic one. What is more, these views are often far closer to those held by members of the government than *either* government or business would be ready to concede.

Revolution in Government Thinking

If there has been a revolution in corporate thinking on world affairs, the same holds true in government thinking on the role of the private corporation, which may provide at least a partial answer to some of the problems at the national-political level.

At the national level, government leaders find formidable road blocks both to European unity and to Atlantic cooperation. There are no easy answers to NATO problems, to the issues of the Common Market and the Outer Seven, to the question of how to reduce trade and investment barriers within and among the various regional groups. Hence many are finding increasing attractiveness in the idea that somehow the Atlantic Community must begin to emerge without waiting for European unity or the resolution of the multiple national problems. As one American ambassador observes from his post in Europe,

I have been increasingly drawn to the thought that this will have to be built up and not down—that is, through functional organization based on technological needs and opportunities—before much of a political super-structure, with constitutions and parliamentary bodies, can be built on top of it.

But this official admits that "this is about as far as I have gone." He asks:

Is it possible for the Atlantic Council of the United States to organize a study group of some kind to take a serious crack at this question? You probably would need a point of departure—some handle to take hold of.

In any case, there is much to be said for approaching the question of institution building—which is what makes for community building—from a management viewpoint. And it seems not unlikely to me that an examination of the problems and successes and failures of sharing a piece of American power through international corporate arrangements might shed some interesting light on how to share other pieces of our disproportionate power without waiting for an "Eastern Pillar" [a united Europe] which is not yet designed, which may never come into being, and which might or might not be a healthy eventuality anyway.

Key Is Interdependence

If there is a single key to the puzzle, it will lie in finding interna-tional economic policies where joint action will reap greater rewards for each of the participants than if he were to "go it alone." The word is *interdependence.* Treasury Secretary Henry H. Fowler explored prospects for a sound, strongly growing, and interdependent free world economy at the Crotonville conference:

The interdependence of the world in which we live is not a simple two-way street running among the developed nations. There are many side streets, and they lead off from our well-lit world, glowing with promise, into dark precincts where poverty rules.

We are economically interdependent with the developing nations of the world because they provide us with most of our raw materials, and because, as their markets grow, they increasingly will be an outlet for our goods and services.

But it is not enough simply to realize that we have compelling reasons for assisting the less developed nations toward a better life. For one thing, the task is so gigantic that we need a much greater sharing of the task among the developed nations.

One of the long-term solutions to the world payments problems lies in placing payments surpluses back into circulation. Increased assistance to developing nations by countries with balance of payments surpluses would help solve the problem.

Many concrete channels already exist for such cooperative assistance to the developing world, such as the International Development Association (an affiliate of the World Bank), the various bilateral and regional financial institutions, and in particular, the Asian Development Bank. Each country in a position to help should determine how best to respond to the needs, in light of its own capacity.

What we need for a stronger free world—including, at the very heart, a stronger Atlantic Community—is to put these lessons together. Let us develop our trade and investment policies, public and private, in ways that permit maximum sound economic expansion, as a growing pool of economic resources—for the use of each, for the benefit of all.

3

The Question of Technology

PART 1 *Introduction*
by Dr. Antonie T. Knoppers

Author of approximately 60 scientific papers on pharmacology and endocrinology, Dr. Antonie T. Knoppers is an accomplished international scientist and businessman. He holds an M.D. degree from the University of Amsterdam, and a doctor of pharmacology degree from the University of Leyden. He joined Merck–North America, Inc., as manager of medical services, and later became director of scientific activities for Merck, Sharp & Dohme International. He is currently president of that division of Merck & Co., Inc. A member of the Council on Foreign Relations, the National Foreign Trade Council, and the board of directors of the American Management Association, he is also a trustee and member of the executive committee of the U.S. Council of the International Chamber of Commerce. In addition, he is a member of a number of other international private organizations.

Photo by Fabian Bachrach

Any study of U.S. private investment in Western Europe must give major emphasis to the present differences in technological development between the two sides of the Atlantic. America's leadership in technology is a fact, and it is increasing. Furthermore, in my view, this leadership is greater than is generally realized in Europe.

The "technological gap," as it is called, is undoubtedly one of the principal reasons for the continuing high level of U.S. direct investment in Europe. On one hand, these investments offer the recipient country access to new technology, training of labor in new skills, monetary inflow, and an escalation of competitive ability. On the other hand, the U.S. firm is afforded an international outlet for its superior technological know-how.

The essential problem, therefore, centers on the transfer of

39

technology and Europe's need for it. If there is indeed a widening of the technological gap, Europe would be unwise to deter U.S. direct industrial investment, because it does insure a flow of technical knowledge. At the same time, Europe must develop a sufficient technology of her own to maintain a manageable balance of the two-way flow.

Management Is the Key

The key point for Europeans to grasp in trying to develop their own technological prowess is this: Superior technology is the result of superior management and superior management concepts. It is management attitude which has to pave the way for effective European technological development.

Note these comments from an issue of *Science* magazine:

Amid all the questioning, it is recognized that much of the story of supposed technical mastery is really a story of the organization of firms. In an age of rapid technical advance, one of the most potent organizations for rapid applications of research discovery is a force of salesmen and sales engineers like the one that has helped IBM, a late-comer to the electronic computer business, get and keep over 70 percent of the world market. It is beginning to be appreciated in Britain that organizational problems may partly explain why Britain, which has not lacked for ideas about aircraft and computers, has not been able to slice out a secure piece of the world market in either industry.*

Similarly, it was a management concept that put Merck and Company, Inc., into the forefront of new drug development. In the late 1920's, Mr. George W. Merck decided to create an atmosphere which would attract the very best scientists (the Merck "campus"), and to spend money to achieve important advances. This management decision was successful in creating outstanding technology.

Quality and Quantity in Technology

In the development of new technology, one can discern three major phases. The first is the idea stage, where an individual or group of individuals interpret available data in a new arrangement, and speculate on the consequences. The second is the basic evaluation stage, where numbers of people, laboratories, and instruments check out the idea and determine its possible success. In the third phase, a proven idea is pursued in practical application. Here,

* Victor K. McElheny, "Europe Considers Industrial Mergers," *Science* magazine, April 22, 1966 (published by the American Association for the Advancement of Science).

40

imagination, consumer orientation, trained people, and money will influence the outcome.

It is therefore readily apparent that the development of new technology has both qualitative and quantitative aspects. It is estimated that in 1962, the United States spent $17.5 billion on research and development, while Western Europe spent $4.4 billion. To be more specific, in the drug industry in 1965, about $360 million was spent on R&D in the United States. In Great Britain, $32 million was spent on R&D. During 1966, Merck and Company alone spent about $40 million.

In terms of people (also for 1962), 436,000 scientists and engineers were involved full time in R&D in the United States. Comparable Western European figures show 148,000 people. Since 1962, U.S. expenditures have probably risen to approximately $25 billion, and the essential relationship to Europe's efforts may be even larger today in favor of the United States.

How Much "Fallout" from Space Research?

One of the most significant factors in the technological revolution in the United States is the enormous "fallout" from the large government and industry expenditures on space and military technology.

This is particularly true for developments in physics—the science which, more than any other, will affect the technology of the next 50 years.

Let me mention just a few glamorous catch words like "gravitation," "relativity," "quantum theory," "elementary particle physics," "superconductors," and "cryogenics." In these highly theoretical areas, one begins to see the shape of things to come in exciting new developments in communications, for example, and in information management, storage, and retrieval.

In fact, entire fields which did not exist at all a few years back are now the life interest of many young American researchers. A few examples are telemetry, satellite navigational control, meteorology, radio astronomy, terrestrial magnetism—or, if you prefer to stay on earth: superconduction, semiconductor lasers, and the fabulous new research field of materials science, where new materials are tailor-made to withstand the awesome vacuum of outer space, with its great temperature and pressure differences.

Clearly, the European effort is not of the same magnitude. Although European scientists match their American counterparts in the quality of ideas, the numbers are logically in favor of the United States.

41

Gaps in Chemistry R&D

The fact that most of the spectacular space-related developments are in the field of physics should not comfort the European chemical industry. Chemistry has become so much a science wherein many disciplines have to be integrated that the consequences of the technical revolution in physics will also revolutionize chemistry. The same is true for the biological sciences.

However, both quantitatively and qualitatively, the situation in chemistry is not totally unfavorable for European research and technology. There is no doubt that in nearly all fields of chemistry, some excellent work is being done in Europe. Yet in many a field there is a distinct and growing gap. And in some fields where a balance exists today, there is also the danger of a gap developing. Europe has excellent and massive research in chemical technology, but an alarm signal is in order even for its giant industries.

I have the impression that in the heavy chemical industry (high volume, low profits) an equilibrium of competitiveness exists. Yet significant shifts have occurred in the theoretical field, and Europe is having difficulty catching up. For example, the field of quantum chemistry is being pursued with great vigor in the United States.

Its ultimate goal is to arrive at computational methods which will allow the prediction of chemical reactions in hours or days, where it takes months or years to run the experiments.

In this case, one sees an example of an idea based on European theory which developed into a wide, revolutionary application in the United States—a sequence of events which has become the pattern. The greatest impact on the rate of chemical research has been made by new instrumentation, which gives new, faster, better insights. And it is the United States which is producing and selling such useful and needed laboratory instruments.

The development of holography is an object lesson in the development of science and technology as far as the United States and Europe are concerned. This is a new form of three-dimensional photography which is uncannily realistic. It was originally conceived in 1947 by Professor Dennis Gabor at Great Britain's Imperial College. Yet Professor Gabor and his collaborators had available only feeble sources of monochromatic light, essential for holography's practical application.

The invention of the laser (1960) in the United States provided a new, intense source of coherent light, and this innovation put holography on a practical basis, with new applications to come. These new applications are naturally being done in the United States.

Holograms can be produced in color and this fact could lead to realistic, three-dimensional color television. It might lead to reading machines which could convert human text into computer language, cutting out the laborious process of coding everything on punched cards. If X-ray holography should be developed, it would offer a powerful tool for crystal structure analysis, and might revolutionize molecular biology. It would influence quantum chemistry. And its defense use is obvious.

What happened? A basic idea was developed elsewhere (in this case Great Britain). But its further development and practical applications are carried on in the United States.

Flow Sometimes Favors Europe

In a few fields of technology, the two-way flow between Europe and the United States has been in favor of Europe. For example, Great Britain developed the Pilkington floating glass process, which has been licensed to several American glass manufacturers. And there is one interesting and illuminating example where Europe is ahead— natural product chemistry. One

need only mention the names of Watson and Krick, of Perutz and Hotchkiss.

Let us return for a moment to the three successive stages of research: ideas, basic experimentally proven theory, and development and application. It can be said that whereas Europe originally dominated the first two phases, nowadays a shift has taken place. In the establishment of basic, experimentally verified theory, the United States takes advantage of its multitude of institutions and superior equipment.

This general development is the cause of the so-called brain drain, the migration of scientific talent (often the best) from Europe to the United States. The belief that the brain drain is caused solely by higher wages and more affluent living is not accurate.

This loss of scientific talent is serious. During the three years 1961, 1962, and 1963, about 16,000 scientists (half from Europe) entered the United States. From 1956 to 1961, West European countries exported about six percent of their graduate engineers and scientists to the United States.

The cause of the brain drain is clear and the correction of it should be part of an integrated effort to keep the technological gap in reasonable balance.

It is clear that Europe should do several things:

1. Remain aggressive (and especially, allow no economic nationalism) in acquiring technology through attracting U.S. direct investment.

2. Organize research and development on a European scale rather than national concentration, particularly through total mergers.

3. Create a climate for American industry to carry out large research projects in Europe, which, through increased social mobility, will also enhance the level of European-owned research.

Is Europe on the right track? In some instances, yes; but the problem is, in my opinion, bigger than is generally appreciated.

1. Acquiring Technology through Direct Investment

As stated earlier, Europe has acquired American technology by permitting and even encouraging direct industrial investment. Sometimes such an investment is in the form of a fully foreign-owned undertaking, either subsidiary or branch; at other times in the form of a joint venture, from majority to minority interest. If the contributions—technology, financing, available infrastructure, local management know-how, long range compatability—are balanced with the division of profits and good growth policy, joint ventures can be ideal. This is often the case when the production of a specific product group is involved. Some joint ventures of this type in Holland are very well conceived.

A direct investment by a foreign company through an acquisition of a local company presents both favorable and unfavorable aspects for the host country. Acquisitions which are based solely on cost reductions through a combined infrastructure often do not make much sense. There should be a better rationale, such as that a national company with a good marketing group needs a flow of technology, and consequently new products, which it cannot provide itself.

Both joint ventures and direct investment bring needed technology and raise the competitive level. But if, at the same time, nationally financed technology is not developed in some reasonable ratio, they create a danger of future dominance.

Nevertheless, European nations cannot afford to forego them, as France has learned painfully. Says a French economist: "Aren't we Europeans really trying to get the best of two worlds? Aren't we trying to get the advantage of mass markets, mass production, competition, and modern technology, while at the same time trying to preserve a way of life more attuned to 19th-century nationalism? We'd better realize that fight is lost."

It is deplorable that the political impasse of Europe, created mainly by France, has a retarding and sometimes thwarting effect on European economic integration at the time it is most needed. The French are, however, beginning to get the message. One U.S. auto manufacturer put a new, 5,000-job assembly plant in Antwerp instead of Alsace. A petroleum company shifted a proposed polyethylene factory from Bordeaux to Belgium. And another auto maker is about to build a new production complex a few miles across the French border in West Germany, from where it can sell in the Common Market, including France.

Thus French policy toward foreign direct investment has been liberalized, for it is realized that French nationalism would mean economic dependence or an unacceptable retardation of the growth and standard of living.

2. Organizing for Europewide Research

Recently, some studies have indicated that the movement of European firms is more in the direction of national concentration than toward transnational European mergers. As one analyst summarized: "If the Common Market repulses the American giant corporation and fails to establish European incorporation, the European movement may fall short of real integration."

Although this general thesis is acceptable, there are some points of argument. First, the traditional movement for integration in Europe has followed lines that are less acceptable in the United States, mainly because of antitrust restraints on such things as R&D interchanges, cooperative sales arrangements, joint parts production, reciprocal marketing in home countries, and so on. Some of these European methods of cooperation are being challenged by the new EEC antitrust rules, but by no means all. In this technique of operation, the United States–based international company is at a disadvantage since the constant threat of U.S. antitrust laws is a much more limiting factor than Europeans realize.

Secondly, the transnational corporation cannot fully develop in Europe without a supranational company law, now under recommendation by the European Economic Community. For instance, the cumbersome structure of the Agfa-Gevaart merger is about as far as the two companies could go under national laws.

Many of the obstructions to European mergers are functions of time. But time is of the essence. If, due to political stagnation or to lack of initiative or boldness of the managerial class in Europe, too much time is lost, the gap may become difficult to manage.

There are hopeful signs. Concentrations in the electronic and appliance markets are taking place. The merger and integration of Hoesch A.G., Dortmund-Hoerder-Haelbenunion A.G., and Hoogovers-Staalfabrieken is a signal event. Last but not least, the research cooperation between Bayer and Rhone-Poulenc in the virus and cancer fields might be an initiative which will trigger similar moves.

3. Encouraging U.S. Research in Europe

Much could be done, I feel, to create a climate for America to conduct large research projects in Europe, to be combined with a fostering of social and economic mobility of scientists and managers. Europe could develop incentives for American and European firms alike, through tax exemptions or even indirect support.

Examples in the United States overwhelmingly prove that personal mobility of scientists and managers is essential for accelerated growth. If European and American researchers could work side by side, such mobility would benefit Europe immensely. At the same time, Europe should also review its educational system, which puts too great an emphasis on excellence and does not give enough attention to the mass education

necessary to support that top group.

In conclusion, although Europe is taking steps to remain open for direct investments as a method for transferring technology, and although initiatives are being taken for European transnational mergers, integrations, and research cooperation, the total picture as projected into the future is not satisfactory. Acceleration is necessary.

Steps could be taken by the Atlantic Council directly (or by stimulation of other institutions) to foster all the actions possible to support the major corrective suggestions outlined above.

1. The council could initiate or support a qualitative and quantitative study of the Atlantic scientific and technological gap, by identifying those sectors of science which will dominate future technology. It could then evaluate the present balance or gap and also look into the future.

2. This basic information could be studied by economists and sociologists in order to evaluate the consequences for the United States and Europe.

3. The total picture should be used to alert governments, industry, and the public to the realization that the scientific and technological gap is a lasting problem, and one which should be tackled and reduced to manageable, balanced proportions.

3 PART 2 *Atlantic Council Report*

As former United States Commerce Secretary John T. Connor brings out in a later chapter, America has continuously welcomed the inflow of foreign capital, industrial techniques, and new technologies since its founding days in the late 1700's. Seasoned economists, businessmen, and government officials openly acknowledge this injection of fresh ideas and fresh resources as the primary cause for this nation's phenomenal progress from a traditionally agrarian society to the world's leader in science, technology, and living standards.

Similarly, knowledgeable Europeans credit the influx of American capital, technology, and management resources following World War II as the essential ingredient for the miracle of their own reconstruction. Indeed, European progress was so swift that by the early 1960's the basic theme and concern of American industry was "keeping America competitive." One American manufacturer was so dismayed and distraught that he threatened to dismiss employees if they were found driving foreign cars. The words, "cheap foreign competition", did not die easily on the lips of those who saw their very corporate existence threatened—in particular, by the tough new brand of German and Japanese entrepreneurs who in just two decades had created highly efficient and automated world trade companies out of the ashes of World War II.

Need for U.S. Technology

The postwar priority of all European countries was to persuade American industries to come to Europe. Their overwhelming need was to build a new economic foundation based upon the new technologies. American direct investment was the fastest and most logical answer.

In Britain, where the Treasury and Bank of England must authorize all direct investment, permission has never been refused in the 20 postwar years. Italy, Belgium, West Germany, and Holland pursued equally liberal policies.

Italy, for example, has guaranteed foreign investors the right to repatriate capital and earnings. Similarly, the Dutch and Belgians made a special point of advertising tax benefits provided under their regional development plans. West Germany assured complete freedom for all capital movements, and tiny Luxembourg made special efforts to attract American investment in order to break away from its single-product (steel) economy.

Even France, which up to 1958 had followed a protectionist policy, freed capital movements as she entered the Common Market. In 1959, France virtually eliminated restrictions on both imports and exports of capital. One result of such liberalized policies was that by the end of 1961 there were 250 new American investments in France, more than in any other country.

American motivations in setting up new businesses in France, rather than merely exporting to French markets from factories in the U.S., have been obvious. One reason related to the high return on capital in Europe. A second concerned itself with the tremendous business growth potential in the European market as it entered the era of the consumer economy. A third reason has been the obvious advantage of becoming part and parcel of the European team, learning the local differences in cultures and buying patterns, the unique characteristics of labor and technical manpower resources. Above all, there has been the desire and need to hold actual membership in the European Economic Community itself as it moves from a vision to a practical, multinational, mass-market reality.

In short, American companies recognized the economic facts of life: that to remain competitive at home, they had to meet their international competitors on their own shores.

Research and Development in Europe

In introducing this chapter, Dr. Antonie T. Knoppers convincingly illustrates that the impact of U.S. direct investment in Europe is substantially greater than the cold statistics would indicate. Country by country, the size of corporate investment usually does not exceed 1 or 2 percent of total investment. But in company after company, plant after plant, one finds whole new industries, in basic chemicals, pharmaceuticals, aspects of electronics and engineering—and whole new processes and techniques for conventional industries.

For example, the $10 million investment by Libby, McNeill & Libby in canning and food processing in a 10-year period in the Rhone Basin promises to revolutionize not just food processing but the marketing and distribution methods of French agriculture. In Britain, a long list of new productive processes and materials introduced by American firms could be cited, from the manufacture of automatic car transmissions to pneumatic road drills. In addition, whole new geographic regions are coming alive, as, for example, when 130 American firms opened new operations and new payrolls in Northeast Britain. Competition by regions and by countries for new American investors is a matter of record.

Why then do Europeans worry? If through foreign investments Americans were able to shortcut the industrial revolution two centuries ago—and Europeans today are able by the same means to shortcut the technological revolution—then what is the problem?

The Atlantic Council's eight-nation survey of the business climate in Europe endeavored to "target in" on this problem. But in truth, it was not until our last meeting of European businessmen, in Milan, Italy, that the issues were put in sharp focus. The spokesman was Dr. Aurelio Peccei (who introduced Chapter 1)—formerly a driving force of Fiat, a World War II leader of the resistance against fascism, and today the vice chairman of Olivetti.

During the closing minutes of the meeting, those of us who had been conducting the survey asked: "Is there any final observation or request which you would like us to take back to the United States?" To put Dr. Peccei's reply in context, it is well to note his responsibilities with Olivetti, a company in a front-rank position in world competition. Hence, his comment is significant because it is not from a European "protectionist" but from a foremost proponent of free competition:

Even you Americans don't realize the speed and scope of your technological revolution, and the speed with which the gap is widening between America and Europe. You must make Americans recognize that fact.

Referring to the outer evidences of a European consumer economy
—the shiny cars, the abundance of motor bikes, new steel and glass
buildings, and roadside drive-in restaurants more modern than those
in the United States (as seen on Italy's autostrada)—he added:

But this is surface, a facade. In the areas that really count, Europe still
lags far behind America and, in truth, is slipping farther and farther
behind, perhaps dangerously so. The gap—the real gap, the technological
gap—is increasing. And it won't be good either for you or for us if America
completely eclipses Europe in new developments. A partnership and an
alliance must be formed upon a relationship that is at least somewhat
equal.

The answer, in the Italian executive's judgment, lay in joint ventures and other cooperative efforts.

Later, in Rome, this thought was amplified by another Italian businessman, Dr. Paolo Rogers—also associated with Olivetti, but perhaps
better known for his worldwide economic background, including frequent service as a delegate of the Italian government to the U.N. Conference on Trade and Development and other international meetings.
Dr. Rogers cautioned that unless prompt and energetic action were
taken, the gap might turn into a dangerously divisive factor. It was
inconceivable that Europe could fill it by her own means and resources
alone. He concluded:

Close cooperation between the United States and Europe may offer the
only solution. The alternative would be stagnation of the European economy, with tremendous and widespread implications.

Change: Not Always Welcome

Although fresh approaches and new technologies are sorely
needed to rejuvenate sagging industries and economies, it does not
automatically follow that such changes will be welcomed. For example, in France, the food industry represents one of the more back-
ward sectors of the economy and precisely the kind of sector which
could most benefit from the spur of new competition and new
methods. (In the biscuit industry alone there are some 450 firms
operating along traditional lines, and until recently not challenged by
"the new competition.") It is here that change is most painful to con-

ventional ways of doing business. In his Atlantic Institute report on foreign investment in Europe, Christopher Layton quoted an official in the French food industry who advised, "Our industry is linked to agriculture, one of the bases of the nation's life. You cannot have an upheaval in buying, processing, and methods of distribution without great change in the structure of agriculture itself. Do not go too fast."

Mr. Layton pursues this point with the interesting case history of how one international firm, Libby, McNeill & Libby, has proceeded with wisdom and good results. At first there were protests from competitors, and fears from the farmers that Libby would import American raw material when it established itself in the Rhone Basin. But, Mr. Layton stated,

> . . . the French government had the wisdom to bless and guide the project. The farmers are now delighted with the regular contracts, efficient distribution, and technical help which they get. And some guarantee of a French say in the future running of Libby has been assured by the purchase of a 20 percent holding in the parent company by the Banque de Paris et des Pays bas.

> It is interesting to note that in this case the scheme was facilitated by the choice of an agricultural zone which was already being transformed. This was not a backwater, but an area where the state itself had put in money and the farmers themselves were struggling towards more effective cooperative marketing.

Is a Cooperative Approach Practical?

How practical is the idea of cooperative R&D efforts so as to gear Europe's immense potential for development into U.S. development expertise? Are Europeans prepared for this faster pace? Are Americans in a position to benefit?

Raytheon's success in Italy would indicate *yes* on all scores. Charles F. Adams, the chairman of the board, outlined his company's experience to the Atlantic Council investigators:

> What the Europeans have been looking for, in Raytheon and other U.S. companies, is to upgrade their technology. Sometimes we have gone to them; often they have come to us to work out arrangements. As for results, right now it can be said that in Italy the work we have done, say, on electronics for the Italian Navy, has not only brought the quality of work up to par with the U.S. Navy, but carried the Italians beyond in certain areas. In

51

some cases, this infusion of basic technology from the United States has been applied to specific design and engineering projects over there so successfully that the joint operation has actually leapfrogged the United States and gone ahead at a very fast clip.

It did not worry Mr. Adams that the speed of progress by the host-nation partner has sometimes exceeded that of the United States. For instance, in the case of the NATO Hawk missile program, Raytheon worked not just with Italy but with a five-nation consortium to provide technological assistance to produce this American-developed weapon in Europe. Mr. Adams noted:

> There is no question but that this has enriched the technological base of all countries. Now, five years after the Hawk program started, our associates are talking about developing something more advanced on their own. I am sure that in many aspects of the design, they are capable of doing very competent work, indeed—in Italy, France, Germany, Holland, and Belgium.

Are the benefits all one-way, flowing from the United States to the recipient nations? The Raytheon board chairman did not think so. The U.S. company has rights to the product, he said, and can take advantage of this.

Mr. Adams predicted a growing role for NATO in the sharing of technological information. "We're going to see more of this kind of thing, and it will have the effect of creating a somewhat closer political unity." This prediction is based on the growing number of joint activities, such as the German–U.S. effort in battle-tank development, the British–French development of the Concorde airplane, and the development of the Atlantic antisubmarine airplane.

Encouraging Participation

It is not just a question of whether or not U.S. companies can "do something" to strengthen Europe's technological base. Failure to take action is, in essence, "doing something" by default: namely, fanning the fears and triggering nationalistic sentiment among that vocal minority which feels that the answer lies in taking the line suggested in an Italian newspaper: "European industry must merge in order to compete with the world giants."

In December 1965, at the Crotonville, New York, meeting of corporate officials and government leaders (as explained in General Norstad's foreword) there was considerable discussion of what should be done. Opinions varied as to the extent of the gap. Some participants observed that the U.S. lead was not across the board, but existed chiefly in certain identifiable areas such as electronics and nuclear power. Where there was no problem, obviously no action was needed. Examples were also cited of specific European companies which could more than meet the American competition. And in certain fields, European industrial research and development was described as being ahead of that in the United States. On the other hand, it was agreed that the fears, whether justified or not, could not be ignored. As stated by Ambassador Walter Dowling, director general of the Atlantic Institute:

> Some are exaggerated and even unreal; but even these, unless actively corrected, can have a devastating effect on the Atlantic Community and all of its participants.

The conclusion was that constructive answers lay not in pitting countries against each other in technological tests of strength, but in helping to break down nationalistic barriers as companies increasingly share R&D through investment, licensing arrangements, partnerships, consortia, and other ways.

Careful observers also agree that besides doing more to increase European participation, American companies should explain more— make publicly available more information on their R&D programs already under way in Europe. Such data should demonstrate the extent to which the American company is relying on and strengthening the host country's scientific and technological manpower.

The Europeans themselves have said specifically what they would like Americans to do. In November 1965, at the Atlantic Institute's Fontainebleau conference, a distinguished group of European industrial and financial leaders summarized their suggestions to Americans. These suggestions often paralleled those made by the U.S. businessmen at Crotonville:

1. Operate research and development facilities in the host country, thereby strengthening its technological base and combating any brain drain.

2. Permit early participation by Europeans in new product development. This will counteract any fear that new products of American technology may be developed initially in the U.S. home market and only belatedly sold or manufactured in Europe.

Dual Initiative

At Fontainebleau the European conferees took stock of their own responsibilities. They recognized that to a large extent the fear of American supremacy was due to the slowness of the European side to make the adjustments required by the new markets being created. Their suggestions to themselves and other Europeans embraced such measures as better marketing, tax and cartel legislation, development of an integrated European capital market, and increased efforts and incentives toward R&D—all aimed at speeding up European progress.

In short, Americans and Europeans are becoming increasingly aware that new initiatives are needed and expected from both sides. Perhaps the most profound point emanating from many private discussions with Europeans in a number of countries is that a very high percentage of individual businessmen, if given a choice, would prefer to join with Americans, rather than with other Europeans, in building multinational enterprises. The reason lies in the benefits to be derived from U.S. technologies and corporate resources.

4 The Question of Size and Power

PART 1 *Introduction by David Rockefeller*

As president of New York City's largest bank, the Chase Manhattan, David Rockefeller is the closest of the famous Rockefeller family to the current mainstream of American commerce. He was named 1964 "businessman of the year" by **Saturday Review** magazine, which called him a "spokesman for creativity in management" and "a reasonable champion of change." A Harvard graduate, Mr. Rockefeller holds a Ph.D. in economics from the University of Chicago. He is chairman of several important committees, including the Council for Latin America, The International Executive Service Corps, New York's Museum of Modern Art, and the Rockefeller University.

Photo by Jan Jachniewicz

Although it is a deeply misleading and thoroughly prejudicial way of introducing the subject, most discussions of big business, and the power that is assumed to go with it, begin from a negative point of view—the view that big business is at worst an impossible ruffian and at best a slightly disreputable character who, if only he can be domesticated and civilized, may prove a useful citizen yet.

The foes of big business have excellent reasons for beginning in this manner. A good offense will generally beat a good defense, as most sports fans are aware.

But why many of those with friendly feelings toward big business frequently start off in much the same negative way is not equally clear. Perhaps they are simply following convention. Perhaps they like to wrestle with straw men. Or perhaps—and this is more likely—they are not truly informed of the facts as they relate to the world in which we live.

Certainly the air must be cleared in America, because all too many Americans have grown up with a vague mistrust of bigness wherever it is found—whether of big business, big government, big labor, or that memory from childhood, the big bully of the playground.

Misconceptions of Bigness

But there are many kinds of bigness, some good and some bad. Bigness, for one thing, is meaningful only if it is thought of in relative terms. It is not always easy to correct erroneous ideas about the place and role of big business in the United States—partly, I suspect, because it is much more difficult to unlearn an old idea than it is to learn something new, which is why we find it much easier to accept the fact that the earth is round than did our ancestors of the middle ages, and why our children seem to be better equipped to accept the idea of interplanetary travel than their parents.

But if it is necessary to correct America's misconceptions about big business, it is doubly necessary to correct European misconceptions about big U.S. firms doing business on the continent. Three misconceptions in particular stick in my mind.

Follow the Flag. The first of these is that the U.S. flag follows slavishly the migration of large U.S. companies abroad—that U.S. firms in their operations overseas are in some sense merely an extension of U.S. foreign policy, that they pursue the national interests of the United States while ignoring the welfare of the country in which they are located. Such fears may have had some foundation back in the days around the turn of the century, when O. Henry was writing short stories about the "banana republics," and gunboat diplomacy was an accepted element of international relations.

But there is no reason for such concern today. In fact, the worry of many businessmen operating overseas has been that they get too little support from their government—far less, for example, than the businessmen of other countries such as Britain and Germany. As pointed out in an earlier chapter, only very recently has this attitude on the part of many of our foreign missions started to change in a favorable direction.

In any event, old-fashioned "dollar diplomacy" runs directly contrary to national policies, interests, and goals. Moreover, the long-run self-interest of any business enterprise is itself firmly rooted in the community in which it does business. Therefore it is only reasonable to expect firms to have a concern for the communities in which they operate. Most companies go to great lengths to try to be good corporate citizens of their host countries. It is getting harder and harder to identify these companies as being purely American. It is to their best interest, and at the same time it is quite consistent with broader U.S. interests.

Americanization of World Culture. The second notion is that the move of large U.S. companies abroad leads to the "Americanization of world culture," turning the rest of the world into suburbs of the United States. And to be sure, American ideas—from food fads and business techniques to books, TV shows, advertising, and art—are being bought, sold, used, and admired all over the world. What is called the Americanization of the rest of the world should more properly be looked upon, however, as the spread of modern industrialization, which is identified with a growing number of nations. But since the United States is in the vanguard of the new industrial technology, it has found itself the most conspicuous nation carrying the new techniques around the world.

Greater uniformity of customs and techniques, which goes along with industrialization and vastly improved communication, is not an indication that other countries are losing their unique characteristics and becoming pale imitations of the United States. Nor does it mean that cultural exchange is a one-way street. Of course, many young people of France drink Coca-Cola and dance "le twist," but at the same time many young Americans are drinking French wine and dancing in "discothèques."

Nor is there anything new about the international exchange of everything from popular fads to basic ideas. If there is any one artifact that characterizes the United States, it is the automobile. Yet the first cars were built on the European continent. Indeed, car imports from France gave the United States its basic automobile vocabulary. Words like "chauffeur," "garage," "coupé," and even "automobile" itself have all been domesticated from the French language. This most certainly did not result in the "gallicization" of the United States any more than the introduction of such U.S. business terms as "marketing" and "public relations" will result in the Americanization of France.

Destruction of Smaller Firms. The third notion is that giant U.S. companies will gobble up and otherwise destroy the smaller European companies. This is a concern, it seems to me, that cannot be dismissed lightly, but should be discussed with our European friends with all the patience and prudence we can muster. After all, the same fears were expressed not so long ago in the United States. Around 1900, discussions of big business in the United States were full of dark forebodings about how a handful of mammoth corporations would soon dominate the whole of American life.

Now that we have had 75 years of living with big business, analysts no longer make the same frightening projections. The reasons for the change in attitude are clear. For one thing, the forecasts of doom simply haven't come to pass. Industrial concentration ratios haven't changed in over 30 years. There are now over 5 million independent business firms, the vast bulk of them family owned and operated, doing business in the United States. Proportionate to population, this is about the same number as in 1900. At the same time, the public has been made aware that the steepest rise in mass living standards and individual opportunities in any nation at any time has occurred in the United States during the time when the economy has been strongly influenced by the efficiency and productivity of big business. Our economic growth, and the change in family income patterns that accompanied it, has raised all but a relatively small part of our population to a level on the income scale which is well above that of any other major nation.

It is true that many of the U.S. companies investing in Europe today are larger and more powerful than their European counterparts. In the absence of a common market in Europe, European companies in the past did not have the opportunity to grow the way the larger, homogeneous market of America has enabled our concerns to expand. But the specialized skills and worldwide experience of our big companies have much to contribute to the European economy and consumer. The question is whether they behave themselves as good corporate citizens. If not, measures should be taken against them by the host country, which, after all, is not powerless in such matters. If they are good citizens, as is the case with an ever-growing number, the benefits to the host country flowing from their investment will far exceed any adverse impact of their competition with local firms.

Moreover, a growing number of U.S. companies today are seeking partnership with European firms rather than outright acquisition. In this way many of the real or imagined threats to the European entrepreneur are eliminated. Large scale production and marketing demand bigness in many industries. Our European friends, through reasonable regulation and initiative, should seek to enjoy the benefits of size. Restrictive policies against U.S. investment will only tend to perpetuate the gap between our industry and theirs.

This is particularly true in the area of technology. There is growing evidence that the United States is gaining an impressive technological lead over European industry, as discussed elsewhere in this book. And there is growing evidence that this lead depends heavily on the large corporations that have both the management philosophy and the massive resources required for major research and development efforts. Europe cannot hope to share in this advance by severely restricting the larger U.S. companies or by otherwise opposing the growth of big corporations. Much study remains to be done to measure the impact of what has come to be known as the technological gap between the United States and Europe. But preliminary research in this area strongly suggests that the large U.S. companies operating in Europe are the best and most active avenues for the flow of technology.

In the remainder of this chapter, Gene Bradley shows how large U.S. companies can introduce more competition, know-how, and financial resources that will redound to the advantage of all Europeans.

4 PART 2 *Atlantic Council Report*

Corporate members of the American Chambers of Commerce in Europe—those already in place and in operation in Europe—would be the first to endorse David Rockefeller's conclusion; namely, that U.S. companies can and must so compete that the end result will "redound to the advantage of all Europeans."

Several years ago, the Council of American Chambers of Commerce in Europe felt compelled to produce a short paper on "The Posture of American Business in Europe." It gave heed to increasing anxiety from European producers and officials about not only American exports, but investments in Europe as well. It noted a deliberate campaign in some countries to tarnish the public image of American business, stating: "This is a concern that the American businessman can neither ignore nor lightly dismiss, in spite of the fact that antagonism toward American operations can by no means be identified as a general, or even widespread, attitude throughout Europe."

Whether European fears are justified or not, the AmCham report pointed out, they nevertheless constitute a factor which U.S. firms must seriously bear in mind.

What Fears Exist?

At an AmCham Belgian luncheon in Brussels on October 9, 1964, the Honorable John W. Tuthill, then U.S. Ambassador to the European Communities, defined reasons why there is so much talk in Europe about the size of American firms. Some Europeans fear that U.S. companies are so large that they can set their prices so low as to destroy their European competitors. He added:

> In part, this anxiety is promoted by those who fear *any* competition and who, for many years, have had little to worry about. And like their counterparts in any country, including the United States, they find it easiest to identify foreign competitors as the source of evil. . . . But mainly, Europeans worry that American business is so powerful that, whether located in the United States or abroad, it will eventually change the whole way of life in Europe.

In reality, as the AmCham report concluded, the fear of U.S. dominance would appear to be exaggerated. There are extensive national controls in every European country with respect to foreign investment, quite apart from regulations being developed within the European Economic Community. In the eyes of these seasoned American observers, present European fears of "colonization" by U.S. industries would seem to stem from a reluctance to accept what Americans have begun to consider as one of the new basic facts of life for all companies. Specifically, most American businessmen consider that a "one-world concept" is essential for all companies if they are to stay competitive in the world race for markets. They believe that resistance to foreign companies merely reflects a continuing nationalistic effort to perpetuate protectionist tendencies—the same kind of protectionism which the Common Market is attempting to eliminate within its own walls.

There are cases, of course, where fear of U.S. dominance can be substantiated by the facts, as the AmCham report observed:

The U.S. companies concerned undoubtedly are aware of this, and in their own interest should be ever heedful of the antagonisms that such a situation arouses—and align their policies accordingly.

From America, Dr. Alfred C. Neal, president of the Committee for Economic Development, also cautions that European companies and countries are frankly awed at the power—financial and managerial—which U.S. companies can muster:

We must face the fact that in the eyes of most foreign governments, even in Western Europe, American companies are frightening by their sheer size.

He noted statistics which are preoccupying much of Europe, such as that it takes the total sales of 13 of the largest European companies to equal sales of General Motors Corporation. (The validity of such comparisons is questioned, later in this chapter, by Chase Manhattan's Otto Schoeppler, operating in Germany.)

Total U.S. Investments in Europe

As noted earlier, concern over the total of U.S. investments in Europe is not a matter of overall magnitude. Direct U.S. investments account for about 1 percent of all investments in Western Europe and for only 1.4 percent of total investments in France, the center of greatest concern. But in specific fields, the proportion can run extremely high. French sources say that U.S. investment accounts for 90 to 100 percent of the total investment in several of that country's industries, including computer, synthetic rubber, and photographic products, and for about 50 percent of the investment in the agricultural equipment, elevator, oil, and cosmetics industries.

The practical implications of all this were summarized by Dr. Neal as follows:

63

The anti-American attitude toward major investments in important industries is now stronger than it has ever been before. The foreign control of American investment can be counted upon to be a growing problem in all of the developed countries. It should receive attention at the highest levels and should probably be a major factor in the work of the Organization for Economic Cooperation and Development.

Building Larger European Firms

The increasing talk of building exclusively European corporations is not just a threat by French nationalists, as is often supposed. It is true that the French are among the most concerned. But as Dr. Antonie Knoppers has pointed out in his introduction to the previous chapter, the French are seeing with increasing clarity the limitations on their own powers to act unilaterally. They recognize that any restrictions must be applied through the EEC. To shut the Americans out of France would merely shunt new investments (with their new technologies) to other Common Market countries, thereby strengthening their technological positions vis-à-vis France.

Because of its strategic position in Europe—in geography, size, and power—Germany presents a particularly interesting case study. Otto Schoeppler, vice president of Chase Manhattan Bank for Germany and the most recent president of the Council of American Chambers of Commerce in Europe, provided a useful vignette of the investment picture:

1. The total direct American investment in Germany at the end of 1964 was estimated at $2.3 billion. This represents about 3.5 percent of the direct investments in Germany.
2. The number of American firms doing business in Germany has been exaggerated. A reliable estimate is 1,100 companies, a somewhat misleading figure because the number of American companies with manufacturing facilities was estimated at just over 400. Of these, 171 were listed with a capital investment DM 1 million (one million deutsche marks) or more.
3. Of these 171 companies, 110 were reported to have exclusively German management. In other words, 65 percent of the American manufacturing subsidiaries with a capital of DM 1 million or over are managed exclusively by German personnel.
4. In terms of labor, a very scarce item in Germany, it was estimated that all American companies doing business in Germany employ about 290,000

people, which represents approximately 1 percent of the total German labor force.

5. In terms of sales, American companies in Germany accounted for $3 billion which represents only 3.2 percent of the German GNP. These, in turn, provide a substantial boost to German exports. Opel and Ford, for example, export about 45 percent of their production, International Harvester about 50 percent, and Deere-Lanz about 40 percent.

6. In terms of size, of the 35 largest companies in Germany (based on 1963 sales), only 3 American companies were listed. The largest of those was Esso (Standard Oil of New Jersey), in 10th place, followed by Opel, which ranked 18th.

Mr. Schoeppler then dealt specifically with the question of size, noting that it has recently become fashionable to compare large American companies with some small country's national budget or GNP. "Such comparisons make a vivid impression," he said.

But playing with statistics is a two-edged sword. Today this technique is being used against large American firms. Who knows where it will be used tomorrow? Moreover, the fact that the comparisons are irrelevant does not seem to dampen the enthusiasm of the users. Let me give you a few examples of how the game works:

It has recently been mentioned in the press that the sales of the top 20 U.S. corporations are as large as the GNP of the Federal Republic.

The insignificance of a statement like this can be emphasized by a counter-example. The sales of the top seven European firms are greater than the GNP of all of Australia ($19.5 billion); those of the top two greater than that of Austria ($7.6 billion). While General Motors' sales are roughly equal to the sales of the top 13 German firms, at the same time, the sales of Europe's largest company (Royal Dutch Shell) equal those of the top 10 French firms.

Another example:

It has been said that the sales of the top five U.S. firms are equal to the GNP of Italy. Picking a country which has one fourth the population of Italy (for Italy has one fourth of the U.S.) we find that sales of the top five Italian firms are well above the GNP of Portugal (i.e., $3.6 billion versus $2.9 billion).

One more example:

To say that the sales of GM are greater than the German budget has as much meaning as to say that Volkswagen's sales are greater than the Swiss budget; Siemens' sales greater than the Spanish budget; or Daimler-Benz' greater than Denmark's.

Large European Firms Also Giants

Mr. Schoeppler assumed that the purpose of making comparisons such as these was to point out the fact that America has some large corporations:

No one would deny that the United States does have large corporations. But we must not forget that U. S. corporations are large because the American economy is large. American firms serve a domestic market of 200 million people in an economy which generates tremendous disposable income. By comparison, the large European corporations are really giants when considered within the framework of their respective national economies. Switzerland supports a Nestlé, Holland a Royal Dutch Shell and a Unilever, Germany, a full third of the top 50 European companies.

Moreover, European firms are much more internationally oriented than the oft-castigated U.S. corporations. Volkswagen makes 60 percent of its sales outside the borders of Germany—GM only 19 percent outside the United States. Farbenfabriken Bayer sells 49 percent of its production to foreign purchasers, versus only 17 percent for the largest U.S. chemical corporation, Du Pont. Comparing the largest food packagers of the United States and Europe, Nestlé makes the vast majority of its sales outside of Switzerland, whereas General Foods sells over 90 percent of its output in the United States.

I could go on and on with comparisons like these, but I hope the point has been made. If anyone in Europe begins talking about restricting the free flow of goods and capital in the international sphere, it appears to me that he is striking a blow at the very heart of his own economy. Bear in mind, the United States exports only 4 percent of its GNP—Germany exports nearly 16 percent.

Mr. Schoeppler then came to grips with a somewhat popular complaint that American companies are so powerful, with a preponderance of their strength anchored back in the United States, that they could afford to "dump" their overseas operations at the first sign of recession, depression, or other trouble. He recalled that since 1914 Europe has been embroiled in two major world wars and in the world's most serious economic depression. During this period, the 13 top U.S. firms in Germany have weathered at least two, and in most cases three, of these catastrophies. All are still in Germany, growing and contributing to the German economy. These companies represent at least 75 percent of the total American investment in Germany. "What better proof could one have," Mr. Schoeppler asked, "that the

American companies do not pack up and run home at the first sign of a dark cloud?" These companies are Esso, Opel, Mobil, Ford, IBM, SEL, Esso Tank-schiff, Titangesellschaft, International Harvester, F. W. Woolworth, Deutsche Maizena, National Cash Register, and Singer.

Essential Issue Is Psychological

Reduced to essentials, the basis of the movement to isolate American business in Europe is much less economic and political than psychological. Politically, most Europeans continue to favor strong ties across the Atlantic. Economically, there are far greater needs for new investment over the next decade than there are capital funds available in Europe.

The psychological concern is illustrated by the criticism received by many European firms who have found that foreign mergers, joint ventures, and other arrangements are the honorable alternatives to going out of business. Such criticism scarcely seems just, as Otto Schoeppler pointed out in Germany:

> Would you criticize a person in distress for accepting help—a drowning man for reaching for a life belt—or would you accept the life belt only if it happened to be thrown by a fellow national? What real difference is there in whether a company is purchased by a British, French, American, or another German corporation? Is not really the only important point whether or not a corporate life has been saved and continues to exist in the interest of the national economy?
>
> I would also like to observe here briefly that there have been a number of incidents where both a German and an American company were competing to purchase an existing German corporation. In many cases the German company was the successful bidder, from which you can draw your own conclusions. However, I am not criticizing this—for this is simply the force of competition and free enterprise at work.

In Britain, to illustrate a lack of psychological concern, the vice president of a large international bank reminded us of the lack of British opposition to American business, even though U.S. investments there are heavier than anywhere else in Europe. He recalled that he had not seen any publicity on a statement made by a British official that more than half of the 150 firms in the United Kingdom which account for 85 percent of the nation's total exports are American subsidiaries. There was no complaint, apparently, because these U.S. companies are exporters, contributing significantly to the U.K.'s balance of payments. "The United Kingdom is trying to alleviate its economic problems by promoting exports, and the people who are doing the best job are American subsidiaries," the banker added. "The only people who have been hurt are the inefficient operators."

Even though the United States and Britain have a common language and similar cultural traditions, it nevertheless is significant that we enjoy such good relations despite the magnitude of U.S. investments on U.K. soil. This volume now exceeds $4.5 billion (or approximately three times the size of U.S. investments in France). A case could be made to prove the opposite point: that relations are good because of—not in spite of—these cooperative ventures. In fact, all over Europe, relationships are often best at the private, business-to-business level.

68   *Dimensions of Good Public Relations*

The conclusion is that it is not so much a question of size and power as of how they are employed. In its deepest sense, it is a question of common interest and of acceptance within the community. Olivier Giscard d'Estaing, former managing director of the European Institute of Business Administration at Fontainebleau, recently underlined the importance of public opinion and the value of identifying the company with the host community rather than with its foreign home of origin:

As a child, I thought that Esso was a French firm closely related to the oil (essence) business, not knowing that it meant S.O. for the Standard Oil Company of New Jersey. Singer had always been used in our childhood life around the house, and became a part of our personal life. At a recent London automobile show, 30 percent of the people interviewed thought that Ford was a British-controlled company. For old, established firms in foreign countries, the foreign image is practically unknown and unharmful. However, for newcomers, specific action has to be taken to give a familiar concept to the product, the branch, and the company name.

There is ample evidence that good public relations is part of the answer. We hear few, if any, major criticisms of Kodak, Coca-Cola, and several score of others that long ago refined their psychological and social approaches to overseas communities and markets. Most important of all, such companies have participated in the host country, so as to give its government, industry, associations, management, labor, consumers, and investors the feeling that the company is operating in their interest.

A good public relations approach begins with country and site selection. It includes motivation for joining the community in the first place. It embraces a new concept of "identification" which relates more closely to the business than to the United States (or any other country of origin). It can and often should involve a more energetic public affairs program per se. And it should enlist the support of all individuals and organizations, government and private, with a stake in U.S. business success. These dimensions are vital if "bigness" is to be understood and accepted. Let us review each one briefly.

Choosing the Location. Potential investors have a very attractive psychological advantage as they shop for plant location. There are still many countries and companies competing for their business. This "seller's market" has helped to curb some of the anti–U.S. business tendencies that might otherwise go unchallenged.

Motivation. Once the location is selected, the job is to become a part of it. How much does the newcomer company want to "belong"? The problem is essentially the same whether the company is a European one going into the United States or a U.S. company going into Europe. Here is an example of each:

Italy-based Olivetti has established itself in the United States quite successfully. According to Sergio Pizzoni-Ardemani, special assistant to the president: "We could very easily have continued to manufacture our typewriters wherever we wanted and import them free of duty to the U.S., but our thinking went beyond tariff restrictions. We believed that if we really wanted to be part of the industrial scene in the U.S., we could not merely sell products made elsewhere. This placed us in a marginal position. We wanted to be here as participants in the U.S. industrial and commercial life. The basic element must be the will to belong, not to just happen to be in a country to overcome some artificial barriers."

Raytheon chairman Charles F. Adams would appear to agree, based on his company's experience in Italy: "We haven't gone in very much for trying to build up an image. We have built up an organization that could bid successfully on communications systems against tough competition. The reputation we have acquired has been built around being a good competitor. In close government relations I think we have come out very well. In fact, the Italian government has given us certain recognition for what we have done to help build a strong electronics activity in Italy."

Identification. An important part of the correct psychological or diplomatic approach is to avoid identifying the company with the "greatness of America." According to John V. Deaver, vice president of the Chase Manhattan Bank, many companies are becoming almost "a-national" in character in the sense that the flag doesn't really follow the company. Mr. Deaver believes that as more and more American corporations go overseas, they are increasingly recruiting their top people abroad. "Those who don't do this still go to great lengths to try to be corporate citizens of their hosts' countries. It is getting harder and harder to identify these companies as being purely American."

In the judgment of a U.S. international vice president formerly heading one of America's largest subsidiaries in Canada, host-nation identity is the key. "If we achieve this, in time the degree of foreign ownership will be forgotten, just as we don't know the ownership of many companies that are operating in this country. We judge them by what they are. An ideal foreign enterprise in time loses its foreign identity, gains its own identity, and lives by its own citizenship." Americans have long forgotten that at the beginning of this century approximately 30 percent of the value of American industry was owned by Europeans, which certainly did not retard U.S. development or jeopardize the national interest.

The theme "stress the company, not the country" was sounded again and again across Europe and in America during the course of our Atlantic Council study. Building a company identity is considered good business—and not disloyal to the United States. To extol the virtues of an American company or an American product—or of any foreign company or product—often tends to roughen rather than smooth relationships. (There are cases when a broad nationalized approach *is* good business—e.g., Swiss watches, French perfume, Belgian lace, German cameras, and perhaps American computers. But these are the exceptions.)

Building the Public Affairs Program. There is a real need for thoughtful, factual, and persuasive public relations to communicate the fact that many of the uncomfortable adjustments now under way would have been inevitable—even without the American stimulus—as Europe proceeded to create its own integrated mass market.

The starting point is broader understanding within the company. But a number of authorities believe that, in parallel, the story can be carried to the consumer, who should be, after all, the ultimate beneficiary. As the treasurer of a large U.S. manufacturing company stated, "One of the great voids is that we say nothing about the consumer." He added that American business, probably because it has not been broadly enough based, has not done a good job in public relations in Europe. "I think that we and other large companies should constantly keep before the nationals of the countries in which we operate the benefits which we contribute. We are not doing this, probably because we are too new there."

Reaching the consumer means direct advertising as well as institutional public relations. The American vice president of a group of manufacturing businesses observed that Europeans, in contrast to Americans, are used to "buying" rather than "being sold." European marketing methods still leave much to be desired, he added. "The consumer doesn't have the same opportunity to see products displayed or to get a purchase serviced. Tools such as display, advertising, servicing, and leasing, are not well known in Europe, and it's this marketing know-how which would be of great benefit to many European companies and consumers."

The Atlantic Institute's Ambassador Walter Dowling concurs that Americans, reported to be the masters of public relations and advertising, have failed to get their message across to the European people, to the business community, and above all to the intellectuals who, as in most countries, are among the key opinion molders.

"Certainly American investment has brought growth, new technology, tax revenues, technical skills for the labor force, and many other benefits to Europe," Ambassador Dowling points out. "And this is freely acknowledged by those who have studied the matter; but you would never know this if you listened to many Europeans today." Ambassador Dowling then quoted one of his European colleagues:

Business, including American business, operates in a fundamentally more hostile atmosphere in Europe than does business in the U.S. Many of the key assumptions which you make without question—the desirability of profitable enterprise, the importance of serving the consumer, the value of mass production and distribution—these ideas must be constantly fostered in Europe; particularly the American contribution to them must be well told.

Enlisting Support from Others. An international banker headquartered in New York suggested that American Chambers of Commerce do more to show how U. S. business activity benefits both the United States and Europe. He acknowledged the danger that such efforts could appear self-serving. But the danger can be minimized if the focus is on economic rather than political issues. American companies cannot duck responsibility for bringing facts into the open. He added: "I do not think that the French fully understand the benefits which multinational competition has brought to them. We should illustrate and publish how these benefits have been achieved. These facts have not been brought before the public in any of the European countries, as far as I know."

The proposal for a concerted public relations program may seem at first to run counter to the earlier proposal for companies to "work themselves into the landscape." If thoughtfully worked out and applied, however, the two proposals should supplement, not conflict with, each other. At the one extreme there are mass communications, needed to win consumer acceptance for new products and practices which may have had their origin in America but their impact in Europe; this does not mean boasting of them as American. At the other extreme are selective public relations, needed to gain understanding from a relatively few individuals, perhaps no more than a dozen officials from government, labor, and industry associations. In all instances, whether promoting a new product or resolving a labor dispute, the messages should deal with facts and issues, not countries and nationalities. Understanding is wanted not for the country, but for the company, doing business in Europe. A grievous error would be a "Made in America" campaign to sell U.S. products, policies, and people into the hearts of Europeans.

Is "Big" Business "Bad"?

Preaching the benefits of mass production and modern marketing does little to calm the anxieties of the corner grocery store owner as he sees a giant supermarket being built in the next block. Extolling the virtues of superhighways finds a rather unreceptive audience among the merchants whose stores are being bypassed and home-owners whose houses are being bulldozed away. But do these personal hardships mean that there should be no supermarkets and no free-ways?

Change *is* painful; and to many, it seems particularly objectionable when related to big companies.

In introducing this chapter, David Rockefeller discusses the pop-ular notion that it is automatically "bad" to be "big."

Such a notion dismisses lightly—and with dangerous implications —the basic truth that it takes large companies, in partnership with medium-sized and small companies, to tackle the giant industrial programs (and social problems) of this century. As already noted, meeting humanity's urgent needs will require a "systems approach" by large world corporations, working independently and in consortia —and in concert with the public sector—on a scale far surpassing today's boldest corporate ventures. This is the need, the trend, and the probable outcome. But this does not relieve the corporate execu-tive from painstaking care in helping to usher in these changes as painlessly as possible.

In Europe, what can American companies do about their own "big-ness"? One suggestion, which sparked little enthusiasm among the U.S. executives who examined the problem at the Crotonville con-ference, was that the American companies should "exercise dis-cipline" in expansion plans until "European companies have built up resources more equal in nature." In short—tread water while the competition swims forward. Leaving U.S. companies out of the equa-tion altogether, European companies will still face the psychological problem of bigness as they find larger and still larger corporations an absolute requirement.

It might, therefore, be useful to review the rationale of two American businessmen—M. J. Rathbone, former chairman of Standard Oil of New Jersey, and Joseph C. Wilson, president of the Xerox Corporation—who analyzed the "big business" and "small business" story in the January–March 1966 issue of *The General Electric FORUM*, devoted to business and economic growth.

Mr. Rathbone, an acknowledged spokesman for big business, stressed the importance and permanent place of small business, and the interdependence of large and small businesses in our diverse economy. "My company, and most other large companies, depend on small businessmen not only as customers, but as suppliers of countless products and services which they can provide effectively and expertly, often at lower cost."

In turn, Mr. Wilson, representing a small business which had obviously found the key to swift growth, defined the success formula in just three words: a "fiery entrepreneurial spirit." His whole point was a plea to "forget the statistical approach in evaluating business, big or little, and turn instead to evaluations of individuals." He also refuted what he termed "an almost unconscious, subtle assumption that big business, per se, is evil." He then outlined the program followed by Xerox which can put large and small companies into productive partnership.

Continuing the dialogue, Standard Oil's Rathbone outlined five positive economic and social values that go with bigness:

1. Big manufacturing plants, up to a point, enjoy certain economies of scale which can mean lower unit costs, lower prices to the consumer.
2. Large firms, because of the size of their financial, personnel, and physical resources, can engage in ventures beyond the reach of smaller firms.
3. Because of their greater resources, large firms are often better able to withstand short-term adversity. They thus exert a stabilizing effect on both the economy and the society.
4. Large firms which are integrated vertically have the advantage of a steady, reliable flow at each stage between raw materials and retailing. This enables them to plan their expansion with greater assurance, and thus makes them a more efficient source of expansion for the whole economy.

5. Because of their greater capability to do independent research, large firms are a major source of technological progress, which directly benefits the consumer in price, quality, and range of choice.

Mr. Wilson, whose company bridged the gap between small and large companies in quite a short time, urged that mutual suspicions between associates of larger and smaller elements of business be swept aside so as to permit growth of all businesses, large and small. While the small businessman should have wholehearted encouragement, he does not want special privileges. On the contrary, Mr. Wilson suspects that the small businessman would much prefer an attitude of helpfulness on the part of the stronger. "All of us," he concluded, "should have the common sense to work with the new entrepreneurs and share experience with them. Our economy needs efficiency on all levels of commercial endeavor, and the greater efficiency we achieve, the healthier our society, the better for us all."

These points are especially applicable to the current discussions of American bigness in relation to European companies.

Alternatives for Europeans

Recognizing the formidable competition coming from powerful American companies, what are the alternatives for Europeans in "the new competition"?

First, they can form a tighter European "club," without Americans: mergers among Europeans only. Although in the minority, there are strong proponents for this approach. In essence, it is a larger form of the kind of nationalism which seeks the benefits of larger business units, but still within the confines of a limited geographical area.

This concept disregards a wide popular sentiment within the business community which would actually prefer an association with an American company, all things equal, because of the experience and resources which the American company can bring into the partnership. There is a modified "Common Market approach" which advocates eventual partnership with Americans, but not until European corporate units have been built up to be more nearly equal to those in America. In the judgment of many, this postponing of American partnership is equivalent to the postponing of progress.

The *second* alternative is for mergers on an international scale regardless of nationality (including with Americans). As the next chapter, "The Question of Management Attitudes and Practices," will show, a convincing case can be developed that the source of ownership is a minor issue provided the "guest" corporation becomes truly indigenous to the host nation, in terms of management, direction, research and development, labor practices, export policy and goals, support of the national and regional plan, and other considerations of life-or-death economic importance to the nation.

The *third* approach—failure to merge—is "unthinkable" but not impossible. Much in history, including military and economic warfare, is "unthinkable." It is not difficult to construct a series of unfortunate events which could trigger restrictions and reprisals from nation to nation at an escalating rate. As will also be analyzed in a future chapter, a failure in the GATT negotiations would have given much aid and comfort to the protectionist forces in all countries which are seeking ways to return to the trade, tariff, and investment barriers which enlightened public and private executives in all nations have worked so hard to bring down.

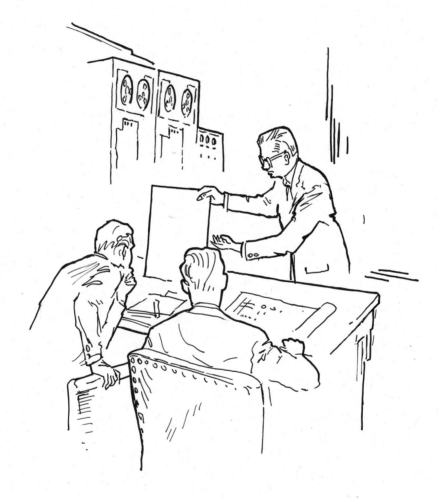

5 The Question of Management Attitudes and Practices

PART 1 Introduction
by Fritz Berg

Mr. Fritz Berg has been president of the Bundesverband der Deutschen Industrie E.V. (Federal Association of German Industries) since its founding in 1950. A strong proponent of private initiative and free enterprise, he heads one of the most modern steel wire factories in Europe. Since the early postwar days, Mr. Berg has been committed to European and Atlantic cooperation. In 1951, he led the first German industrialists' delegation to the International Industrialists' Congress in New York. He also played an important role in the efforts for an agreement between France and Germany, took part in the founding of the Council of European Industrial Associations, and was a member of the advisory and technical committee for the Schumann Plan.

Photo by Jos. Josuweck, Koln

Fortunately for all of us, the economic Atlantic Community is no longer a distant goal, nor a matter for idealistic dreaming. It is a living reality. In fact, the recurring tensions and frictions between the members of this community, especially between Americans and Europeans, are a sign of its liveliness.

It is no secret that these tensions and frictions do exist, and that they center on the so-called "invasion of American capital." Originally, most of the criticism was voiced in France, but now it is hardly less in Germany and the rest of Europe, although it is done with more reserve in public in these areas.

It does not matter whether the criticism is well founded or not.

What does matter is that unless it is corrected, it can have, as Ambassador Walter Dowling has pointed out, "a devastating effect on the Atlantic Community and all of its participants."

In introducing this chapter on management attitudes and practices, I would like to note at the outset that, in my view, the attitudes and practices of industrial management on both sides of the Atlantic contribute less to the tensions and frictions which exist than do the attitudes and actions of some politicians. It seems to me that the main reason for the resistance of European businessmen to American investment is not the over-Americanization of our economies. Neither in France nor in the rest of Europe is this the primary cause of resistance. Rather, I believe the main reason is more likely to be political policies.

Where Business Influence Needed

Thus, management's foremost responsibility should be to persuade the governments that Atlantic deeds are now more important than Atlantic words. There are several areas where business influence should be brought to bear on political policies, with favorable results for all parties.

The first of these is the continuing U.S. balance of payments defi-

cit, where some business concern has already been demonstrated. Many Europeans feel, rightly or wrongly, that the deficit in the American balance of payments exists mainly because of the high level of private American investments abroad. They feel that European nations who hold dollar surpluses are, in effect, "financing" the U.S. deficit and the "invasion of American capital." Thus, the businessman into whose industry American money finds its way, either through a merger or direct take-over, suddenly views the continued financing of the American payments deficit with considerable alarm.

Similarly, U.S. trade policies exercise a stronger influence on the European businessman's attitude toward the Atlantic Community than do the practices of American managers in Europe. Again, rightly or wrongly, many Europeans feel U.S. export and import regulations are quite restrictive. And the trade barriers of excess tariffs or wide disparities in duties have been certainly a greater handicap for both the Kennedy Round of tariff negotiations and for Atlantic Community cooperation than any ill-advised practices by American managements in Europe.

In many respects, European businessmen cannot help thinking that they have succeeded better than their American colleagues in convincing their governments of the measures needed to facilitate national competitive strength and export growth. Even across the unpleasant gulf which exists between the European Free Trade Association and the Common Market, businessmen speak with a single voice on many of the key issues, especially those involving tariff policies.

Laws to Ease Mergers

The question of corporate size has recently occupied a place of importance in the thinking of European businessmen, and considerable attention is being paid to the need for creating European corporate laws to make mergers easier within the Common Market. Thus, corporate coalitions could be formed which would be more likely to stand up against the competition of American "giants."

At the Fourteenth International Management Congress of Conseil International pour l'Organisation Scientifique (CIOS) in Rotterdam in autumn 1966, attended by large numbers of American businessmen, F. H. Ulrich, member of the board of directors of the Deutsche Bank A.G., spoke on, "Adapting Entrepreneurial Size to Economic Growth." In this speech he attempted "to throw a glaring light" on the differences in size. The production of one single American company, General Motors, is larger than that of the 12 million inhabitants of The Netherlands, he said, continuing:

This company's *profit* for the year 1965 was DM 8,500 million, which was nearly as high as the *total sales* of the Volkswagenwerk A.G. group, amounting to DM 9,300 million. U.S. Steel's net worth is roughly three times that of the seven big steel companies in the Rhine and Ruhr area, and its turnover nearly equals that of all these German companies. Four American automobile makers annually produce nearly 8 million passenger cars, whereas within the Common Market 5 million cars are manufactured by more than 20 firms. The quoted stock market value of American Telephone and Telegraph is more than two-fifths higher than that of all German companies listed on stock exchanges.

Under these circumstances it cannot come as a surprise to anyone that European businessmen place particular importance on the construction of internationally competitive corporate coalitions.

Mr. Ulrich also added this comment:

Support for entrepreneurial growth, even if it involves mergers and thus concentration, does not mean that one should reject certain controls in this respect. One can entirely agree with the continued functioning of supervisory authorities such as the Cartels Office in the Federal Republic of Germany and the antitrust authorities in the United States.

However, I would like to supplement this idea by pointing out that national competition regulations no longer meet the requirements of the Atlantic Community. In the European Economic Community the need already exists for common competition and corporate laws. Sometime, the same will probably apply to the Atlantic Community.

Competitive regulations tend to create uncertainties on the national front. Lengthy procedures to find out whether a business measure is permitted or not in certain circumstances are not compatible with the requirements of an economic community such as the Atlantic Community.

It is impossible to require that productivity-improving investments be put off for years, or prevented altogether, by bureaucratic bullying, on the pretense that competition is in danger of being infringed.

The Challenge of the European Businessman

In summary, I would like to say that compared to political obstacles, corporate management attitudes and practices are relatively insignificant blocks to increased Atlantic Community cooperation. The disintegration of NATO, for example, is a greater drawback for the Atlantic Community than U.S.–European differences in the Kennedy Round.

At the same time, the closer the community moves economically, the less the temporary—or perhaps permanent—disintegration symptoms in the military field are likely to affect it. The task for businessmen, therefore, is to endeavor to persuade their governments to remove the political obstacles to closer cooperation. To use a favorite American saying: The European businessman not only feels challenged; he himself is challenging, too.

5 PART 2 *Atlantic Council Report*

As we conducted the Atlantic business climate survey among American executives, we found three kinds of response to our query, "What are some of the major antagonisms or problems which you have found in doing business in the new Europe of the mid–1960's?"

The first and largest group supplied problems of the nature developed at length in this book. This was the norm. Even the most seasoned executives were aware of the growing European apprehension of American business expansion.

A second group, often with a touch of bewilderment, said, *"What problems?"* This was a legitimate response. They had "worked themselves into the landscape" so thoroughly and so successfully so long ago that their problems were no greater than those of corporations of European origin.

The third group—fortunately a relatively small minority—replied substantially as did the second: "We have no problems other than those normally encountered in doing business in the United States." In truth, these were companies which did have problems, and often in large measure; but they were so new on the European scene that they did not recognize the customs they were breaking, the sensitivities they were chafing, the antagonisms they were creating for everything American.

What Are the Criticisms?

These are some of the main criticisms, most of which center on the question of management attitudes and practices:

1. Reluctance of Americans to learn languages and customs, wives especially.
2. Lack of sensitivity in labor relations.
3. Avoidance of contacts with established local business leaders and failure to join industry associations.
4. Inadequate advance planning and therefore failure to stay in business.
5. Major corporate decisions made by home offices in the United States rather than by subsidiaries on the spot in Europe.
6. 100 percent U.S. ownership instead of joint ventures.
7. Ignoring or even defying a host government's national plan.
8. Buying of companies simply for the sake of quick profit rather than investing in areas where a national need could be met (R&D, employment, exports, etc.).
9. Insufficient hiring of local managers.

Good citizenship cannot be legislated, either for Americans in Europe or for Europeans in America, or for any nationality operating outside its borders. Nor can enlightened management and production methods be abandoned simply because they disturb the status quo. A hard-and-fast "code of ethics" for multinational companies could only serve to freeze both Europeans and Americans to the now-obsolete past at the very moment when flexibility and fresh approaches are needed.

The best that can be said is that the give-and-take play of the marketplace will force changes in management thinking through the sheer process of time and events. But it is the appearance of cavalier methods—more often unthinking than intentional—which spurs editorialists such as Pierre Bernard, writing in *La Nouvelle Republique*, to challenge French manufacturers to "get together to stand up to the menace from America."

In fairness to both Europeans and Americans, we must note that an appraisal of press reports indicates that despite the fears, many serious Europeans would far rather have "the American presence" than try to live without it. For example:

The invasion of American firms is one of the best things that has ever happened to British industry.—*The Observer*.

(French businessmen are) unconcerned with whom they buy from, or with the possibility of eventual American economic domination, as against the immediate advantage of cheaper prices and better quality.—Maurice Duverger, *Le Monde* (citing a poll published in the October 31, 1964 issue of *Enterprise*, which showed 75 percent of French businessmen interviewed would prefer to see a large French firm taken over by foreigners than to see it nationalized).

With respect to foreign investments [in Belgium] it must be said that these have been beneficial in terms of introducing new industries and diversifying the economy, as well as stimulating employment.—Frederic Osterreith, president of Antwerp Chamber of Commerce.

Two Examples: The Netherlands and France

1. *The Netherlands.* The Dutch, above all, should be sympathetic with the growing phenomenon of great world corporations. The most recent *Fortune* listing of top foreign corporations places 3 from Holland in the top 10: Royal Dutch Shell in first place, with 1965 sales topping $7 billion (larger than any American corporation except for General Motors, Ford, and Standard Oil of New Jersey); Unilever in

second place, with over $4 billion; and Philips' Gloeilampenfabrieken, ranking seventh and topping $2 billion. If we were to play a numbers game, which is largely meaningless, we could compute that the sales of these three Dutch firms exceed the combined output of the following American companies:

Firestone Tire and Rubber Co.	Singer Sewing Machine Co.
General Foods Corp.	Deere & Co.
Eastman Kodak Co.	Coca-Cola Co.
United Aircraft Corp.	Colgate-Palmolive Co.
Caterpillar Tractor Co.	Borg-Warner Corp.
B. F. Goodrich Co.	Douglas Aircraft Co.

It would be safe to generalize that the fear of Shell or Unilever would be practically nonexistent in most American communities, thanks to the good business practices of these companies. Yet even the Dutch are worried about large U.S. companies. They are concerned over what they term great differences between U.S. and European philosophies of doing business. This concern exists despite a very special relationship between The Netherlands and the United States—cultural, historical, economic—resting upon a basic love of freedom and democracy. Dutchmen are said to feel much closer to the United States than to most of the major countries in Europe.

Note that the Dutch are not overly disturbed over possible U.S. dominance in Dutch industries. But in the words of one Dutch businessman, they do become concerned that "Americans lack sensitivity." As one businessman told us in The Hague, "Americans live here exactly as they would back in the United States and do not care what goes on in a Dutchman's mind. It is a question of viewpoint. For example, take the question of labor. In Holland, labor 'belongs' to the company rather than to the union. This is a very important point. It is not decent to take labor away from another company and pay 10 cents more, because it is not the money that counts."

Because of Holland's basically sympathetic attitude towards all Americans and their desire to work ever more closely with us, it is useful to review major Dutch concerns over U.S. methods and their proposals for better understanding. These are voiced in varying degrees of intensity in most of the countries studied in Europe:

1. Labor practices as described above.
2. Lack of proper investigation into local laws, customs and regulations before embarking on a new venture.
3. Higher paid U.S. managers working with lower paid Dutch managers.
4. Lack of authority by the Dutch subsidiary to make certain routine operating decisions based on local conditions without first obtaining home office approval.
5. Unwillingness or inability of Americans to abide by established systems concerning price levels and market distribution.
6. Basic conflicts in legal systems, particularly involving antitrust matters (giving rise to psychological and emotional reactions against U.S. business).
7. General lack of sensitivity to Holland's urgent and changing needs.

For example, with acute labor, housing, and construction materials shortages, the last thing the Dutch need is new heavy industry with great demands on all three resources. Should a company devise a plan to satisfy housing wants (where newly married couples have been waiting as long as seven or eight years to get a house), they would be greeted with open arms. The same would hold for companies offering labor- or material-saving methods. American businessmen operating in Holland confirmed the above points, and proposed that businessmen entering the country for the first time use them as guides in establishing corporate policies.

2. *France.* France is often credited—rightly or wrongly—with being at the other end of the "receptivity" spectrum. French industry, historically protectionist, is undergoing drastic reforms requiring new technology and an industrial base geared to the larger EEC markets. This reform, coupled with a shortage of private French capital and the fear of being hemmed in by larger and wealthier U.S. firms, accounts for some of the psychological or emotional reactions of French business towards U.S. investments. Yet, outside capital—including American capital—is openly recognized as a necessity.

The picture in France is neither black nor white. A high French official told us that there is no official policy against U.S. investments, and that investments are encouraged where they:

1. Bring new technology to France.
2. Reduce French imports.
3. Expand French exports.
4. Use French labor.

5. Help to build the economy of a particular region within France.
6. Meet a need of the French government's economic plan.

The only safe generalization is that it is not safe to generalize as to where and how Americans can succeed, country by country and region by region, in Europe. The key is not the place, so much as the methods applied; and these refer most specifically to: (1) labor; (2) supporting the national economic plan; and (3) local participation in management and ownership.

Clashing Labor Practices

No issue is more volatile in Europe than that of labor practices.

Americans, trained in the world's first mass market where productivity has become king, have had to learn to manage labor costs as a matter of straight survival. The same policies which to Americans are just and fair are often considered unwarranted in Europe. A negotiation which in America would be something to be settled privately between the managers and their employees would in Europe be of major concern to the government.

The cases of two American firms illustrate the point. To compete and stay in business, they had to dismiss some employees. The exact amount of advance consultation with the host government has not been revealed, but the reports are that it was inadequate. Such incidents, with their direct social implications affecting the worker in his community, have provoked a more widespread concern over U.S. investments. Referring to such instances, an international banking vice president said:

In closing down plants and releasing large numbers of employees, it is indeed unfortunate not to be aware that this isn't done without first having substantial advance consultation with the government. This is in order that operations can be phased out in such a way that they do not create political problems for other Americans in the host country.

He stressed the political effects, observing that such examples have been used frequently by protectionists as an outlet for other misgivings.

Obviously, a skillful policy in labor relations is of central importance to a new company. But this does not mean following by rote the often conservative European customs. As one Britisher emphasized, new management techniques and methods, after all, are often America's biggest contribution to European productivity—more important than technology itself. He illustrated as follows:

> At Fawley and Coriton refineries in Britain, American managements have pioneered a revolution in productivity and labor relations by bargaining on a plant basis with the unions and persuading them to sweep away a mass of restrictive practices and overtime in return for massive wage increases.

At the Crotonville conference, U.S. businessmen stressed this same point—that there are two fundamentally different concepts which have been brought into contact and sometimes into conflict in Europe. The European shift from a producer-oriented to a consumer-oriented economy is forcing a shift from a former emphasis on security to a new emphasis on productivity. As one conferee phrased it, "Any policies which inhibit productivity are bound to give way to policies which enhance productivity."

What can Americans do about this clash of concepts for which they are at least partially responsible? First, let us assume, with the Britisher, that to live with outmoded methods would negate the benefits of having Americans in Europe in the first place. This being the case, the answer has to lie in accepting responsibility which goes well beyond the average encountered in the United States. When it is necessary to break with precedent, the company must make clear, in advance, the need, logic, and advantages of its action. Americans experienced in the European climate do this as a matter of course. However, the newer companies often do not—and on them falls the burden of increased consultation with local officials. As U.S. businessmen affirm, it is usually possible to operate within the social framework of a country and still follow sound business practices.

Supporting the National Plan

Historically, American businessmen have considered their role to be that of satisfying the needs and wants of the people with a minimum of government interference or even coordination. Despite closer government-business contacts, the principle still holds in U.S. thinking that private companies do not look to the government for guidelines on how to work with public officials and with each other in developing new markets. On the contrary, the U.S. competitive system is often thought of as "dog-eat-dog," with the antitrust laws assuring the liveliest competition.

By contrast, European businessmen live with a precedent of working with the government and with each other for mutual progress and profit. An American investor unwilling (by nature) or unable (by law) to adopt this concept remains an outsider. The U.S. businessman who is suspect in America if he joins or forms a "fraternity" is suspect in Europe if he does not.

Clearly, the U.S. business leader can make things a good deal easier for his company if he can, in all good conscience, follow more closely the local example in this respect. The fact that some U.S. corporations have done this successfully—and without violating either the letter or the spirit of U.S. laws—should encourage other American businessmen.

The American businessman gets help from the U.S. Chamber of Commerce, the National Association of Manufacturers, and individual industry associations, but he does not expect them to negotiate for him with the government on specific corporate problems in labor or market development. By contrast, the European businessman does rely for such help on France's Patronat, Germany's Bundesverband der Deutschen Industrie (BDI), Belgium's Federation of Industry, and the other national trade associations with their vertical components for each separate industry. Not surprisingly, European business and government officials become upset at what they consider the independent, "standoffish" Americans. Thus:

Belgian Employees Association officials are said to resent the fact that U.S. businessmen do not take a more active part in the Belgian professional and employer associations which concentrate on labor practices, export drives to developing nations, and similar goals.

German businessmen believe that there should be more cooperation, more coordination, and more contact between U.S. companies and German executives. They would like to search out new methods with Americans to ensure "a smoother entrance of U.S. capital into Germany." Perhaps the most surprising statement we received in Europe during our Atlantic Council survey came from the head of one of the largest business associations in Germany. He said that not a single U.S. business manager, when shopping around for joint ventures or new business opportunities, had ever asked for his suggestions. He assured us that Americans would not prejudice their case even if they only listened to and then ignored German advice.

In Spain, during our Atlantic Council study, we were advised of American insensitivity to the Spanish temperament. It was explained to us that American attitudes which might be only minor irritants elsewhere could result in a major failure for a U.S. company in Spain. The proposed answer: "More contact between Spanish and U.S. businessmen to increase mutual confidence and to maintain Spanish receptivity to U.S. investment."

Contact does not have to be personal. It can be made through a third party. Americans can research their opportunities through sources other than the host country—for instance, their own overseas offices, U.S. banking institutions abroad (already "wired into" the local market), U.S. embassy officials, the American Chambers of Commerce in Europe, and a growing number of consultants and private organizations.

Many seasoned executives prefer exploring through U.S. channels because (*a*) this approach is more familiar; (*b*) they fear that dealing directly with host-country associations might result in prejudiced advice or might stir up opposition to their expansion plans; and (*c*) they are concerned that collaboration might lead them into an unhappy situation with U.S. antitrust laws.

However, other experienced Americans in Europe feel that it is possible and desirable to work closely with the associations and still avoid the pitfalls just described. One of the immediate advantages of the joint venture is that it automatically introduces the new effort into the European business stream.

Local Participation

Finally, deeds must match words. If Europeans are concerned about "domination" by American companies, at least one significant act can be offering them the opportunity for ownership in the company. This could include issuing for sale in the host country corporate bonds that are later convertible into common or preferred stock. A number of companies have done this in recent months, giving the host-nation citizens a feeling of participation in the company's operation. (Incidentally, such action does not go unnoticed by government officials in the United States, who see overseas bond sales as a constructive way to help America's balance of payments program.)

There is also a body of opinion which holds that managerial direction is more important to Europeans than ownership. James H. Goss, former international group vice president of General Electric Company, which has been operating on all continents since the turn of the century, has stated this view as follows:

If you're going to operate in a foreign country, you must have management that's competent to make the 98 percent of the decisions which must be made locally. I know of very few countries where we have been operating for 20 years where this isn't the case. We try as far as we can to have nationals participate to the fullest possible extent in the management of the companies. We try to bring the companies into harmony with the economies under which they operate. We try to have nationals on the board of directors and encourage their equity participation in the company. We try, as far as we possibly can, to respect the corporate status of these companies and exercise control only through our representation on the boards of directors of these companies.

An executive of a more recent entry in the European market, a U.S. aerospace-and-defense company, stated:

Our Italian business is run by an American-speaking Italian who was with us for many years in the States. He completely understands what is happening in the environment. We've used the best of American engineering, American technology, and American methods, but we have trained Italian people to put these methods into effect. This infusion has had to be done carefully, slowly, and selectively, with due consideration of what's good about our methods. All the know-how isn't on our side.

Another U.S. company which hung up its new-business shingle recently in France made the immediate decision to manage the operation out of Paris rather than New York. Management policy flows from the Paris-headquartered board of directors, consisting of Frenchmen and Americans in approximately equal proportions. The advanced planning and marketing organizations are also binational. The front-line management staff is largely French, although most top positions are backed by a competent American. To date, this joint venture with joint ownership and joint control is "on target" in its business plans.

The Personal Equation

Having stated the issues and cited cases, it is well to reduce the problem to its basic essential: the Golden Rule. John S. Andrews, vice president of Ford's European automotive group, summarized it as follows:

The achievement of Atlantic cooperation, without which the full potential of Atlantic economic growth cannot be achieved, depends in large measure upon minimizing the friction resulting from the day-to-day contacts of individuals from each of the nations making up the Atlantic Community. The essential lubricant required to minimize this friction is the universal understanding of and compliance with the differences in culture, traditions, practices, and languages within the community. In other words, let there be no "ugly Americans," nor, for that matter, "ugly Europeans," but rather a true community bound together by common aspirations and mutual understanding.

United States Ambassador John W. Tuthill sounded the same theme in his luncheon address to the American Chamber of Commerce in Belgium, cited earlier. What is happening in Europe does not mean that Americans should renounce honest and fair competition. "But we must be especially regardful," he said, "for local problems, for local tradition, and for local pride. These are problems which American firms face in the United States and which are often very successfully resolved. We can be no less attentive to them abroad."

New Breed of International Management

Many companies—but by no means all—have now passed the era where international managers were a separate group, spun off from the parent company, usually small in number, and too often forgotten when the time rolled around for promotions to key positions in the executive office. (For those companies which continue to hold to such concepts, the Council of European AmChams has some well-chosen words, included at the close of this chapter.) In a growing number of companies, international business is becoming one of the best approaches to "the front office," instead of a sometimes neglected commercial foreign legion. For every manager tapped for service abroad, there will be literally hundreds of others who will be measured and promoted on how well they accomplish their total mission, part of which will relate to international business.

As a result, today's world companies are attracting a higher and higher caliber of management. Europe is creating its own brand of "Eurocrats" who, in the eyes of one executive experienced in employment trends on the continent, would rather work for an American company in Europe than one of their own native origin. The reason is plausible. Young Europeans see their own national operations struggling to throw off nationalistic practices and prejudices, while American companies in Europe are logically freer of ties to any single nationalistic set of customs.

The above appraisal may seem to be contradictory. On one hand it is noted that the key to success in an international operation is for the local managers—regardless of their country of origin—to mold their operations into the host-national environment. On the other hand, it is noted that more and more Europeans are striving to throw off their national loyalties in favor of a truly international corporate operation. Both points are valid. At the end of the long haul (which is arriving more swiftly than most prophets would have dared to predict a decade ago), all people from all nations will be developing more kindred tastes, just as we have seen U.S. regional barriers disappearing since the beginning of World War II.

What is fervently hoped by many Americans as well as Europeans is that the unique, distinctive, and delightful national tastes and customs will not blur together into a melting pot of mediocrity as the consumer age arrives for all nations. Preserving individuality—indeed, enhancing and capitalizing on it—will no doubt be one of the great challenges for international corporate innovators and entrepreneurs from all nations.

Living and Working Abroad

In contrast to the part-time internationalists who are headquartered in the United States but who may spend several weeks or months abroad each year, special attention needs to be directed to the man who transplants himself, his family, his future, to an overseas corporate post. To this observer, who had the good fortune to spend some time with the Peace Corps, it seems shortsighted that the American businessman should receive, relatively, so little training to help adjust for what will be the most dramatic (and often most jarring) experience in his lifetime.

More than 100 companies do send executives and their wives to the four-week orientation courses sponsored by the Business Council for International Understanding, under the able leadership of John Habberton. In collaboration with American University, BCIU conducts five of these courses every year. Language training is additional and optional, and is strongly recommended for executives assigned abroad. Top lecturers are secured for all the basic subjects which an executive must understand in depth if he is to represent his company effectively, including an objective study of the United States in foreign perspective. Each executive also receives special "area training"; appropriateness of area material on Europe, for example, can be seen in the following list of topics: The New Europe; Diplomacy and Power (changes in the European state system); European Political Parties; Britain in Transition; Germany and the New Europe; Europe and the Common Market; EFTA "The Outer Seven"; The European Businessman and Economic Planning; European Labor; Americans and Europeans. Sessions are also arranged on a personal interview basis between the business executive participant and a variety of country specialists from U.S. and foreign governments and internal agencies.

These four weeks are all to the good. But by comparison, the Peace Corps provides approximately 12 weeks of intensive training, often including an environment physically similar to the foreign country in which the volunteers will be serving. Three hundred hours of language are provided. Students are advised that they will be living with host nationals on an equal basis, not as an American elite or "gilded ghetto"—a practice which has brought fierce criticism of Americans too often in the past.

The attitudes of both the Peace Corps volunteers and the communities in which they live testify to the effectiveness of this effort, which admittedly is tough, costly, and time consuming. But if the Peace Corps feels (and has proved) that there is value in investing three months in intensive training out of a total service commitment which spans a mere two years, it would seem that the same basic principle should apply for businessmen who will be making a permanent change of undefined tenure.

AmCham Survey of Business Conditions

It is axiomatic that the informed businessman, the man who knows what to expect and how to adjust accordingly, will be the most productive for his company and make the best impression in his new foreign community. With this in mind, the Council of American Chambers of Commerce in Europe conducted a survey among its members to get the facts as to conditions under which American businessmen live and work in Europe. The survey concluded that the "handicaps of a U.S. businessman in living and working in Europe are of a number and kind unknown in the United States."

The survey recognized the popular notion of a life filled with glamour, where the American reaps substantial financial rewards on an American salary which goes farther in paying European prices. This, however, is not the case.

In the world of financial reality, the American businessman stationed abroad soon realizes that the romance of Old World culture cloaks the practical problems of coping with new-style taxes plus old-style conveniences. The process of adjusting to life in Europe is for him an expensive one and he is laboring under significant hardships in living abroad. These hardships fall into three general categories: (1) United States and European tax burdens; (2) standard and cost of living burdens; and (3) career and other personal hardships.

Those wishing a copy of this brief paper, entitled *Essential Role of U.S. Businessmen Abroad*, should write to the Council of American Chambers of Commerce in Europe, 21 rue du Commerce, Brussels 4, Belgium. It pinpoints problems; it does not attempt to develop them at length. Highlights include:

1. Tax Burdens. Until recent years American citizens working and living abroad did not pay U.S. income taxes on income earned overseas. Since

1953, the American Chamber paper states, "Repeated inroads have been made on this exclusion during a period when the U.S. businessman abroad has done an unparalleled job in expanding and promoting American business overseas. The maximum exclusion now available for long-term residents abroad is $25,000." Also analyzed are European income taxes, other European taxes, absence of deductions, and inadequacy of foreign tax credit, all of which, in the judgment of the Chamber of Commerce officials, add up to burdens and unwarranted penalties for Americans abroad.

2. Standard and Cost of Living Burdens. Recognizing that no American can live abroad precisely as he can at home, the Chamber report offers counsel on how to attain the many elements of "a good life" in Europe virtually impossible to realize in the United States. The report touches on:

a) Living quarters—the problems of European housing shortages, local financing, rent controls, and exorbitant prices.

b) Related residence expenses—heating, appliances, and the "nightmare" of the American's utility bill.

c) Food—with caution on luxury items.

d) Medical and hospital expenses—including doctor's quality of care and costs.

e) Household personnel—an essential part of the European way of life for the middle-class family.

f) Education—of utmost importance for the average American parent.

3. Career and Personal Hardships. This thumbnail sketch points to opportunities for advancement and the risks involved, problems in investing, and personal hardships which loom large to many businessmen, including one of the most annoying: ineligibility to vote in local or national elections at home.

Conclusions of the AmCham Survey

What does all this add up to? The council finds the following conclusions inescapable:

1. There is an inherent contradiction in the income tax policy of the U.S. government and its policy of furthering its foreign trade relations in the national interest. On the one hand the government is intensely interested in promoting and protecting our trade and investments with other nations, receiving in that endeavor a great amount of practical help from business. On the other hand the government's tax policy toward these businessmen—the only men who can bring realization to U.S. foreign policy through the expansion of trade and investment with other countries—has the result of discouraging their

efforts. Any further tax burdens would constitute unwarranted penalties against those Americans who are flying the flag abroad and who are already carrying many burdens, simply because of residence outside their own country, which their counterparts in the United States are not called upon to bear.

2. It is evident to the council that many companies are having trouble in persuading executives to work abroad. Being away from the eye of management at home might be considered to carry certain advantages, in one sense, to a man's career; but the disadvantage may be "out of sight, out of mind" with the consequent chances of missing out on promotions. The emoluments offered are not sufficiently attractive to compensate for this risk.

3. To retain its present enviable posture in international trade, the United States must continue to recruit executives and responsible employees of the highest order. Such men must be guaranteed conditions of livelihood and employment that in no way would be inferior to those they could reasonably expect at home. Inordinate federal taxation of, or other burdens upon, American business personnel working abroad must, in the long run, inevitably weaken their tremendously important capacity to serve the foreign policy interests of their country.

97

These are the kinds of issues which have been emerging during the various dialogues between government and industry and between Americans and Europeans. The climate for progress is encouraging.

6 Stimulating U.S. Investments in Europe

PART 1 Introduction
by Ambassador Attilio Cattani

Ambassador Attilio Cattani was a member of the Italian Diplomatic Service for 40 years. In his career, he served in Paris, Athens, Mexico City, and Zurich, and in 1948 became Italy's representative to the Organization for European Economic Cooperation (OEEC). From 1952 to 1955, he was president of that organization's executive committee. Instrumental in the drafting of the Treaty of Rome in 1957 which established the European Economic Community, he later became Italy's representative to the EEC. He was serving as secretary general of the Italian Ministry of Foreign Affairs when he became chairman of the newly formed Olivetti–General Electric joint venture in 1965.

The flow of U.S. private investments to Europe, almost nonexistent in the 1950's, has increased vastly during the first part of the 1960's. It has been a natural manifestation of the very vigorous and expanding U.S. economy to look outward to the external world as an increasing opportunity to expand. And the European Economic Community's rapid growth and need for capital have made it attractive for U.S. businesses.

One of the principal results has been to give the Europeans a sense of tremendous challenge. U.S. investments have stimulated European enterprises to face increasingly the rigors of worldwide competition, and to appraise their own methods of doing business. In addition, the new inflow of capital has provided a strong catalytic element in Europe's own economic growth.

In my view, the time is now right to begin to study how long-lasting economic and political gains can be realized for the whole world out of the increasing U.S.-European economic ties. There are three major reasons:

1. The flow of U.S. capital and new techniques is already large enough to constitute a major factor of economic growth in Europe. We must carefully promote the steady and continuing inflow of these investments, not only to stimulate the European business community but also to improve the prospect for true interdependence between Europe and the United States.

2. Economic unity in Europe, which was in some doubt in the second half of 1965, is now under way again. And it appears that the common agricultural policy which has been worked out and the results in the Kennedy Round could lead to new political developments in Europe.

3. The movement toward closer solidarity between Europe and the United States has underlined the need for some type of action to insure a proper play of competition in a constructive way.

Modernizing the Rules

Now that we have been successful in generating the economic forces which are drawing us together, we have to devote ourselves to studying ways of sustaining these forces and of maximizing their benefits—to organize the best ways of collaborating harmoniously toward integration.

One of the ways to facilitate such cooperation is to modernize the "rules" governing Atlantic business relations, much as a modernized business structure was set up in Europe to govern the operation of the European Economic Community. In the modern business world, the free play of "pure competition" is largely an abstract concept. Certainly competition guides business decisions, but most governments have set up structures to modify pure competition in order to protect various elements of the business community, as well as the consumer. Thus, we need to find some way of harmonizing the business laws and customs among the various nations of the Atlantic Community.

Of course, the development of new institutional frameworks for Atlantic cooperation will not happen tomorrow; such frameworks presuppose dynamic action by governments to reappraise their objectives, as in NATO. But what seems to be most important to understand is that we must at least begin to bring the idea into constructive focus on both sides of the Atlantic. In so doing, we may be doing no more than simply appraising the situation, broadening our knowledge and understanding, and proposing possible ways of solving complex problems. But at least this is a start, and it must happen now.

Therein lies the great value of the recent conferences of the Atlantic Institute and the Atlantic Council. Some very valuable and concrete suggestions were formulated, which provide a starting point for the needed reevaluation. Some of the recommendations were already being followed by the larger companies. The spreading of understanding from the conferences can also help other companies blend more easily into the economies of foreign nations.

Patient Efforts of Persuasion

As a European I might comment about some of the things Europeans should be doing to facilitate the evolution of their societies into broadly based consumer-oriented economies. To be sure there are certain developments in Europe which are logical and desirable in the economic area such as improved capital markets, increased research, and merging of companies across borders. But human history has not normally been dic-tated to any great extent by logic. We must realize that fundamental and historic changes do create painful adaptations and difficulties which cannot be overcome overnight or imposed by force.

These difficulties will be solved, with a patient effort of persuasion. After all, the bold idea of a united Europe took patience, clear political determination, and sustained action. The idea started with the European Coal and Steel Community in 1949, became an objective of general economic character with the Common Market in 1958, and is now a lively and revolutionary enterprise overcoming immense difficulties.

I say "revolutionary" even if this is a peaceful revolution. We are passing from centuries of a long history of national policies to a new history of federal character; and it is being done by mutual consent—not through force of war, which has always been the traditional method of unification, even in such a relatively new country as the United States.

Some of the needs so evident to our American friends—and which may also be obvious to us—can frequently create psychological difficulties which can only be solved with patient persuasion. Again, the example of the European Common Market is useful. We have had to proceed with great care in creating the EEC and making it work, in order to maintain the cherished and valuable diversities of the different nations which make up Europe. The tremendous task of unification will succeed only if we are careful not to damage any national, moral, or economic feelings. A premature and excessive unification thrust could set in motion a reaction which might undermine the entire objective.

This word of patience applies to the integration problems between the United States and Europe. The key which unlocked the door to the Common Market—and which can unlock the door to a true Atlantic Community—is an arrangement in which all partners grow stronger while each contributes needed elements to the partnership. For example, in many fields where U.S. technology has outpaced Europe's, it is foolish for Europeans to try to rediscover what already exists. In other fields, such as chemicals, Europe's advanced technology can be built upon by Americans. Certainly the consistent flow of American investment to Europe is the fundamental lever which has enabled Europeans to take advantage of the new technical advances, and which may enable us to close the so-called technological gap.

Start with NATO

If we are to make Europeans equal partners of the United States in an independent free world, some more imaginative and bold actions must be devised. In my view, we should start with NATO. It should be reinforced as a political organization, with a widened economic and political scope in the spirit of Article II of the NATO charter. NATO is probably the only existing institution where bold action and innovative programs could be formulated in bringing together U.S. and European governments, with the cooperation of R&D institutions, universities, and private and public enterprises.

Of course, we should not pretend to charge NATO with all the complexities of economic cooperation between the United States and Europe. Many international organizations are already properly set up and competent in various fields, such as the IMF, GATT, OECD, and the EEC. But only NATO encompasses all areas. It could establish in R&D programs, for example, the lines of a bold program of action and knowledge-sharing.

Businessmen Must Take Part

Since the business community has the fundamental capacity—and responsibility—to play its part, it is not too ambitious to imagine that businessmen should participate in an economic and social council, an advisory organ of

NATO. Their function would be to pool their experience and talents, examine policies and programs, and give advice to governments toward fulfillment of the common objectives.

In the modern world, any action of government must be sustained by continuous understanding and support of those people whom the action affects. In this case, businessmen are especially affected—on both sides of the Atlantic—by actions to improve Atlantic cooperation, and they have the responsibility to get involved. Indeed, many want to get involved.

Too often, however, the business community feels it ought not to interfere with government action, which is, of course, a respectable attitude. But I feel strongly that in the new world we hope to create, and which we must create, governments will appreciate increasingly the contribution of the businessman and the private citizen.

For these same reasons, I heartily support the recommendation, which resulted from the Geneva conference, for an "Action Committee" to give continuing attention to the problems and opportunities of Atlantic cooperation. There is a serious need for a regular review of the progress toward closer Atlantic cooperation. Problems of trade, for example, must be studied with realism, goodwill, and care. Perhaps entirely new approaches, new objectives, new methods of reducing trade barriers drastically, should be explored.

But above all, I am convinced that there is a fundamental role for the businessman to play in our challenging assignment to foster closer Atlantic cooperation. The most important question we are facing is: How can we best pool our energies, our capacities, our knowledge, to meet man's basic needs around the world? With his economic tools of investment, research, production, and trade, the businessman will be one of the chief architects of this effort.

6 PART 2 Atlantic Council Report

Just voicing the theme of this chapter, "Stimulating U.S. Investments in Europe," can provoke disturbed and sometimes emotional responses among both Americans and Europeans. This is illustrated in the incredulous reaction expressed to the Atlantic Council survey team by a New York executive when asked how he felt overseas investments could best be encouraged for the mutual benefit of America and Europe.

"That's the last subject which should be investigated," he replied. "In the first place the United States government does not want Americans to expand into Europe because of our balance of payments problem. In the second place, the Europeans have made it equally obvious that they simply do not want any more American investments on their soil."

It would be difficult to phrase a more succinct reason why the business climate survey was needed.

The first fact is that the United States government has said explicitly and repeatedly that it is *for* continued business expansion across the Atlantic, including investments, within the bounds of national solvency.

The second fact is a continuing European need and demand, particularly in certain sectors, for the great benefits which U.S. investments can help them to realize.

From the U.S. Viewpoint

The U.S. balance of payments dilemma is how to moderate investment-dollar outflows without shutting off a major source of U.S. revenues. American businessmen can document, in company after company, that America is more than repaid for any temporary payments imbalances as the overseas operations get established, start making profits, and begin returning money to the United States in the form of purchases and profits to the parent organization.

As one manufacturer stated:

We have made a very substantial contribution to the balance of payments over the years, and this contribution has been possible only because we had investments abroad. Our experience has been that we do a great deal more business in a country in which we have our own investment than in a country in which we allow an independent distributor to handle our business. The independent distributor just doesn't have the same expertise in marketing and professional know-how, nor the same motivation.

A second manufacturer developed this same point on an industry-wide basis:

Overseas 'direct investments have been running at a rate of approximately $2 billion per year; however, U.S. overseas investments are now bringing in $4 billion a year. It is simple logic that American companies do not invest abroad simply for the pleasure of the exercise, but that they are concerned ultimately in bringing more dollars back to their American shareholders.

In this connection, it is interesting to read that the Ford Motor Company estimates that since 1960 its contribution to the balance of payments has been in excess of $3.3 billion; and General Motors has estimated its contribution to the balance of payments at over $2.2 billion in the past five years. I would express the hope that the various efforts to improve the U.S. balance of payments will not cause the kind of restriction on U.S. foreign investments which would diminish the flow of return on such investments to the United States. This would indeed be "killing the goose that lays the golden egg."

From a third manufacturer:

There is nothing mysterious about American companies' balance of payments. The more they have in foreign operations, the more they are able to export. The biggest single item in our favorable balance of payments situation is our exports. These wouldn't be possible without our foreign companies to generate them. To the extent that we don't have these companies, we won't export anywhere nearly as great an amount as we do presently. And the second source of inflow is, of course, dividends and royalty payments. It's impossible in many cases to get royalty payments without investment in the company. We have several situations which we are presently studying in which the principle income will be from royalties but the royalties won't be obtainable without an investment in the company.

Why Support for Investment Restraints?

In the face of such documentation, it might seem surprising to some that an overriding conclusion gathered from the Atlantic Council survey is that the large majority of American businessmen and financiers rallied vigorously to the President's appeal for voluntary restraints. "I go along with these voluntary measures taken, as it is stated, in the emergency," commented one banker. "Certainly something was needed, and these measures are at least a movement in the right direction."

Another banker, taking a national viewpoint, concurred:

We have gone along, to a large extent, with the President's balance of payments program, because we believe that the United States must obtain a stronger international position. We must be able to negotiate from strength in the discussions concerning the international monetary framework which are bound to come up in the next year or two.

This rallying of businessmen to the national cause resulted, naturally, in business adjustments which could be quite painful from the corporate standpoint. One chief executive was questioned by his own staff on the wisdom of his being so outspoken in support of the President's program. To this he countered:

Put yourself in the shoes of the President of the United States and the Secretaries of Commerce and the Treasury. Suppose you were facing a continuing deficit which weakened the country's ability to remain solvent at home and meet its international obligations abroad. What would *you* do under these circumstances? What alternatives would you propose?

The chief concern of both government and business leaders is not over short-term measures, but over long-term policies. One U.S. manufacturer believed that part of the answer might lie in educating medium-sized companies (along with the large companies) to expand abroad in such a way that the turn-around time for their investments could enable them to bank rather early net gains to the U.S. economy. (By "turn-around time" he referred to the time it takes a company to get back to this country the money it had to send abroad to start up a new investment. In short, how long does it take a company to "get back its bait?"—through repatriated profits, increased exports, and so on.)

One pharmaceutical manufacturer was particularly articulate on this point, urging that the long-term solution may be to get more and more companies involved in trade and investment than are involved today:

The turn-around on foreign investment, at least in the developed countries, is much quicker than people seem to realize. It is hard to generalize, but in some types of investment, certainly, it could happen in 18 months or so.

Not all businessmen agreed that the flow of dollars could be reversed so quickly. An international industrialist in the heavy equipment field estimated that the total time cycle could run as long as eight years. "First you have to finance the thing to get it started," he said:

Then you borrow as much as you can borrow and keep a respectable balance sheet. Then you get into the profitable aspects. Then you have to pare these borrowings down to a minimum level so you've got a comfortable balance sheet before it would be wise to bring back any of this. You boot-strap the thing as much as you can and let it go on its own—send a minimum amount of capital over, just stretching it as far as you can go—and then reducing that down to the point where the company is in good shape financially. Then you repatriate some dollars. And in a business like electronics where the R&D part of the budget is very high, sometimes it takes you quite a while before you get through with all this pump-priming and make a profit.

In summary, the main disagreement becomes not one of principle, where nearly all parties favor the most liberal possible flow of investments, but one of timing. The government view was expressed as follows:

Our position has been, not that we want to eliminate the outflow of capital, but that we need a pause in the increase in these outflows to allow our payments to catch up. While a curtailment of these increases will also curtail somewhat the increase in our investment income, these receipts will, nevertheless, continue to grow.

From the European Viewpoint

An almost audible sigh of relief could be heard in the capitals across Europe as America began its determined effort to end its balance of payments deficit. While some individuals were concerned that the voluntary restraints would cause a capital shortage in Europe (thereby putting a damper on future expansion), most European businessmen and government officials welcomed a pause in the flow of U.S. dollars abroad—for a temporary period. They felt that this would have a moderating effect and relieve inflationary pressures.

As in the United States, however, many feared the long-range effects. In Belgium, businessmen felt that a long-range program could hurt their competitive position and plans for expansion. In France, the feeling expressed through American Chamber of Commerce representatives was that any restriction by any government is regretted and should be temporary. In Spain, there was an official worry that the U.S. program might limit its ability to expand at the very time when the country was trying to "come from behind." In Germany, a leading banker summarized the attitudes of many: namely, that America had the maturity and capability to handle its finances effectively, once it put its mind to the problem, and that the whole Atlantic Community would thereby benefit.

Removal of the balance of payments irritant has done much to improve the climate for U.S. investment. While various concerns and misgivings can be heard across most of Europe, in balance it must be noted that the majority are not pleas for protection, nor are they even anti-American. Although resentment exists in some European circles, there is no Europewide anti-American business sentiment.

Country–by–Country Appraisal

In appraising the European investment climate, it must be quickly noted that the word "European" is not a precise term. Attitudes will vary tremendously from country to country and even among geographical areas within a single country. Further, the climate may shift from month to month, depending upon political-economic developments. And there may be wide variance even among political and business leaders within a single country, depending upon the immediate problems and crises at hand. With these disclaimers, we shall venture a country-by-country sketch of the business climate.

1. *United Kingdom.* Britain hopes U.S. investment will be continued at an increasing pace. The climate for foreign investment, particularly U.S. investment, is generally excellent, especially where new technologies will bolster the economy and where American business will foster economic growth of an area in special need, such as in Northern Ireland and Scotland. "The British welcome anything and everything except automotive and pharmaceuticals," as one industrialist put it; "or any investment that de Gaulle doesn't want," as someone else said.

There are certain historical and practical reasons which account for the excellent U.K. climate: the exemplary behavior and good record of U.S. corporations during the past five decades; the common language and similar cultural traditions that exist between the two countries; and the willing and effective adaptation by U.S. firms to the British methods of doing business.

The one concern expressed in U.K. government circles was over possible U.S. dominance in certain industries such as automobile, aircraft, computer, defense equipment, and pharmaceutical. This concern is said to be magnified whenever new acquisitions of leading U.K. firms by large U.S. firms are announced. Lurking in the background are British fears that they might become, as someone said, "like Canada—your 51st state."

There is no evidence of discrimination against U.S. investment where the British government or private agencies are concerned. U.K. government officials are striving to stimulate foreign investment in certain industries having high export potential in order to improve the U.K.'s critical balance of payments situation where a serious trade deficit persists.

2. *The Netherlands.* The Dutch welcome new investments in selected sectors, but no longer offer special incentives. With a booming economy, a labor shortage, and an overstrained construction market, the government has adjusted its policy from one of active solicitation of foreign investment to one of selectivity and no special incentives. Foreign and Dutch investors are now treated the same. The majority of U.S. businessmen interviewed indicated that they had encountered no discrimination; neither do they enjoy the special benefits once afforded them.

The government favors new industries which bring in capital goods and technical know-how; those highly automated and requiring modest labor forces; and those which will stimulate further development, including exports.

Dutch officials do not concur with the merger attitude prevalent in some EEC circles—that European industries must combine together in order to compete on a more equal footing with giant U.S. corporations. A number of observers commented that the Dutch probably would veto any proposals by other EEC members designed to restrict U.S. investments in the Common Market.

3. *Belgium.* At the seat of the Common Market, Belgium is one

of the most favorable investment prospects. It continues to offer incentives and is striving to develop larger industries. The government actively solicits U.S. investments which will meet the Belgian need for more technical know-how. There is no evidence of discrimination against U.S. companies.

Belgium also welcomes new foreign investment because there is a need for large industry. The country is now made up primarily of small and medium-sized firms. Its position as headquarters for the Common Market underlines its need to become an important industrial center.

Belgian laws contain specific incentives for foreign investments, such as interest subsidies, real estate tax holidays, tax-free holding company provisions, easily obtainable construction permits, and the lowest corporate tax structure in the EEC—36 percent on undistributed profits, compared to a high of 60 percent in Germany. U.S. businessmen operating in Belgium generally agreed that U.S. business was treated favorably, and that the long-range outlook for U.S. investment was good.

As with The Netherlands, the Belgian government would be opposed to possible restrictions in the Common Market on foreign investment. Neither Belgian government nor business officials are overly concerned about possible U.S. dominance of Belgian industries. For example, there was no hostility in Belgium toward the establishment of a large automobile industry by General Motors. Belgium welcomes the creation of such an important business within its borders.

Understandably, American business is most desired where it is not directly competitive with Belgian industries in priority sectors. U.S. businesses are wanted particularly in electronics, precision opticals, metallurgy (nonferrous), and chemicals. But one American official cautioned that despite this excellent climate, it could change quickly with an on-rush of unexpected new American businesses. "There is such a thing as indigestion," he added.

4. *Spain.* This historically important nation—today outside both the Common Market and Outer Seven—vies with Belgium for the title of "most favorable climate." It is eager to join the European business community, and is developing its economy as rapidly as it can.

While the Spanish government's approval must be obtained for foreign investment in certain politically sensitive industries, such as petrochemicals and oil, the government maintains a favorable, friendly policy toward foreign investment.

Spain's need is for basic industries that will stimulate the economy, raise per capita income, and provide technical know-how. Its current four-year Economic Development Plan provides for a steady flow of new foreign investment to assist in achieving a 6 percent annual rate of economic growth and in developing a consumer-oriented economy. The Spanish government warmly welcomes U.S. investment, offering certain incentives for investment under the "Polo" program in which the government is encouraging industrial development in seven different areas in Spain. Incentives are applicable not only to U.S. firms but to Spanish and other foreign companies alike.

Spanish businessmen pointed out that U.S. business methods have taught them a method of working (such as care over specifications, precision in techniques) which is helpful to the Spanish economy after its long-term isolation from foreign influences. The absence of the cartel-like "fraternities" encountered in several other countries, and American newness to the Spanish scene, have also helped to create a favorable attitude toward U.S. capital.

5. *West Germany.* By most economic measurements, West Germany is the dominant country in Europe: in terms of gross national produce, R&D resources, and market potential. It continues to attract a high volume of U.S. private capital, due in large part to its tremendous domestic demands, which serve as a powerful magnet.

Although no specific incentives are offered, the German government maintains a favorable attitude toward foreign investment. When a rash of newspaper articles hinted that the government was cooling off toward American companies, German officials quickly reported to the press that such definitely was not the case.

Among U.S. businessmen, mixed feelings were found concerning the true climate for U.S. investment in Germany. Some felt that there were storm warnings; others felt that there was no current problem, but that barriers might develop later. All stressed the need for business sensitivity and judgment in order to preserve favorable relationships in a nation which offers a happy combination of free competition, rising consumption, responsible government, high rate of economic growth, and an advanced stage of technology.

Germans in particular seemed pleased over U.S. efforts to balance its international payments picture. A point emphasized by some (but discounted by others) was that there was a real fear in Germany that the United States might be living beyond its income. Germans remember their own runaway inflation that led to the rise of Hitler, World War II, and catastrophic destruction. And if American prosperity should lead to a boom-and-bust, many Germans would not want to be tied to the United States with joint ventures if and when the U.S. bust should occur. Some German businessmen were found resentful over past U.S. monetary policy which permitted "easy" money, based on lower U.S. interest rates, to come to Europe, while European businessmen had been compelled to use local capital, available at much higher interest rates. It was felt that the U.S. balance of payments deficit had placed European businessmen at a competitive disadvantage with U.S. businessmen.

While apprehensions over U.S. investments were in greater evidence and more pronounced in Germany than in the United Kingdom, The Netherlands, or Belgium, at the same time there were also vigorous expressions of opinion in German industrial circles that U.S. competition was more to be welcomed than feared. German businessmen believe that there should be more cooperation, more coordination, and more contact between U.S. and German businessmen. There is a desire to seek acceptable methods which would insure a smoother entrance of U.S. capital into Germany.

6. *Italy.* The Mediterranean member of the Common Market offers a flexible climate and certain advantages for U.S. investment. The Italian government's policy is to encourage continued foreign investments needed to stabilize the country's economy.

Italy is not, and cannot be, self-sufficient. Its economic balance depends upon its capacity to export finished and semifinished goods to pay for imports of raw materials and machinery.

Investments which will increase Italy's exports are high on the government's list of priorities. Investments that will bring new technology are especially acceptable.

The Italian government especially welcomes and encourages new investments that will help to strengthen the underdeveloped (and often impoverished) South. A glance at a per capita income map reveals that this region rates little higher than most of the developing world stretching across South America, Africa, and Asia; and this disparity between the South and the Central–Northern regions has been a sizable roadblock to building a true sense of unity and nationhood for the whole of Italy.

Italian businessmen stressed that the United States is pulling away from Europe too fast technologically, and that the United States and Europe must stay closer together. They feel that the United States must adopt a true "partnership spirit" toward European industry and that a stronger, more industrialized Europe will create even larger opportunities for U.S. business.

One of Italy's major problems is the Communist influence on labor; Communist demonstrations are aimed against the United States in general, not against U.S. investments specifically. Labor unions are oriented more toward political agitation than economic. Only about half the union members are in Communist-dominated unions and even that half is not all antigovernment.

The Italian government does not share French political concern over the so-called dangerous penetration of European industry by U.S. firms. Italian businessmen believe it is desirable to strengthen the Italian economic structure through mergers, 50–50 joint ventures between U.S. and Italian firms, and new forms of industrial concentration. In this context, it is useful to note the role of the Italian government in business operations, through the Institute for Industrial Reconstruction (IRI), the government holding company controlling many key sectors of Italian industry. It is estimated that about 40 percent of the Italian GNP rotates around industries in the IRI group. The Italian government holds control in all telephone companies, radio and television services, the railway transportation, and has large interests in the mechanical and steel industries. Some companies in the IRI group are partners in joint ventures with U.S. capital.

7. *France.* While France maintains a more restrictive policy toward U.S. investments than most countries, it is well aware that large-scale U.S. potential investments can be diverted to other European countries, and it recognizes what this can mean to its European

colleagues (who are also competitors) in terms of new technology and products, increased exports, and a relatively more favorable position on the world trade scene. Hence, French policies have been moderated.

It may seem a paradox that at the height of political tensions between the United States and France, when the NATO headquarters was being moved from Paris to Brussels, businessmen and trade officials were most outspoken on the need to maintain harmony with Americans at the business level. Again and again French spokesmen have stressed their long-range common bond with Americans as well as their immediate business prospects through collaboration. This is particularly true among younger U.S.-trained French executives who want to do business the European way, but within a more dynamic American context. There is need for more contact and more communication between French and U.S. leaders to discuss matters of common interest.

U.S. businessmen in France have emphasized that while it may be more difficult for American firms to make direct investments in France and establish themselves in the French economy, there are compelling reasons for doing so. U.S. companies have found, for one thing, that although resistance to their entrance may have been substantial, once this has been overcome and the hurdles of establishing a new business have been vaulted, compatible relations with French business then commence.

Even more compelling are the advantages of setting up business in France as a base for preparing to serve EEC markets:

a) France itself is a major national market.
b) The French are competent workers and labor conditions are therefore comparatively good.
c) There is a pool of trained talent or potential talent for research and development work.
d) France is still a developing economy.

8. *Switzerland.* This attractive country is in a unique class. It was not analyzed in the Atlantic Council study on the same basis as the other nations because its importance is not measured by the size of market, gross national product, availability of trained manpower, and the other standard criteria. It has been and continues to be of

TABLE 1
New Operations of U.S. Companies in Europe
January 1958–January 1966

	Bel.-Lux.	Fr.	Ger.	Italy	Neth.	ECC	U.K.	Switz.	EFTA	Western Europe
Chemicals and drugs	115	99	99	99	74	486	36	36	82	595
Petroleum and other fuels	26	25	38	26	18	133	17	5	31	167
Textiles and clothing	31	24	25	21	24	125	15	14	33	163
Nonelectrical machinery	76	98	81	69	43	367	74	53	139	516
Food, beverages, and tobacco	22	34	34	29	23	142	19	17	39	187
Paper	15	24	16	13	5	73	9	11	28	104
Office machinery	8	15	18	5	7	53	10	15	29	85
Transportation equipment	22	45	15	24	12	118	17	17	37	157
Heavy equipment	16	22	11	9	7	65	13	5	19	87
Electronics and electrical machinery	56	96	73	79	42	346	54	42	101	455
Basic metals and metal products	47	35	51	37	21	191	20	12	38	239
Instruments and watches	11	21	36	18	22	108	19	20	41	150
Household appliances	5	20	14	11	4	54	9	10	20	76
Rubber	9	14	7	13	4	47	4	4	8	57
Glass	7	2	5	8	3	25	1	1	5	31
Research and engineering	18	29	13	11	16	87	10	12	23	112
Other industries	26	25	30	16	10	107	14	13	36	147
Services:	(77)	(87)	(55)	(44)	(30)	(293)	(21)	(47)	(80)	(385)
Finance	21	33	21	13	6	94	5	17	27	128
Retail and wholesale trade	4	7	3	4	1	19	3	1	6	26
Hotels	7	6	3	1	1	18	1	3	4	24
Marketing and publicity	17	17	10	12	10	66	6	11	20	87
Other services	28	24	18	14	12	96	6	15	23	120
TOTAL	587	715	621	532	365	2820	362	334	789	3713

Source: Chase Manhattan Bank.

strategic importance as a headquarters for other European operations.

Hence, the comments of American businessmen interviewed in Switzerland relate more to the larger countries already discussed.

9. *European Economic Community.* A few words are in order on the Common Market as a whole.

The EEC needs a sustained flow of outside capital because the European capital market is not large enough to meet current and future industrial needs. U.S. companies continue to be sought for specific investments or enterprises, particularly those involving advanced technology. This is expected to continue.

In the military or defense industries, EEC countries wish to build and continue to control their own companies, but want and must have advanced U.S. technical know-how. It is in this area that the European attitude toward U.S. business is notably responsive. But the movement of business expansion is by no means confined to a few selected industries, and American companies have joined European companies on the widest possible front. Table I (p. 115), which concludes this chapter, reveals the broad spectrum of new business operations set in motion by U.S. companies in Europe from January 1958 to January 1966.

All of the evidence is that Europe is no longer a "have-not" area—in financing, capital resources, management competence, production capabilities, and marketing expertise. Indeed, with this new strength, signs of business nationalism are visible in some sectors and could spread to others, creating a trend away from the very internationalism which has gotten the European economy into high gear.

For the future, the climate for transnational investment will depend just as much (if not more) on psychological factors as on economic. The basic question is not whether there is too much movement of investment capital between nations, but whether there will be enough. The key to progress is whether businessmen from all nations can learn to team up in international ventures that unite the resources of several nations to the benefit of all.

7 Stimulating European Investments in the United States

PART 1 Introduction
by John T. Connor

Former Secretary of Commerce John T. Connor has directed the major effort toward promoting the Administration's goal of correcting the U.S. balance of payments deficit under the voluntary restraints program. Before assuming his Cabinet post in January 1965, he devoted 25 years to law, government, and industry; the last 10 years as president of Merck & Co. In 1942 he served as general counsel to the Office of Scientific Research and Development, then headed by Dr. Vannevar Bush. Following World War II service, he became counsel to the new Office of Naval Research, and later, special assistant to the Secretary of the Navy, James Forrestal. His current responsibility is president, Allied Chemical Corporation.

EDITOR'S NOTE: *Since the preparation of this statement, John T. Connor has resigned as Secretary of Commerce. However, the principles and ideas he has set forth have been reaffirmed by the present Secretary of Commerce as a continuing part of U.S. policy.*

When the Atlantic Council made its recent survey of the climate for American business in Western Europe, interviewing businessmen and government officials of eight countries, two questions often asked were:

Do you want to invest in the United States?

If so, what can the United States do to help?

The immediate response to the first question usually was complete silence, the council's investigators reported. Then would come polite, guarded comments that invariably meant "no."

Subsequently, questions and problems of stimulating European investment in the United States were discussed by continental and American business leaders in conferences at Crotonville, New York, and at Geneva, Switzerland.

The Crotonville conference formally reported that:

Additional European direct investment in the United States would be welcome and more should be done to attract it. . . . Portfolio investments are attractive to individual European investors and provide some participation in the growth of the American economy, but much more could and should be done to interest European corporations in mutually advantageous opportunities for direct investment.

The Geneva Conference expressed the same general recommendations with the additional observation that an "information gap" exists in Europe in regard to investment opportunities in the United States, particularly among medium-sized and smaller European companies.

European business spokesmen at both conferences raised practical questions about basic matters such as limitations of European capital resources, insufficiency of European technology, a dearth of managerial talent to send to the United States, uncertainty as to application of U.S. antitrust laws to joint ventures and acquisitions, and U.S. tax policies.

What Advantages for Both Sides?

With businessmen on both sides of the Atlantic now approaching the 1970's in their planning and programming, I welcome this opportunity to discuss, in the words of the Crotonville report, some of the "mutually advantageous opportunities for direct investment" in the United States.

Why advantageous?

We have all known the answer for generations. The first U.S. Secretary of the Treasury, Alexander Hamilton, expressed in 1791 a basic attitude concerning foreign capital —adhered to ever since in the United States. He stated:

Instead of being viewed as a rival, it ought to be considered as a most valuable auxiliary, conducive to putting in motion a greater quantity of productive labor, and a greater portion of useful enterprise, than could exist without it.

This can be translated into today's dictum: the United States believes in two-way investment as well as in two-way trade and two-way travel.

Alexander Hamilton was emphasizing the advantages to the United States of new capital investments. The advantages to foreign investors, of course, would be the profits to be gained and the enrichment of their knowledge about doing business in the world's greatest market. These are separate advantages. What are some of the "mutual" ones referred to at Crotonville?

For one thing, an increase in European direct investments and in the number of European companies in the United States would tend to counterbalance direct U.S. investment in Europe. The U.S. capital flow into Western Europe and the resultant competition it is engendering give rise to concerns and fears within the Atlantic community of nations.

(U.S. direct investment—book value—in Europe increased from $1.7 billion in 1950 to $12.1 billion in 1964. European direct investment in the United States increased from $2.2 billion to $5.8 billion in the same period. The average amount of European direct investment in the United States has been about $257 million annually while U.S. direct investment in Europe has been increasing at an annual average rate of $743 million.)

For another thing, "a greater portion of useful enterprise"—as Hamilton put it—from Europe participating in the U.S. economy would put European companies physically into the American market. It would enable them to see firsthand how U.S. business operates, particularly in the areas of technological development. By acquiring more of the American know-how in these departments, European businesses would gain in competitive knowledge, as already has happened in a few cases. And this would further counterbalance competitive strengths.

These are some of the mutual advantages. There are, of course, others.

Positive Moves toward a Balance

There are two ways to move toward a balance. One is negative, by measures to restrict or cut down the high side of a flow, reducing everyone's economic progress. The other is positive, to make special efforts to build up the low side of an equation, bringing everybody to a higher economic plateau.

We in the United States do not like the principle of restrictive approaches in investment any more than we do in trade. We much prefer to try to build up the influx of capital investment, and we are intensifying our efforts to do so. In this connection, an increased two-way flow of investment capital occupies an important place in the U.S. program to strengthen its balance of payments position on an enduring basis.

If I were to sit down with a group of Europeans and discuss why we believe it would be sound policy for their businessmen to increase direct investments in the United States and to suggest in general terms how they could do so, I would start by setting aside momentarily the name "United States."

I would begin with the basic proposition of stimulating investments outside Europe to strengthen the European economy. Suppose we were to find a country in which:

a) Private capital from abroad has been welcomed uninterruptedly for 175 years.
b) Foreign investors had consistently received in all that time the same consideration as citizens of that country.

A country in which:

c) The economy is self-generating, self-sustaining and self-expanding.
d) Population is increasing rapidly toward 220 million within 10 years.
e) Gross national product (all goods and services provided yearly) is climbing toward the trillion dollar mark.
f) Spendable income and personal savings are rising year after year.
g) Businessmen, regardless of citizenship, operate under a tax structure as favorable as anywhere.
h) Workers are among the most productive in the world.
i) Conditions for doing business offer reasonable assurance that attractive profits can be made on a sound investment.

If there were such a country, I would ask: "Wouldn't you consider making a direct capital investment there?"

And suppose that in this country one would also find:

j) Conditions for starting a business more easily and with less government red tape than in most other places.
k) Supplementary capital available to help anyone get started.
l) All kinds of free professional services at hand to help in locating a plant and working out its special needs.
m) A pool of trained business managers available.
n) An established and versatile commercial distribution system serving all types of business.
o) Research and development services obtainable for all kinds of products (about which I will have more to say below).
p) Freedom to dispose of company profits as desired, either remitting them to the country of origin, or reinvesting them.

Given all these inducements, wouldn't anyone seriously consider such a country as a place to make direct investments?

A Banker's View

Let me share with you what a banker has to say about a country such as this as an opportunity for business investment. Here is part of a letter he sent overseas recently to some prospective investors:

First are the factors that indicate an unusually good, self-sustaining economic trend and also the favorable official environment for foreign-owned investments. Total consumer expenditures, for example, amount to over half of (the country's) gross national product. . . . The basic general official policy is to treat foreign capital on a basis of complete equality with domestic capital. That includes even the bidding for the Government's own substantial purchases.

Total business taxes compare very well with those abroad and in some instances are lower. . . . Cost factors here are surprisingly favorable. Funds and earnings are freely repatriated without any regulatory formalities. . . .

For the background information usually required by a foreign-owned company considering setting up production in an area with which it is not familiar, the government offers a series of free services. . . . It makes available listings from many of the country's 300,000 manufacturers for opportunities for direct investment, joint-ventures, and licensing arrangements. It helps assess possibilities for particular products.

By now anyone would probably have decided that the country I am talking about is the United States after all. Is the United States as attractive for the foreign investor as I make it sound? Investors will find this the largest and richest market in the world. Moreover, as the governor of one of our largest industrial states said recently, in this country "profit" is not a tarnished word. And as one of our leading business magazines also has said within recent weeks, "there's plenty of privacy left in private enterprise" in the United States.

Opportunities in the U.S. Future Marketplace 123

If anyone were to ask *why* he should invest in the United States, I would begin with the future American market. Americans comprise about 7 percent of the people of the world, but they use:

70 percent of the automobiles.
Over 50 percent of the television and radio sets.
30 percent of the railways.
50 percent of the highways.

The population is rising: 4.5 million new births a year; new marriages, new families, increasing every year throughout the 1960's—all of which adds up to sales for more housing, furniture, appliances, clothing, and consumer goods.

A majority of the 195 million Americans today purchase a broad range of nonessential or semiluxury goods. In 10 years they will spend one third again as much. And the typical American consumer of 1975 will be younger and wealthier than he is today.

The rate of growth will require 2 million new business firms over the next 10 years to meet increased demands for goods and services. A large number of these, of course, will be service companies and retail outlets.

U.S. industrialists say that the maximum potential of any growing market cannot be realized unless production takes place within particular marketing areas and unless product designs, sales, and distribution are directed toward local demand. Similarly, many foreign companies exporting their products to America already have found that it is more profitable to manufacture and sell the same goods from a U.S. location.

By producing through a subsidiary here, a foreign manufacturer can:

1. Eliminate most of the problems involved in exporting to the United States.
2. Gain freedom from U.S. tariffs.
3. Have a more effective means for expanding his U.S. market through the main commercial distribution and communications systems.
4. Be better informed on technological trends.
5. Have direct access to large government markets such as federal agencies, defense production, 50 state governments, numerous large city governments.

How to Enter the U.S. Market?

If a businessman were to ask *how* to get started in the United States I would suggest:

Licensing Arrangements. U.S. firms constantly are seeking new products to add to their lines and are looking for improved production processes. Foreign companies that possess technological know-how will interest American firms.

Joint Ventures. These often prove feasible in the United States. Many American organizations seek partners with a salable new product or production technique and who can provide fresh capital for expansion.

Wholly Owned Subsidiaries. An overseas firm with adequate capital and other resources can operate effectively in the United States by starting a new firm.

Purchasing a U.S. Firm. This enables a foreign investor to obtain established production and distribution facilities and begin operations immediately.

(The four above suggestions are

not listed to suggest an order of priority or desirability, but only in the probable amount of investment that would be required.)

We have sometimes been told that the U.S. market dismays Europeans because of its geographical size, complexity of regions, states and cities, and numbers and varieties of people. I do not think anyone need be discouraged by these concerns. The businessman new to the United States will find here efficient, well-organized marketing services of many types readily available, whatever his product.

As to capital, the foreign businessman will find the U.S. private internal money market efficient, fluid, and relatively free of controls. Cost of money here is as reasonable, and the supply as ample, as anywhere in the world. Of course the capital markets in most countries, including the United States, are tight at the time of this writing. Even so, loan and supplementary equity capital is available to assist foreign industrial investment here.

Local Development Groups Can Help

In addition to the abundant sources of private capital, loan capital is available from many state and local public and semipublic development groups. In a few places, capital grants are available to new industries locating in the area.

While every investment is an individual matter, and no two are alike, various combinations of arrangements have been and can be made through private, federal, state, and local capital-type contributions to finance the start of a new industry. Twelve thousand organizations are engaged in industrial development in the United States: agencies of state, county, and city governments; railroads, utilities, and commercial banks; and associations of local businessmen, such as chambers of commerce.

All are seeking new industrial plants for their particular city or region. All have something to offer. Reasonable requirements for purchasing, or building and equipping, a new plant can be met through the help of these organizations.

A request to the nearest American embassy or consulate, by those abroad—or a telephone call to the Commerce Department's Office of International Investment by those who may be in the United States—will provide personal and confidential attention to a caller's investment questions.

A foreign business executive would have no difficulty in sending top managers or special technicians to work in the United States if his country has a commercial

125

treaty with the United States, as most European countries do. These treaties include provision for liberal rights of entry.

If a foreign firm has a shortage of executives to send to the United States, it could recruit junior and more senior managers locally. U.S. colleges are turning out something like 54,000 business and commercial graduates every year, and over 6,000 more from advanced business and financial schools.

Forming a U.S. Company

If you were to ask me *what* a foreigner should do about forming a company in the United States I would offer the following.

First and foremost, creating a corporation in the United States is relatively easy and inexpensive. There is no national or general corporation statute qualifying companies to do business. Each of our 50 states regulates the establishment of business within its own jurisdiction. And U.S. business law generally is free of administrative whim.

All states generally follow the policy of equal treatment for companies organized in foreign countries, and foreign companies are free to organize wholly owned subsidiary companies. Most states do not require that a specified number or percentage of incorporators or directors must be United States citizens. Therefore, foreign investors are at liberty to use their capital in any way they may wish, subject only to those regulations applicable equally to American citizens. There are few exceptions to this.

The federal government avoids interference with the right of companies (foreign or domestic) to engage in particular types of economic activity in the 50 states. However, restrictions are imposed on foreign-owned companies in a few special types of business such as coastal shipping, radio communications, air transport, mining, banking, insurance, and public utilities.

Once granted authority by one of our states to do business, a company organized in a foreign country is regarded as having the same rights and privileges, duties and obligations as a company organized within any state.

There are 5 million businesses of all kinds and descriptions in the United States, and most of them service local or regional markets. Approximately 304,000 are manufacturing establishments or single plants, producing $400 billion worth of goods annually.

One sixth of the 304,000 have a net worth of $200,000 or less. Over 96 percent have fewer than 250 employees; 91 percent have fewer than 100; and over 52 percent have fewer than 9.

In terms of value added by all manufacturers, approximately 40 percent, or more than $160 billion, was contributed in 1965 by plants employing less than 250 workers.

Many large U.S. producers buy most of their semi-manufactured and finished components from smaller, independent companies.

Doing Business in the United States

If you were to ask about doing business in the United States, I would say this:

First, consider various cost elements. Overseas firms considering production in the United States will find that some cost elements are greater here than in other industrial countries. But they will discover also that for some products other costs are considerably lower.

Material costs for manufactured products average about 25 percent higher abroad than in the United States. The appreciably lower cost of materials in the United States is due to the wide diversity of domestically produced materials available, and to our efficient processing and distribution systems.

Availability of raw and semifinished materials in all parts of the country is an important factor in making it possible for a new firm to go into production quickly in the United States.

High productivity of labor makes possible the prevailing high hourly wage rates in the United States. It is the high output per man-hour—the low labor cost per unit of production—that makes this possible. Wage rates, in other words, are geared to high productivity. In recent years labor costs have been very stable here in contrast with some other countries where wage rates have been increasing rapidly. The labor cost gap between the United States and Europe, about which we used to hear so much, is being reduced steadily.

The supply of labor in the United States will continue to increase rapidly, and tomorrow's labor force will be more highly trained than today's. By the end of the 1960's there will be nearly 11 million highly skilled workers in America. At present about one third of all workers are members of trade unions. The degree of unionization varies substantially industry by industry.

U.S. business generally pays less income taxes than those in comparative business in other developed countries .

Tax laws help a new company starting out in America to write off costs of new machinery rapidly. In addition, depreciation allowances for plant and equipment are liberal.

Competing in the U.S. Market

If we were to discuss selling in the United States, I would make these points:

Any company which has a useful product or service of any kind that is newer, different, more useful, more attractive, or less expensive than competitive products can, under normal circumstances, profitably enter the U.S. market.

There is also a profitable market in this country for manufacturers of those more standard products for which demand is expanding rapidly, such as service, food processing and packaging, new engines of all kinds, home furnishings, and a wide variety of products in the retail field.

The U.S. market is made up of nine regional markets, including from 130 to 140 large cities or metropolitan areas. Within these regions there are literally thousands of local markets. With planning and care, an investor can establish a plant in a marketing area of sufficient size and accessibility to absorb his initial production. Naturally, he can expand his activities as sales warrant.

In fact, the continuing success of the medium and small manufacturer in the United States is attributed to his ability to plan his sales and distribution on a local basis, instead of trying to cover every market in every region in every state.

Narrowing the Technological Gap

Perhaps we should discuss briefly the desirability of direct investment in the United States as a means of narrowing the technological gap between American and European industry.

The extent to which a technological gap exists may be debatable, but not the fact that it exists. This is affirmed by the record. Companies in other countries pay U.S. companies $5 for licenses to use U.S. industrial processes for every $1 that American companies pay foreign companies for rights to use their processes.

Pick up any issue of a business magazine in the United States today and you probably will see articles and photographs of new technological developments in industrial processes and products. For example, a recent issue of one of our magazines carried an article about the stream of new products coming from U.S. industry, such as:

New flame-resistant, radiation-resistant, cold-resistant film for encasing wire, for use (at present) in missiles and space instruments.

A machine that picks up mowed hay and presses and packages it into bite-sized cubes for beef cattle, at the rate of 5 tons an hour.

The use of "vaporized" aluminum to coat steel strip, for ultimate use as corrosion-resistant material for containers, replacing tin.

Many on both sides of the Atlantic believe the technological gap between the United States and Western Europe is growing. A broad application of new technology on both continents is desirable, because it will help maintain the sound economies and steady growth that benefit all the Atlantic trading countries.

A few European companies already have proven that an investment in an American company is an effective way of keeping the European parent competitive. An American subsidiary provides a window through which U.S. development in technology and management systems can be watched and adopted by the European parent.

Powerful Support of Business Growth

Obviously, it is not possible to cover in these pages all aspects that must be considered when a European company prepares to make a direct investment in the United States.

For example, I have not discussed U.S. antitrust and other laws affecting competitive practices. This is a difficult and complicated subject to master, as everyone knows. These laws, however, are not as difficult as sometimes pictured. They are a protection in most cases to the overseas investor, rather than otherwise; for essentially, they are designed to keep U.S. markets competitive. As we have seen, the United States is a land of medium-sized and small businesses, notwithstanding its giant corporations. Competition is vigorous and is carried on within a framework of rules designed to combine fair play with economic growth.

Nor have I discussed the detailed aspects of our tax laws, federal, state, and local, as well as the taxes for social security and unemployment insurance. These also require special knowledge to master the fine print. But there are no hidden clauses therein to upset the main point of this introduction that, as a general rule, tax laws are designed in the United States to foster—not to hinder—business development and new investment.

That philosophy goes to the heart of our political and governmental system. For undoubtedly

129

there is today the most powerful combination of forces supporting, abetting, promoting, and protect- ing business initiative and invest- ment in the United States to be found in the world.

---

7 PART 2 *Atlantic Council Report*

There is much to be gained by proving to the Europeans—and to our- selves—that they have a lucrative market on this side of the Atlantic and that they can compete in it successfully. In his introductory mes- sage to this chapter, John T. Connor outlines the advantages to the Europeans, and suggests an action approach, more completely and convincingly than has yet been presented by any American official to date.

The benefits to the United States of a successful "reverse invest- ments" program can be summarized as follows. Such a program would:

1. Increase U.S. exports.
2. Produce a fresh flow of investment capital and technology to the United States.
3. Reduce U.S. imports (as products are licensed and built within the country rather than shipped in from the outside).
4. Create jobs and tax revenues.
5. Cement Atlantic relationships on a business (and businesslike) basis. (It is belaboring the point to note that a Frenchman with a profitable plant interest in Peoria would find it difficult to be anti-American.)

While economic benefits would be long range, there can be imme- diate returns in improved transatlantic relationships. Through deeds, not words—even in the feasibility study stage—America can begin demonstrating to policy leaders across Europe that we are sincere about the idea of partnership; that we encourage a two-way flow of ideas, dollars, and technology; and that the "Americanization of Eu- rope," the "second invasion of Europe," and "Yankee economic im- perialism" are catch phrases, not the national policy of the United

States of America. A number of our embassy officials in Europe would be gratified with the diplomatic gains that could be registered should such a reverse investment approach prove feasible.

What Are the European Attitudes?

During the business climate survey in The Netherlands, Atlantic Council representatives found members of the American embassy suggesting U.S. initiatives in this field. They suggested that the U.S. Commerce and Treasury Departments devise a program to demonstrate what the American government is doing to encourage foreign investment and business expansion by Europeans in the United States. This might include citing the large number of European success stories in the United States, and detailing guidelines to success for new investors. Such a program would provide an effective rebuttal to criticism from various European circles that the United States is only interested in what it can achieve for itself in Europe.

Although Dutch government and business leaders agreed that a flow of Dutch capital to the United States could be of benefit, and viewed the United States as a solid and profitable market, they expressed the type of pessimism described by Mr. Connor in his opening comments. A Dutch official pointed out that while the Dutch are free to buy U.S. securities, it would be difficult for a Dutch firm to start a new enterprise in the United States of sufficient size to enable it to compete. In addition, since the need of The Netherlands is to emphasize exports, a transfer of investments to the United States would drain off management and capital still badly needed at home. He suggested that perhaps there was not enough useful information on the subject. Officials in country after country voiced much the same comments.

The Belgian government would not oppose investments in foreign countries such as the United States. But it could not be expected to be enthusiastic about a U.S. "investment drive" while Belgian industrial problems continue to require attention. Again, more information is needed on how European companies could take advantage of American capital, management, technical, and labor resources.

In Germany there is, first of all, a shortage of capital. This fact, combined with huge demands for money for new investments in Germany itself, leaves little surplus capital available for export. In addition, Germans fear that their money would not go as far in the United States as in Germany because of the exchange rate. "Haircuts alone cost $2.50," was one comment.

Italian businessmen favored in principle investing in the United States. They held that Italy and Europe must be built up, but that this should not exclude entirely doing some business in the U.S. market. Two spectacular examples demonstrating that "it can be done" are: first, the Washington, D.C., Watergate luxury apartment development overlooking the Potomac River, a new enterprise which will have a total value of $66 million when completed—a project spearheaded by Italian management and Italian money; and second, the Olivetti Underwood example. The Watergate project is a joint venture with Americans; the Olivetti Underwood business started as a joint venture, but is today entirely owned and managed by its parent company in Italy.

Case Study: Olivetti

The dramatic Olivetti Underwood venture has become a popular industry case study, and is now part of the Harvard Business School program. Beginning with an initial $8 million, Olivetti built its equity step by step into a $100 million investment. Its ownership jumped from 30 percent initially, to 66 percent, and finally to 100 percent.

The overhaul was painstaking and complete. It meant redoing a factory which had not been equipped in 10 years. It meant complete training and retraining of personnel. It meant setting up a special school for salesmen and servicemen (with teachers from the Olivetti school in Florence, Italy) which trained some 7,000 people in the span of about a year.

When Olivetti began the overhaul in 1959, the first estimates said it would take from three to five years to put the U.S. concern back on its feet. This, in fact, was the case. As Sergio Pizzoni-Ardemani, special assistant to the president, recalled, "As five years expired in November, 1964, we made it." He added that 1964 was the first profitable year since 1955. "It was a tremendous success if you consider that the year before, in 1963, we still had a $5 million loss. As for 1965, the profit was over $1 million." Olivetti Underwood's current share is slightly less than one fifth of the market, and to them the future looks bright. The greatest benefit is that this experience has internationalized the company, enabling it to compete anywhere in the world with the same skill and marketing resources generally credited to American companies.

While Olivetti's plans for rejuvenating the sadly lagging U.S. typewriter company did not go entirely according to plan, and while the final investment was far more than originally envisioned, Olivetti officials consider the operation a success. They would do it again. They are perhaps the strongest advocates in the United States of more reverse flow investments.

Can only European giants follow suit? Chase Manhattan's vice president John Deaver does not believe that the smaller size of most European companies automatically rules them out. "We would like to see more Europeans doing this," he emphasized, "and we are doing everything we can to encourage them."

A vice president of a U.S. firm representing several score of industrial and consumer products agrees. His company would be interested in joint ventures with foreign companies, depending upon what the potential partner might have to contribute. "If the company has something to bring that would be a real contribution to technology or something new, the answer would be definitely yes. This thing has to work both ways."

New York State Success

One of the most encouraging proofs that reverse investment flow is possible, and benefits both parties, is found in New York State's Department of Commerce sales promotion program.

This has been a twin drive that has stimulated New York exports to overseas markets and, at the same time, has persuaded foreign manufacturers to set up shop in New York State. Former Commerce Commissioner Keith S. McHugh has been the power behind the drive with, of course, full support from Governor Nelson A. Rockefeller.

To convert interest and inquiries into business transactions, New York's Department of Commerce opened a Brussels office several years ago and has achieved, in its judgment, "dramatic" results. In terms of exports, Mr. McHugh estimated that 1965 sales to Europe which could be credited to the program were between $60 million and $70 million. "This brings total additional sales since we launched the program to close to $200 million."

While the program's primary thrust was (and still is) to increase exports, New York officials soon realized that the same machinery designed to create interest in American products could also stimulate inquiries into New York investments. This has been a most interesting development which, according to Mr. McHugh, has "just grown like Topsy" out of the export program. In suggesting that New York offers important opportunities for European enterprises, Governor Rockefeller lists the state's unique advantages "in natural resources, water supply, transportation, ample skilled labor, and the largest supply of consumers in the entire 'Common Market' of the 50 United States."

Two–Pronged Approach to Executives. The approach has been direct and personal. Department of Commerce officials headquartered in Brussels seek out chief executives in key industrial concerns across the continent, to explain the advantages and mechanics of New York State investments. The Brussels staff has found that the most appealing approach to European executives is first, to invite them to explore the American market, and second, to describe the advantages in buying New York products. Thus, rather than calling first on the purchasing agent, besieged by salesmen from all companies, the New York representatives start at the top with their two-pronged approach.

The results have been far beyond what even the promotion staff expected. For example, the following are the results of a single two-and-one-half day visit to one German city:

a) 22 German company officers received letters requesting appointments.
b) 2 declined; 20 offered interviews.
c) 15 were interested in licensing agreements or plant establishments.
d) 8 offered to buy New York State products.

New York's experience has been twofold:

First, even when company officials are taken aback by the thought of U.S. investments, they are interested—and flattered. Thus, the seed is planted.

Second, the investment appeal is substantially helping U.S. exports, because the U.S. representative is then able to approach the purchasing director on more solid ground, with a recommendation from the purchasing director's boss. Stressing investment in the United States, then, is stimulating sales from the United States.

The groundwork for the European program was laid through cooperative ventures with Canadian manufacturers, with some 25 Canadian companies setting up branch plants in New York State during the past half-dozen years. But there is a difference between conditions in Europe and in Canada. In Europe, most countries face serious shortages of skilled labor and long-term capital, with no immediate relief in sight, and the New York appeal is keyed to those shortages. New York representatives explain that the United States (and their state) has two economic advantages that other countries cannot offer: abundant labor and ample long-term money. Therefore, why should Europeans try to do all the manufacturing at home? Why not use New York State resources? Without these resources Europeans have less opportunity to expand and take advantage of growing markets in both Europe and the United States.

Further, Mr. McHugh continues, European companies can get better terms on money in New York than in Europe. He explained to the Germans, for example, that a company with good credit could secure 10- to 20-year loans for New York plant construction or expansion, and at lower interest than the short-term money available in Europe. He noted that it is almost impossible to get long-term funds in Germany at any price.

The Follow Through. Negotiations and study by prospective investors in New York take time, up to two years and beyond, before decisions can be made. Mr. McHugh stresses that quick results are not in the cards, and that meticulous support back in America is necessary if there are to be any results at all. New York officials tell foreign manufacturers that if they will locate here, the state government will help them to find a plant site, putting them in touch with bankers and with the New York State Job Development Authority, which can help in financing and in finding skilled labor. If the prospect does not want to risk a full plant operation, New York can get him together with a manufacturer, not directly competitive, but who could make some

135

or all of the product, perhaps doing the final assembly job. As of this writing, New York has between 70 and 80 active prospects from Europe. Lessons learned through the New York program should be useful on a national basis, in Mr. McHugh's judgment.

The federal government would, of course, be involved should this New York concept be carried out on a national scale. If and when the program is expanded, the net result could be a substantial contribution to the U.S. balance of payments problem; and it would also strengthen individual communities, as American labor shares in the new payrolls and American investors participate in some of the financing. Above all, adequate follow-up nationally would have to be available.

Thorny Issues Involved

Throughout the Atlantic Council survey, and through the Atlantic Council and Atlantic Institute conferences in the United States and Europe, U.S. Commerce Department officials have analyzed the thorny political and psychological issues involved in a reverse flow of investments.

No program has unmixed blessings. Europeans could interpret an investment drive as either a public relations ploy or as "another scheme" by America to dominate European business. Conversely, America could complain (with some justification) that inviting Europeans to compete on our doorstep is just plain inviting trouble. Similarly, if reverse investments provide temporary relief to America in its balance of payments problem, the same flow can hurt Europeans, particularly the British, whose problems exceed our own. Finally, over the long haul reverse investments may actually result in more dollars escaping from the United States as the Europeans repatriate their profits and stimulate their own exports to their American subsidiaries. However, to those who believe in the freest possible flow of funds as well as products, these arguments are not warnings to turn back, but rather to proceed with care.

A great deal of research and liaison is in order, beginning with Commerce, Treasury, and State Department officials in Washington. A first step in this direction has come with the appointment by the Commerce Department of a banker with many years of international experience to serve as an industrial development specialist in Europe. As such, this professional is being charged to deal with organizations and individuals throughout Western Europe in an effort to kindle interest in direct investment of foreign capital in the United States. He is to advise and further the knowledge of interested European companies in direct investments, in plant ventures, and in cross-licensing. The U.S. government hopes that his presence in Europe, headquartered in Paris but not confined to any single country, will demonstrate the validity of U.S. official interest in attracting fresh foreign capital to the United States.

Broad Participation Needed

A full program would no doubt involve the efforts of state and private sector trade expansion offices in the United States; U.S. embassies, missions and consulates throughout Europe; host government and trade officials in key countries; and U.S. and European businessmen. The job can be started by the U.S. government, but it requires, emphatically, broad participation.

One leading German banker believes that there are many companies that could be interested in U.S. investment provided they were approached properly. He suggested an informal committee of Americans and Europeans to appraise possibilities. No doubt the several trade organizations representing businessmen could play a useful role—the British Board of Trade, the Belgian Federation of Industry, Germany's BDI, France's Patronat, the Chamber of Commerce and Industry in Spain, and so on throughout Western Europe and North America.

Ultimately, personal involvement must no doubt be the final answer, since convincing cannot be done through brochures, policy speeches, or even direct calls by U.S. representatives. Large transatlantic investments will obviously require transatlantic trips and transatlantic relationships on a scale that exceeds anything experienced to date. Should the effort prove successful, the climate for business expansion could improve for everyone.

8 Capital Markets

PART 1 *Introduction by Dr. Sidney E. Rolfe*

139

Dr. Sidney E. Rolfe has written extensively on monetary-financial matters. His latest book **Gold and World Power** (New York: Harper & Row, 1966) is an analysis of the balance of payments problem and the plans for the reform of the system. He has been on the faculties of Princeton and Columbia Universities and is visiting professor at the New School for Social Research. His business experience includes seven years as chief economist for the C.I.T. Financial Corporation, five years as president of a private group of real estate and investment companies, and consulting assignments with corporations on finance, domestic and international affairs.

EDITOR'S NOTE: *Any discussion of Atlantic economic growth would obviously be incomplete without an appraisal of the crucial subject of capital markets. This issue has become a critical pivot on which economic growth will either progress or stumble, especially in Europe. One of the most knowledgeable spokesmen in this field is Dr. Sidney E. Rolfe, who headed the Atlantic Institute's recent study of European capital markets which culminated in the conference held at Cannes in January 1967 under the joint sponsorship of the Atlantic Institute and the Business and Industry Advisory Committee to the Organization for Economic Cooperation and Development. He has researched the subject extensively in*

The European capital market has at least two faces. When viewed from the American perspective, it once was a giant and can be again. From the European viewpoint it is perhaps resurgent, but at the moment it is still a bundle of restrictions and problems in evolution.

In the American view the Europeans should provide more capital. And since the nations of Europe have now reached advanced stages of economic development, they *should* be able to develop capital markets capable of contributing more capital for European development, for international use, and for the developing countries. Savings in many European nations, in fact, outstrip those in the United States as a percentage of GNP.

In addition, some nations have run considerable balance of payment surpluses recently and thus hold vast resources of gold and dollars. Germany and France combined, for example, hold a stock of gold about equal to that of the United States.

The argument that Europeans should provide more capital has become particularly moving recently in view of the continued difficulties of the American balance of payments. Under the existing rules of international monetary be-

havior, a country with a payments deficit—resulting in a so-called gold drain—has virtually no recourse other than to place controls over capital flows. Consequently, when the United States introduced its capital controls—in the form of the 1963 interest equalization tax, the Gore amendment for banks, and the "voluntary" controls over corporate investment—the United States virtually ended the role of New York as the great capital market for Europe, though not for others such as Canada, Japan, and the less developed countries. In effect, there was an attempt to shift the task of financing European development back to Europe.

But when the same problem is seen from the European point of view, it appears quite different. In the first place, there is no single European capital market in which funds can flow freely among nations. An investor in one country, for example, cannot easily purchase bonds in another.

As one leading European investment banker has put it:

One of the objectives of the Treaty of Rome is the liberalization of the flow of capital, and while remarkable progress has been achieved in freeing trade, very little headway has been made on connecting capital markets in the Common Market or in Europe generally. In the absence of a unified European capital market the capacity for absorbing foreign issues in

140

each national market depends on foreign exchange controls, different issue and withholding taxes, and a variety of other legal and administrative complications. Furthermore, local capital markets are dominated by domestic economic interests and policies.

International Market Does Exist in Europe

If there exists no single European capital market, there does exist an *international* capital market, frequently referred to as the international dollar market because most issues are repayable in dollars. The market has no seat, no locale. John Davenport has written in *Fortune*, "It exists not only in the air, but in the ether." Nevertheless, judging by the amounts of money in it, it is a very effective operation.

In terms of present scale, $132 million was raised in July 1966 (an annual rate in excess of $1.5 billion) in this "international market." While it normally includes a fair proportion of American corporate borrowers, money is also borrowed in it for a wide variety of foreign borrowers, both governments and corporations. Indeed, in July 1966, all but one of the issues were non-American, although most of the funds transacted were in dollars. Interest yields ran between 6 and 7 percent, depending on the features of the issues. The dollar

designation reflects the fact that the market owes its origins to the launching of U.S. corporate issues.

The bulk of the investment—purchase of bonds—in this international market comes from accounts held in Switzerland, the Far East, and Latin America. Only a marginal amount is from European countries. The capacity of Europeans to buy these issues depends on various factors in each country. Germans, for example, are quite free to buy them. In France, while there exists a theoretical right to buy, government authorization is needed before banks will sell the issues.

Do Restrictions Help Payments Position?

Where, then, does the actual money for such investments originate? It is hard to tell, partly because of Swiss banking secrecy laws. Certainly some European funds come into Switzerland to purchase these issues. But it also appears that some, possibly a substantial proportion of the funds, were formerly invested in American stocks or other securities. Because of the declining U.S. securities market, those funds have been put into the new high-yielding issues in the international market.

The international bond issues are sold by syndicates of banks and investment houses, which are partially American and increasingly European. Probably the largest sellers of these bonds are the great American banks through their networks of branch offices in Europe, Latin America, and the Far East. Certainly not far behind them are the Swiss banks, and the various investment bankers who participate in the syndicates. The international market has undoubtedly been a stimulant in teaching European financial institutions to work together, thus providing one of the important components of what may, in the future, be a truly European capital market.

Europe's National Capital Markets—the Challenge

The advanced capital markets, particularly the U.S. and the U.K., for more than a century have had virtually uninterrupted financial development and growth. But the wartime destruction and the postwar currency upheavals in Europe destroyed the stock of institutions and practices. And above all they destroyed the confidence on which a capital market must live. Therefore, the task at hand in Europe is to build almost anew, against a background of very grave doubts which past experience has taught.

The method of financing of European corporations under the aegis of the Marshall Plan required virtually no capital markets. In the postwar years, very heavy reliance was placed on self-financing—the use of internal profits—as a source of corporate investment. But in recent years, as wages in Europe have risen sharply, corporate profits have declined. The Belgian banker, Alexandre Lamfalussy, has described the situation this way:

One of the most striking facts in the development of the main Common Market countries since 1960 has been the rise of the share of wages in the national income. For the period 1955–59, this share was 59 percent in France, 59.5 percent in Germany, and 51.6 percent in Italy. By 1963, the figure rose to 62 percent in France, 64.5 percent in Germany, and 58.6 percent in Italy. . . . Since the shortage of labor is going to be a more or less permanent feature of Continental Europe's economic scene for the years to come, the percentages given for 1963 are more likely to go up than down.

The prophecy has been correct: with labor shortages, the rise in wages has been even more marked in 1965 and 1966. Industrial prices have not risen to offset increased costs, either because of price controls or because of the fear of international competition. Consequently, there has been a vast squeeze on profits, which has forced corporations to seek "external" financing in the capital markets in hitherto unprecedented quantities. This has, of course, placed a priority on the development of capital markets inside Europe to provide the required financing.

Increased Government Financing Needs

At the same time, governments have spent increasingly for their infrastructure needs, to build hospitals, schools, housing, roads, and even swimming pools. Moreover, government expenditures have been financed increasingly by debt rather than increased taxes. Thus, in the EEC, public authority and local authority bond issues, as a share of the total security issues, rose from 9 percent to 17 percent between 1961 and 1965. In some cases, notably Germany, governmental power is so fragmented that the central authority has had no power to coordinate the nearly 26,000 local units, nationalized utilities, and so forth, from going into the capital markets at will without reference to the overall picture.

The decline in self-financing and increase of government debt comprise two elements of demand. Yet a third element is the reduction of the supply of capital from the New York market and the floating of the aforementioned international issues. The reaction of most European governments and central banks (and more recently the United States too) to these increased demands for capital has been a policy-mix which relies heavily on monetary measures—hence higher interest rates—rather than on fiscal measures, such as increased taxes. The consequence for most of Europe has been a soaring interest rate structure, reaching 35-year-high levels. And this has borne particularly hard on private business, especially on smaller firms with lower credit ratings than the giants.

Thorkil Kristensen, secretary general of OECD, has stated the prevailing criticism of this policy-mix forthrightly:

In a number of European countries there have been inflationary tendencies in recent years, mainly due to excess demand. In fact, governments and parliaments have not been firm enough in resisting the pressure for higher public expenditure without sufficient increase of taxation at the same time. In the absence of sufficiently firm fiscal policies, some central banks have had to restrict credit and try to curb inflation through high rates of interest. This, however, is unfortunate, not only because such policies are harmful to productive investment, but also because the very high rates of interest in some European countries have had a disturbing influence on the international monetary system.

It was evident that interest rates could not long be sustained at the high level of late 1966 without serious dangers of recession. It was also evident that major reductions in any one country alone would give rise to fresh balance of payments problems. The January 1967 meeting of the finance ministers of France, Germany, Italy, the U.K. and the U.S. was instrumental in stimulating a general trend toward lower rates.

Can Stocks Fill Financing Gap?

The discussion of interest rates and bonds leaves open the question of equity shares, or stocks. Clearly stocks are the best substitute for corporations for the lost internal income as a source of financing. But while the issuing of new shares has been fairly active in Europe, it is judged inadequate to the need. Indeed, one of the major capital market problems is to create an active share market so that funds can be easily raised this way.

The barriers to this type of financing are many and varied. But high on the list is the decline of stock prices in every country from their 1962 highs. In France, for example, the index average (1947 = 100) stood at about 800 in 1962, but is now below 600. A falling or stagnant market is obviously no stimulus to mass buying.

In general, the European stock markets lack so-called "secondary support." Whereas in the United States and the United Kingdom this secondary support comes steadily from such sources as pension funds and insurance companies, these are negligible in Europe, except Holland. On the contrary, households account for some 40 percent of all share purchases in both France and Germany.

Thus under existing conditions —the alternatives of high-interest rate bonds, the lack of capital gain prospects, the expectation for continuing low profits—share buying is not as attractive as it might be. Consequently European bourses (stock exchanges) have been depressed since about 1962, when the interest equalization tax cut off American buying and the profits squeeze reduced European buying.

Much is made of certain noneconomic factors as deterrents to a stock market in Europe. These are said to be the lack of disclosure of information, the so-called "insider-dealing," the lottery atmosphere as opposed to investment, and so forth. While better disclosure procedures are needed, it is easy to make too much of these factors. Their presence (or absence) did not, after all, deter the 1955–62 rise in stock prices. On balance the short-run prospects for active bourses in Europe is not very strong, even with certain reforms.

Future of European Capital Markets?

It is, of course, impossible to predict precisely what the future of the European capital markets will be. Yet certain trends are clearly discernible. Perhaps the first noteworthy trend is a profound level of concern. This is illustrated in a series of studies and analyses which obviously deepen and widen Europe's understanding of its own capital market problems.

Apart from the monumental study and recommendations by the OECD, there is in creation a similar study by the EEC. On the American side, Professor Ira O. Scott, Jr., dean at Long Island University Graduate School of Business Administration, has made a study for the Comptroller of the Currency which should eclipse previous U.S. data, and be a major contribution. Private sources have also contributed numerous articles and studies, of which the 1966 joint analysis prepared by four European banks (Midland-Amro-Deutsche-Societe Generale) stands out. A study and conference jointly sponsored by the Atlantic Institute and BIAC, under the chairmanship of Mr. Wilfrid Baumgartner (formerly governor of the Bank of France and ex-Finance Minister, now president of Rhone-Poulenc), provide a private, high-level source of analysis and recommendation for the future of Europe.

Apart from studies, new laws and regulations are being prepared in most countries of Europe. As noted, one of the major problems in every country is the weakness of the stock market. To rectify this, a number of countries are taking various steps. Perhaps the most interesting, if yet untested, is the Norwegian law permitting dividends to be tax-deductible to a corporation, as interest payments now are. In France new tax laws have been put forward which make it more advantageous to buy French, but not international, shares. In Italy a new law is being debated to permit investment trusts to function in an attempt to move toward contractual-savings forms, going into shares. In Germany a better disclosure law—a need in every European country— has been passed and other steps taken. Moreover, a reduction in interest rates will clearly make share-yields relatively more attractive than bonds and should serve to stimulate some buying.

145

International Capital Arrangements

On the international scene, perhaps the decisive battles are yet to be fought. For while there is strong pressure for the liberalization of international capital movements from the "internationalists" —including the OECD, the EEC, and other supragovernment authorities—there is equally strong resistance from the nationalistic forces in Europe.

If it is vain to think in any near-term future of a single European currency which would facilitate international capital flows, it is less vain to think about two other possibilities now being discussed. The first is the harmonization of taxes on all varieties of investments among the Common Market countries. This would leave differential interest rates as the sole determinant of investments among the countries.

The second is a *tranche*, or quota, which governments *must* allow their people to invest in the securities of other nations. Some stipulated figure which governments could not nullify and which is free to go into international markets would be a giant step forward and may well come into being in the future under the "Third Directive" of the EEC Commission.

---

8 PART 2 *Interview with Secretary Henry H. Fowler*

As the chief monetary officer for the United States, Secretary of the Treasury Henry H. Fowler is deeply involved in efforts to end the U.S. balance of payments deficit. While Under Secretary of the Treasury, he headed the Presidential Task Force on investment aspects of this problem. He began his government service in 1941 with the Office of Production Management and the War Production Board. From 1946 to 1961 he returned to private law practice, except for a two-year period from 1951 to 1953, when he was associated with the National Production Administration as Deputy Administrator and Administrator. He was Under Secretary of the Treasury from 1961 to 1964, and was recalled from law practice again in 1965 to assume his present Cabinet position.

Photo by Fabian Bachrach

EDITOR'S NOTE: *Few issues are followed so closely by the U.S. government as the development of European capital markets. Treasury Secretary Henry H. Fowler is the U.S. Cabinet officer most directly concerned. In the interview which follows, he points out that improvement of European capital markets bears not so much on* whether *the United States balances its international payments, "but on* how *we achieve that equilibrium."*

Q. Why has the United States taken such an interest in the strengthening of European capital markets? Your predecessor, Secretary Douglas Dillon, raised this issue with the Monetary Conference of the American Bankers Association in Rome in 1962. You laid great stress on this point in your address to the Atlantic Council Conference in Crotonville, New York, in December, 1965; and the United States has been a strong supporter of the studies of this subject by the Organization for Economic Cooperation and Development.

A. Some flows of capital across the Atlantic, in both directions are, of course, desirable. For some years Europe has been a major importer of capital from the United States. In the years 1960–64, outflows of U.S. private capital to Western Europe averaged $1.6 billion, reaching $2.3 billion in 1964. Even with the interest equalization tax and the voluntary restraint program in effect, these flows from the United States to Europe amounted to $1.2 billion in 1965. I feel that if the European countries wish to maintain high levels of investment and rapid economic growth, they must find ways to draw to a greater extent on their own savings for this purpose and that they should not continue to depend to such an extent on U.S. capital.

Q. But doesn't Europe have a higher rate of saving than the United States? If this is so, why do they depend on U.S. capital?

A. Europe does indeed have a higher rate of saving. In 1965, the ratio of savings to gross national product in the OECD countries of Western Europe averaged over 23 percent, as compared to a figure of 18.5 percent in the United States. But we have to keep two facts in mind:

1. The rate of investment in Europe is also higher, and tends to place pressure on savings. In other words, you have to look at both sides of the equation, the demand for capital as well as the supply.

2. Inefficiencies in European mechanisms for matching up savings and investment make the final cost of European savings to some users unduly expensive or leave pockets of unsatisfied or only partially satisfied demand. The result is that you have European borrowers looking to the U.S. for capital.

Q. Is it correct to say that European capital markets should be improved so that the United States can balance its payments?

A. Not precisely. That would be an oversimplification. The degree to which European capital markets are improved will bear not so much on *whether* we achieve equilibrium in our balance of payments—for this we are going to do in any case—but on *how* we achieve that equilibrium. In fact, you have only to look back to see the truth in what I say. We have had to use governmental intervention—through the interest equalization tax and the voluntary restraint program—to bring capital outflow down to its present level. We would

147

like to see an improvement in Europe's capital markets and an increase in the availability of savings relative to demand, to the extent that our governmental restraints could be eliminated without resulting in an excessive flow of U.S. funds to Europe.

Furthermore, most European countries recognize that they should contribute to the capital needs of the developing countries. To do this they have to be net *exporters* of capital, and good capital markets are needed to supplement the flow of official assistance.

Finally, Europeans must realize, and I think they do, that since U.S. capital is not going to be available to fill all the gaps, they must develop their capital markets in order to finance their growth. If a bond issue can't be financed in the United States, it is simply going to have to be floated in Europe, or not be floated.

Q. What is the basic problem with Europe's capital markets?

A. They are not as good as they should be at delivering the right amount of financing, in the right form, and at the right price. This causes problems for the person trying to get a mortgage for the home he wants to buy, for the corporate executive looking for funds to build a new plant, and sometimes even for the government seeking to finance its budget deficit.

Q. What is required to improve European capital markets?

A. Many things. The task involves a restructuring and strengthening of capital markets. New attitudes and habits of savings and investment will be necessary. For example, in the past the European saver has all too frequently placed his savings in a simple, semirigid pattern, be it in real estate, or the local savings bank, or elsewhere. In the future he must become a better-informed investor, diversifying his placements flexibly and according to the incentives offered him. Further liberalization is also necessary, of both governmental and institutional rules and restrictions governing capital transactions. In addition, more progress must be made in developing investment marketing networks to float the large-scale issues required by modern industrial enterprises.

In sum, it is not a single measure which is called for, but a modification of governmental policies together with a broad-scale attack on legal, traditional, and institutional arrangements which now prevent capital markets from operating with the efficiency and at the lowest rates of interest of which they are potentially capable.

Q. What lies behind these problems?

A. This question deserves a book-length answer — and the OECD is producing one right now.

But if I had to point to one factor that I considered most important, it would have to be the fact that European governments are in a position to, and frequently do, stake first claim on available funds. For example, official actions of European governments too often circumvent healthy competitive practices to give private housing a priority position. The businessman who wants to build a plant or buy some equipment must, therefore, make do with the leftover scraps.

Q. Doesn't the size of the market have much to do with explaining the problems of European markets? In other words, isn't there only so much that can be done as long as Europe is made up of a number of separate and distinct countries?

A. Size is of course a factor, and this is why the work that is going on in developing links between national markets is important. However, size is only one factor, and you must remember that there are some well-developed markets in smaller countries—for example, in Switzerland and The Netherlands.

Q. How far away is a unified European capital market?

A. A wholly unified European capital market would involve a very substantial degree of harmonization of economic and financial policies, some of which are in prospect within the Common Market. But in the meantime, there is no reason why there could not be a great deal of valuable progress achieved through harmonizing institutional practices and procedures, and through reducing administrative obstacles to capital flows among European markets.

The situation varies from country to country. The capital markets of the several European countries differ markedly, and it is important to make clear that most of the European countries do have sizable capital markets, some of them highly efficient. However, I would say that attention should be concentrated on the following areas:

a) *Institutional investors:* Such investors have a vital role to play in a well-developed capital market. In many instances, a high priority should be given both to facilitating the growth of these institutions and to increasing their freedom of choice in selecting their investments.

b) *Flow of information:* Better information about the financial position and operations of business is especially important if wider participation in corporate security issues is to be achieved. A broad class of investors can only be developed on the basis of more regular, consistent, and comprehensive information than is now available in many instances.

c) *Flexibility of market instruments:* The availability of capital market instruments closely fitted to the needs of borrowers and lenders has been a striking feature of those world capital markets which are most efficient. Some welcome progress has been made in this direction in recent years, for example, by facilitating the formation of mutual funds, but more can be done.

d) Liberalization of international capital movements: I believe there has been a lag in Continental Europe in this area. Despite the development of strong currencies, European thinking is still heavily influenced by the difficulties of the postwar period. Many European countries are in a good position to carry their liberalization of capital movements much further along, especially in the direction of allowing their businessmen and financiers more freedom to go abroad and compete.

e) Finally, as suggested earlier, something must be done to give the private sector a fairer competitive chance at available funds. I will count on the private sectors in the European countries to spell out the details, since only they can have a full understanding of what is lacking and what is needed.

Q. U.S. spokesmen have been urging this for several years. Do the Europeans reject this point of view?

A. Not at all. I think there is virtually universal recognition of the desirability of improving European capital markets. Several European countries have made special studies as to how to improve their markets. A Common Market group has been looking at some aspects of the problem. Ministers from the OECD countries at their meeting in December 1964 formally recognized the importance of more effective capital markets.

However, I wonder if the Europeans understand the urgency of the situation. I say this because actions taken by the United States to reduce the flow of capital—the interest equalization tax and the voluntary restraint program—were clearly the major factors behind one of the most encouraging developments we have seen on the European financial scene. This has been the transformation of the international bond market in Europe, in size and stature. In 1961–62, for example, the total of new security issues floated by nondomestic borrowers on European markets averaged under $0.5 billion. This was prior to imposition of the interest equalization tax. By 1965, after imposition of that tax, the level of issues was well over twice that figure.

But I do not want to obscure the fact that European governments are giving serious consideration to measures which would increase the efficiency of their markets and increase their accessibility to foreign borrowers as well.

Q. In fact, then, there is a substantial measure of agreement between the United States and Europe on the capital markets question?

A. Yes, I think it is fair to say that almost everyone agrees on at least two conclusions that we have been discussing today: that the U.S. balance of payments should be brought into equilibrium and that European capital markets should be improved. It seems to me that disagreement about the relationship between these two goals has clouded the more important fact that there is agreement on where we should be headed.

Q. How long should it take to accomplish what is necessary?

A. I would not want to get into a guessing game on this. The important point is to be making progress, and not be standing still.

Q. Who will be instrumental in making the progress you regard as being essential?

A. The OECD has been continuing its studies on the subject and a major report is in the offing. I hope there will be a follow-up procedure for assisting in the translation of plans into action. The European Common Market has been wrestling with this question and working particularly on ways to harmonize arrangements within the Six. Several national governments have had special commissions or special studies undertaken to develop recommendations for action.

In this connection, the work of the Atlantic Institute itself is important. In particular, I welcome the contribution of the Capital Markets Conference in Cannes earlier this year, sponsored jointly by the Institute and the Business and Industry Advisory Committee to the OECD, which brought together interested persons from the private sector. We are making good progress in getting governments to focus on the problems of capital markets. Now we need to hear more from businessmen and financiers. They are really the people who suffer most from the inadequacies of these markets.

Many of the needed improvements are not dependent on governments at all. Indeed, they are the responsibility of private institutions, and it is only their interest and concern which will produce the needed changes. Even where the responsibility does lie with governments, not only are views of private parties on the problems and possible solutions useful, but ultimately their support of improvements advocated will be a critical factor in the success or failure of many key proposals.

8 PART 3 *Cannes Report*

EDITOR'S NOTE: *As Secretary Fowler notes in his concluding remarks, the problem of inadequate capital markets cannot be solved by governments alone. For the purpose of stimulating the support of the private sector, the Atlantic Institute and the BIAC to the OECD sponsored a capital markets conference in Cannes, France, January 22, 1967, where the participants were 60 distinguished bankers and industrialists from Europe, North America, and Japan.*

Mr. Wilfrid Baumgartner served as chairman; Dr. Sidney E. Rolfe, as conference director. Three areas of actions were identified:

1. Improvements within the several national capital markets;

2. Improved international links to permit a greater international flow of capital; and

3. Changes in certain government economic policies.

Because of the significance of this conference as a major first step by the private sector, the full text of the conference recommendations are herewith printed as follows.

I. The national capital markets must be stimulated by cooperative action between government, industry, and financial institutions.

II. To stimulate and expand private contractual savings should be one of the primary policy objectives of governments. In order to implement this recommendation, the following proposals are made:

A. Pension funds, insurance, and other forms of contractual savings should be stimulated by tax and other inducements, and by further enabling legislation in those countries where it is now lacking.

B. Governmental regulations restricting institutional purchases in capital markets should be relaxed as much as possible.

C. In the field of insurance, the use of funding techniques should be encouraged.

III. To promote and increase household savings, with a view to overcoming the preference for excessive liquidity, it is essential that inflationary tendencies be continuously controlled. It is also necessary to improve the methods and formulae likely to encourage earners to save.

IV. For their part, governments should adjust their borrowing policies by limiting their demands to a level commensurate with an orderly functioning of the capital markets; by coordinating all types of public borrowing; by aiming at financial equilibrium and self-sufficiency for state enterprises; and finally by limiting the activities of public and semi-public lending institutions to the purpose for which they were created.

V. Governments should rely, in carrying out their general economic policies, on budgetary policy to a greater degree than has generally been the case. Too heavy a reliance on monetary measures can have a detrimental effect on the economy as a whole and particularly on the capital markets.

VI. The appropriate authorities should reconsider and reduce those rules which restrict the freedom of action of existing financial intermediaries; these restrictions were often designed to meet problems no longer extant or of questionable priority. This involves increased competition for long-term loans and flotations in the financial markets, and a reasonable development of the use of bank deposits for medium- and long-term loans. Investors and those seeking capital should have access to markets of their choice.

VII. The conference wishes to emphasize the importance of measures recently taken by certain governments to strengthen their capital markets, and particularly to improve the supply of equity capital to enterprise by appropriate tax inducements. The creation of high standards of disclosure is also recommended.

VIII. To assure the most effective use of available resources, measures should be taken aiming at the complete liberalization of international capital flows. The simplification and the eventual elimination of the presently high complex foreign exchange regulations would contribute to this end.

IX. The use of restrictions on international capital movements to correct economic disturbances originating in areas other than capital markets should be avoided as such practices result in fragmented national capital markets.

X. The recommendations put forward by a group of experts appointed by the EEC Commission to study the development of a European capital market should be carefully considered by all OECD countries. It is particularly urgent to assure fiscal harmonization at the cost level; the abolition of multiple taxation; and the free access of foreign issues, including Euro-issues, on all markets and the development of secondary markets. The use of a single official exchange rate for all financial transactions is recommended.

XI. The work performed by the OECD with respect to the liberalization of capital movements should be actively pursued and implemented.

9 Atlantic Community and the Developing Nations

PART 1 *Introduction*
by Ambassador Willard L. Thorp

Ambassador Willard L. Thorp's position as chairman of OECD Development Assistance Committee caps a long and distinguished career in public service and economic affairs. He joined the State Department in 1945, having previously been editor of the financial publication **Dun's Review**, and director of economic research for Dun and Bradstreet, Inc. He served first as Deputy Assistant Secretary of State for Economic Affairs, then as Assistant Secretary. In 1952, he moved to Amherst College as professor of economics and director of the Merrill Center for Economics. In his long career, he has headed a number of private and governmental delegations to international conferences, and has authored several articles and books, including **Trade, Aid, or What?**, and **The New Inflation**.

Photo by Leo Jouan for OECD

Living standards in the Atlantic Community are at new highs. But in the great majority of countries —the so-called less developed nations—the people are still faced with poverty, disease, and ignorance. Discontent constantly threatens governments with unrest and revolt.

The new political independence recently achieved by so many of these countries has not provided them with increased economic resources or greater ability to produce the goods and services which they desire. In fact, some new burdens are likely to have been added, such as the cost of foreign representation, the support of a full-scale government, and a complete and generous social security system.

157

Nevertheless, their ambitions have been released and the new emphasis on economic development is beginning to produce results. In the first five years of this decade, their overall average rate of growth in gross national product (corrected for change in price level), was 5 percent per year, almost exactly the same as that of the industrial countries during the same period. However, since their rate of population increase is higher, their rate of gain for the average man has been lower than in the richer countries.

Boosting Productivity

The problem of economic development involves many elements. Basically, it must be achieved by increasing the productivity of the country, which means the productivity of its citizens and its capital resources. The nations of the Atlantic Community, to illustrate one side, could not stop their economic growth for long even if they tried to, because research and development, and institutionalized savings and investment, are built into their economic life. The institutions in a less developed country, on the other hand, are often centered on maintaining the status quo, on resisting interference and change.

Any poor country, therefore, is faced by a number of obstacles to growth. Assuming the priority requirement of law and order, there are three points where there can be serious bottlenecks: (1) shortage of knowledge and skilled manpower; (2) shortage of domestic savings for investment; and (3) shortage of foreign exchange.

The requirements in these three areas can be met, at least in part, by foreign assistance to the domestic effort. Furthermore, foreign assistance can not only help in dealing with these existing difficulties, but it should be aimed at building up the process whereby the country can itself meet its requirements in the future. Thus, while teachers may be supplied through Peace Corps and other assistance programs, it is equally important to provide teacher-trainers and then teacher-trainers to train teacher-trainers. At some point, the whole process of foreign assistance can be dismantled and the country can proceed with full reliance on its own resources.

Trade Is the Key

By all odds, the most important way the less developed countries obtain goods and services which they want from the outside world is through trade. Such exports as they are able to make, plus various services such as tourism, are paid for in foreign exchange which can then be spent for goods. Presumably, the more foreign exchange they can earn, the less foreign aid will be required. Depending upon who and what are counted, the figures for imports or exports by less developed countries, excluding trade with each other, is between $30 billion and $40 billion per year, and has been growing at 5 to 10 percent annually.

While primary products—such as agricultural and forest products, and minerals—make up the basic core of the exports of less developed countries, they are paying more and more attention to the possible development of trade in manufactured goods. In many less developed countries, manufacturing output is growing at between 5 and 10 percent annually, although usually it is still only a small fraction of total economic activity. Much of the development to date has taken the form of import substitution—where a market has already been created for a product through importing it. In these cases, transportation costs and a high tariff may give an infant industry an assured market. However, this may merely lead to a high-cost product made possible by a tariff wall.

Somewhat more than this is needed to produce an export industry. It seems clear that certain manufactured goods have a potential for export, particularly those which depend more on labor than

on capital. Given an appropriate foreign exchange rate, they might be sold in foreign markets, if they can get into them. For this purpose, the less developed countries are seeking certain modifications in trade policy from the industrial countries. In the first place, they ask that their products not be barred by tariffs from the markets in the industrial countries. Secondly, they ask that, while barriers are lowered to them, they not be lowered equally for the same goods when produced in other industrial countries. This would give less developed countries preferential treatment as compared with other external producers.

159

Reaction from Industrial Nations

These new proposals have not been welcomed by the industrial countries. Trade policies have long histories, and have varied from time to time between two objectives. One is to make the lowest cost goods available to the consumer, whether foreign or domestic. This approach implies a large volume of trade and a minimum of barriers to it. The other objective is to protect established producers from foreign competition, and this implies barriers to imports on a selective basis.

The new objective which has been suggested is to arrange trade barriers so as to encourage the economic development of less developed countries by encouraging their export trade. This new problem has been taken under consideration by the GATT. A wise policy might be for the industrial nations to permit the growth of new foreign sources of supply, but to make certain that it happens gradually, to avoid quick, drastic adjustments.

The notion of expanding trade depends, of course, upon progress in production in the less developed countries themselves. This requires action of many kinds. There are many general requirements to be met—social infrastructure projects, such as education and public health; and economic infrastructure, such as roads, harbors, and electric power. And then there is the specific industry development, with its requirements of technical competence and capital.

For centuries, these elements have flowed from the industrial countries to the rest of the world. Until recently, this was almost entirely in the form of private investment, and it is still true that the flow of private capital is an important source of economic development. It is particularly valuable because such investment usually involves not only a capital flow but various skills—including persons with management, engineering, and operational experience. In ad-

dition, these enterprises become involved in many related activities, such as education and training, hospitals, and community development. In the past, much of this activity involved the developing of extractive industries but today the scope of private investment is much broader.

Private Investment: Over $3 Billion

For 1965, the 15 industrialized countries which are members of the Development Assistance Committee (DAC) reported that new direct private investment in less developed countries was $2.21 billion. About 60 percent of this amount was new capital; 40 percent was reinvested earnings. In addition, another $640 million took the form of the purchase of securities in existing enterprises. Furthermore, securities were sold in the capital markets by multilateral agencies such as the World Bank, which increased their securities outstanding by $290 million. Finally, private export credits, most of which had a government guarantee, increased during the year by $740 million.

Adding all these together, one can say that the net private capital flow to less developed countries in 1965 was at least $3.88 billion. The United States was the source of 45 percent of the total, followed in order by France, the United Kingdom, Germany, and Japan. In proportion to their national incomes, the order was The Netherlands, Belgium, France, the United Kingdom, and Norway, with the United States in ninth place. Private flows have increased rapidly during the last two years, but may be somewhat deterred in the immediate future by balance of payments difficulties and high interest rates at home.

The flow of private capital is determined by a large number of decisions made independently by private persons. The industrial governments can interpose obstacles to prevent investments, but there is little which they can do to make a private foreign investment take place. However, in such an attempt, various actions have been taken by different governments to make foreign investment more attractive. For example, the American guarantee program, which now is available with respect to investments in over 70 countries, offers low-cost insurance against the inability to transfer profits, and against loss resulting from war or expropriation. Some governments give especially favorable tax treatment to foreign investment.

In addition, business itself is engaged in international efforts to promote the flow of capital to less developed countries. This includes policy organizations, such as the International Chamber of Commerce; and action organizations such as the Atlantic Community Development Group for Latin America (ADELA), which started in 1964 and which has obtained capital from enterprises in most Atlantic Community countries. By the end of 1965, ADELA had approved 27 equity investments and had granted loans in 7 Latin American countries.

Trade and Private Capital Not Enough

Trade and the flow of private capital, however, do not fully meet the three shortages noted above— lack of skills and knowledge, shortage of savings, and insufficient foreign exchange. Thus, there has come to be added another flow known as foreign aid. In 1965, the 15 members of the DAC had gross disbursements of aid to less developed countries of more than $7 billion. More than $500 million went to less developed countries via the multilateral agencies, but the remainder went directly to assist one or another less developed country. (It should be noted that the Atlantic area donors, plus Japan and Australia, are the 15 members of the DAC. It meets in Paris under the aegis of the Organization for Economic Cooperation and Development [OECD], and provides a meeting place for off-the-record discussion among donors of matters bearing on the volume and the effectiveness of their several assistance programs. The United States represents about 60 percent of the total DAC flow.)

This is not to say, of course, that there was any such actual flow of funds. Foreign aid consists of the payment for goods and services which are provided on various terms by the supplying country. In the field of technical assistance, experts may come from government payrolls. Most of them, however, are not professional civil servants, but come from universities, engineering firms, or (like the Peace Corps) simply from private life. As far as the goods which are provided, be they power plants, plows, or penicillin, they are almost entirely the products of private farms and factories in the industrial countries. Even when construction in a foreign country is involved, it is likely to be carried out by a private contractor from an industrial country. Thus, private enterprise plays a very substantial role in the operation of public programs; and to the extent that the new facilities or products generate further demands, they contribute to future trade expansion.

Because of the fact that many of the less developed countries are already heavily in debt, and addi-

tional debt service will merely mean that more and more will have to be given as aid so that it can be paid back to the lenders, a major effort has been made to keep charges low. In 1965, about 60 percent of the public assistance was on a grant basis and much of the remainder was at low interest rates with long maturities.

Can We Solve the Food Problem?

Among the newer subjects under active consideration by the DAC is the world food situation. One might think of agriculture as an economic operation which is almost entirely domestic in character, but it is now a matter of major international concern. Present trends are clear and disturbing: world population is growing faster than food production. The surpluses which had been accumulated in the United States—which have been the chief means of meeting the deficits—have now been virtually exhausted. Asia, which had a small export of grain in the 1930's, imported 16 million metric tons in 1960 and is expected to import 30 million tons in 1966. Eastern Europe likewise has shifted from the export column to being a large importer.

The short-run requirement is to make food available to the deficit countries, and this will have to be financed largely within economic assistance programs. The long-run requirements are to increase agricultural productivity in the less developed countries and to reduce the rate of population increase.

The provision of interim food aid requires new policies in the developed world. Programs aimed at avoiding surpluses and maintaining farm prices must give way to increased outputs and new financing procedures. (The nation physically supplying food need not necessarily be the one providing the related financial assistance to the deficit country.)

All countries are involved in the supply problem, for reducing one's imports or contributing specialties like milk powder will be needed on all sides to get through the shortage period. Thus, one can envisage the gradual liquidation of production control schemes, and the wraps being gradually removed from farmers so that they can at last demonstrate their real productive capacity. This involves not only the farmer's operations, but a comparable growth in the vast number of supporting activities which are essential to his effective performance. A few of the deficit countries may be able to finance their purchases, but others who are already receiving foreign aid will either have increased aid requirements or will have to cut back on their development programs.

The longer run problem of improving agricultural productivity centers much more on the less developed countries. In some cases, there is still fertile land to be exploited or made usable through irrigation. But the main activity must be directed at the farms and the farmers. The difficulties are by no means insurmountable. Nevertheless, it is a tremendous task to change production methods developed over the centuries and closely knit into a social and economic structure not necessarily sympathetic to change.

Although the problem is one which each country must solve for itself, the industrial countries can contribute by providing capital and technical assistance. Much can be done by public agencies and private enterprises, including nonprofit organizations. Better seeds and pesticides are needed. Research on tropical agriculture lags far behind that of the temperate zone. Fertilizer factories must be built, and in the meantime fertilizer must be supplied. Agricultural credit organizations need to be improved. The problems of storage facilities, distribution methods, and marketing and pricing arrangements may be of central importance in some countries.

The problem of meeting food requirements is important in the first instance as a matter of life saving, or at least of avoiding such malnu-

163

trition as will reduce the capacity to work and increase susceptibility to disease. Beyond that, the fact is that less developed countries are predominantly rural. Programs of industrialization must have markets and for this we must develop the rural areas. Agricultural development thus becomes strategic in any overall national plan. Finally, the period of large food importation must be made as short as possible since it will divert more and more foreign exchange or assistance away from uses more closely related to economic development.

Confrontation for the Rich and Poor?

This illustration shows how entangled and interdependent are government policies and actions and private decisions and actions.

Yet they can all work together to deal with a specific problem when it is laid before them. For many reasons, one of the great problems facing the industrial countries is how they can contribute to accelerating the economic development of the great less developed part of the world.

It would be most unfortunate if the next decade saw the world split into two groups bitterly confronting each other—the rich and the poor. This may be inevitable because of the enormous size of the gap. The best chance of a happier outcome will lie in the industrial countries' demonstrating again and again their deep and sincere involvement in the effort to break the vicious circles of poverty, and through a common effort to raise the rates of growth in the less developed countries to new high levels.

---

9 PART 2 Atlantic Council Report

Ambassador Willard L. Thorp, in his appraisal of Atlantic Community relations with the developing world, concludes with the thought that it would be "most unfortunate" if the next decade saw the world split into two groups literally confronting each other, the rich and the poor. He acknowledges that this may be "inevitable" because of the enormous size of the gap between the two.

That end result is a possibility. Indeed, many feel it is a strong likelihood if world events are simply permitted to follow present trends.

Yet that need not be the case. Writing in 1962 in *The General Electric FORUM*, Barbara Ward observed:

> Today, for the first time in human history, our Christian duty—to feed the hungry, to clothe the naked—can be physically and actually fulfilled. Modern science provides the material resources to do precisely this. Therefore, to leave disease, starvation, and misery untended is now, for the rich nations, a matter of choice. They have a new freedom added to the dimensions of their liberty—they can choose or not to end the servile poverty of their fellow men.

She also identified the unique opportunity and responsibility of the Atlantic Community nations vis-à-vis the developing world because of the astonishing scientific-industrial accomplishments of the West:

> All these experiments point to the way the West must go—to closer international cooperation in the Atlantic area as the nucleus of world order; to Western support for quicker economic growth in new Common Markets in Latin America, in Africa, in Asia; to consistent Western programs for higher, steadier domestic expansion, for bolder aims in education, in culture, in better urban living, and for prosperous, free economies rolling forward on the two essential wheels of lively private expansion and vigorous public investment.

Industrial Capabilities and Developing World

During the Atlantic Council and Atlantic Institute discussions on economic development, the subject of the developing world has arisen frequently, but nowhere more pointedly than at the Geneva conference, where a special committee probed into the problem. Tom Killefer, formerly U.S. executive director of the Inter-American Development Bank and currently executive assistant for legal affairs at the Chrysler Corporation, summarized the three points that emerged:

1. The relationships between the northern and southern hemispheres are of growing importance for the Atlantic Community.
2. There are many opportunities (as well as problems) for the Atlantic Community through increased collaboration between private enterprise and available public investment.

3. Heretofore, we have neglected the relationship of the Atlantic Community with the developing countries, and this relationship requires increased attention.

In short, the conferees felt that we must define the measures required to direct the immense capabilities of the industrial world to the equally immense needs of the developing world. To do less would mean failure. It would mean failure in terms of human welfare, because much of mankind will face mass starvation unless the food problem is brought under control. In an even broader sense, it could mean failure in terms of the freedom, security, and survival of the entire developing world, which constitutes over half of the human race. In his Montreal address of May 18, 1966, U.S. Defense Secretary Robert S. McNamara linked international violence with underdeveloped societies, noting that traditionally listless areas of the world have been turned into seething cauldrons of change.

Secretary McNamara pointed out that:

In the last eight years alone, there have been no less than 164 internationally significant outbreaks of violence—each of them specifically designed as a serious challenge to the authority, or the very existence, of the government in question. But what is most significant of all is that there is a direct and constant relationship between the incidence of violence and the economic status of the countries afflicted.

Breaking down the statistics, Secretary McNamara said that:

1. The 27 "rich nations"—those possessing 75 percent of the world's wealth, but only 25 percent of the population—have had only one member which has suffered a major international upheaval in its own territory.

2. The 38 "very poor" nations—those with a per capita income of under $100 a year—suffered no less than 32 significant conflicts.

3. There is an irrefutable relationship between violence and economic backwardness, and the trend of such violence is up, not down.

Mr. McNamara concluded:

Whether Communists are involved or not, violence anywhere in a taut world transmits sharp signals through the complex ganglia of international relations; and the security of the United States *is* related to the security and stability of nations half a globe away. In a modernizing society, security means development. Without development, there can be no security.

Obstacles to Development

Development does not mean economic charity in which the "rich" help the "poor," out of compassion tinged with guilt. As the late President John F. Kennedy said, "There is not enough money in all America to relieve the misery of the underdeveloped world in a giant and endless soup kitchen. But there is enough know-how and there are enough knowledgeable people to help those nations help themselves."

The answer must lie in self-help coupled with partnership. In particular, there is enormous scope for individual companies in the developing world. According to Ambassador Livingston T. Merchant, U.S. executive director of the World Bank:

> Most of us in the West accept that the most effective method for achieving economic growth and advancement is through investing capital and skills in return for a reasonable profit. But private corporations cannot operate profitably abroad in a slough of poverty, illiteracy, or political instability and uncertainty. What must be created or developed—as a base from which all the energies, techniques, tools, and capital resources of private enterprise can operate—is an elementary economic and political foundation.

167

At Geneva, Mr. Killefer outlined six basic obstacles to foreign investment which, in turn, discourage private capital and frustrate economic growth:

1. *Political Instability.* In Latin America alone seven governments have been overthrown by force in the last five years, with consequent discouragement and apprehension about changes in attitude toward private investment.

2. *Statism.* There is operation and control by government of key industries, such as mineral extraction, public utilities, and basic steel. Though not uniformly found, this tendency is deeply rooted and firmly held.

3. *Inadequate Mobilization of Domestic Capital.* Potential savings are lost through capital flight or hoarding, as a protection against inflation or political unrest. Another part of the same problem is inadequacy of machinery for channeling equity and loan capital, the scarcity of savings institutions and effective stock exchanges, and at best, rudimentary capital markets in most countries.

4. *Shortage of Managerial, Supervisory, and Technical Talent.* The educational system of these countries tends to concentrate on liberal arts, law, and philosophy, with neglect of the basic sciences, business, and public administration. So there is a technological gap separating the developing nations from the industrialized countries. Latin America has only 250,000 persons with scientific and technological higher education, or 0.4 percent of its population; in the Atlantic Community the proportion is 10 times as large. And the situation is increasingly critical because so many professionals and technicians have emigrated to the industrialized countries. Paradoxically, Latin America is a net exporter of the commodity it needs most—skilled human resources.

5. *Balance of Payments Difficulties.* These impede the ability to remit earnings on foreign private investment.

6. *Unfavorable Government Attitudes toward Private Foreign Investment.* There are still governments which subject foreign firms to harassment, suspicion, and threatened or actual expropriation.

All these problem areas, Mr. Killefer stated, are interrelated and hence cannot be solved by a piecemeal approach. For example, little would be accomplished by mobilizing domestic capital for new plant and equipment if the shortage of trained manpower were not overcome. Obtaining sufficient foreign investment is worthless if the necessary local counterpart funds cannot be raised. A simultaneous attack on all these problems is required, and to a substantial extent, is occurring.

Basic Public Investment Required

The Geneva conferees recognized that there is a vast amount of long-term investment in infrastructure, education, and agriculture to be put in place before the "power train" of private investment can be attracted to do its work. Food aid, too, will be needed in a number of countries. "Clearly, these programs can only be financed by government funds, provided through one channel or another," the report stated.

The source of such funds can be national economic aid programs, multinational consortia, or international banking institutions founded and financed by the governments. The largest of these is, of course, the International Bank for Reconstruction and Development (World Bank) with its affiliates. But there are a number of other regionally oriented development banks. The United Nations, itself, is a vital contributor in creating infrastructure where it is either inadequate or does not exist at all. The important aspect, in Mr. Killefer's judgment, is not whether the aid is bilateral or multilateral, but whether or not it is coordinated with aid from other donor nations. There is room for various avenues of assistance, provided those avenues point toward common objectives and contribute to the building of balanced societies.

Regardless of their source, public investments must build both the physical and social aspects of the host nation's infrastructure. By Ambassador Merchant's definition, the physical infrastructure includes electric power and distribution systems, roads, railroads, air fields, port facilities, and other communications. He notes that:

> Social infrastructure includes the creation of schools and the training of teachers, as well as the introduction of techniques applicable to agriculture, as a fundamental economic support. It also covers the training of civil servants and governmental experts ranging from finance to police.

Such aid and collateral programs can bring an individual developing country, or region, to the point where it has a viable, developing future, the Geneva conferees stated. Only then will private investment come to believe that a particular country or area has a reasonable future, and a climate hospitable to private investment—which must, in the long term, provide a major part of the funds to meet the development requirements of the developing countries. The conferees also recognized the need for discrimination, stating that priority should be given to those governments which demonstrate a desire and capacity for self-help: "Adequate consultative and coordinating machinery for reviewing national and multilateral aid programs should be established under the auspices of the World Bank or the OECD, as most appropriate, in cases where it does not now exist."

Stimulating Private Investments

Mr. Killefer stressed that problems facing private foreign investment in the developing countries are formidable, but not insurmountable. For example, in Latin America the U.S. investment in industry, petroleum, iron ore, copper, and plantations exceeds $9 billion.

The multiplying effect of these investments is illustrated in the loans of the Inter-American Development Bank, which, in the last five years, has loaned $330 million to intermediary institutions including agricultural, industrial, and general development banks. These loans, in turn, have resulted in many thousands of sub-loans to small businessmen and farmers. "I believe this program is sound," Mr. Killefer observed, "and that a strong and solidly based private enterprise sector and middle class can best be created from many such small beginnings."

Yet, the Geneva conferees were nearly of one mind in concluding that much more needs to be done to improve the climate and opportunities for private investment. On the one hand, this includes such actions as national and multilateral guarantee programs for private investors. On the other hand, it includes action by private investors themselves—in conducting business surveys more effectively, in channeling corporate development programs so as to satisfy the most urgent needs, in long-term planning and investing at reasonable profit.

Two specific measures aimed at increasing the willingness of private investment to venture abroad were presented by George D. Woods, president of the World Bank (IBRD), in his address to the Bank's Board of Governors, September 1966, in Washington, D.C.

The first project related to the Convention on the Settlement of Investment Disputes and the new International Center, both designed to commence the following month. The purpose of these new facilities is to settle, through conciliation or arbitration, investment disputes between states and foreign investors. This combination will provide an additional and needed instrument to facilitate the flow of international capital to the developing countries.

The second project related to a multilateral plan initiated within the OECD for insuring private investors against other than commercial business risks. This project was still in draft stage at the time of the World Bank meeting, with its executive directors planning to carry forward the discussions and proposals.

The whole question of attracting investment capital is especially critical at this time. It is ironic that right now—when many of the developing countries are attaching greater importance to improved fiscal and monetary policies and to market incentives—development is threatened by a serious loss of momentum, when it should be proceeding at a swifter pace. As one veteran observer at the World Bank meetings commented, the reason is that the development effort is faced with a crucial finance gap: the difference between the capital available and the capacity of the developing countries to use increasing amounts of capital productively and effectively. This points up the tremendous need for the developing countries to give development finance a realistic priority among their other concerns and responsibilities.

The need, then, is for plans and priorities. In the case of European economic reconstruction after the war, objectives were defined and plans made to achieve them. In the case of present development, we have yet to formulate the plans; and this is of course the job now being undertaken by members of the international financing community. One proposal made to the Atlantic Council was that it give concerted scrutiny to all aspects of development finance, such as objectives, adequacy of resources, mechanisms, and techniques. As Mr. Woods has pointed out, most certainly it is in the enlightened self-interest of the Atlantic Community to devise a coordinated and long-term approach.

Increased Multinational Trade Needed

A related need is for a liberalized trade policy enabling the products of the developing areas to enter more freely into the markets of the developed world. The question becomes, how developing countries can build their export earnings and diversify their efforts where, at present, they are unduly dependent on a single or just a few products. Here, Ambassador Merchant comments:

Preferential admission to the markets of industrialized countries is one approach; commodity price stabilization schemes is another. I may cherish unduly the virtues of a free market system but I personally find little appeal in either of these approaches. Conscious diversification, rigorous attention to lowering production costs, and skillful marketing techniques offer to my mind the best hope for economic salvation. And surrounding such individual national measures of self-help should be a driving, multilateral effort to reduce trade barriers of all sorts. Regional free trade areas or customs unions in particular cases can also bring benefits.

Mr. Killefer endorsed the idea of regional trade areas, citing the Latin American market, with which he is most familiar:

> I believe that the most suitable framework for unity there, is a common market arrangement under which the member nations could not only liberalize trade, but coordinate their fiscal, monetary, and investment policies as well. This would produce a homogeneous community of some 220 million people with a combined gross national product of $80 billion, a foreign trade volume of $18 billion, and international reserves of $3 billion.

New Development Philosophy Evolving

In truth, it may be premature to attempt to define new relationships between the various common markets and free trade areas, to encourage new groupings and relationships, to suggest new systems and practices—governmental, regional, or private. The first priority is stated in the Geneva committee report; namely, "to produce a new philosophy for the Atlantic Community in relation to the developing countries." This has been evolving, of course, but has not yet reached maturity.

America, for example, is the most sophisticated technological-managerial society in the world, but it has yet to apply the fullness of its genius to "society building" at the village and rural level of the impoverished world.

It has yet to deliver a universal water purification system that will help to prevent the diseases which in Northeast Brazil account for an infant mortality rate as high as 50 percent during the first year.

It has yet to apply the "systems approach" to education in Southeast Asia, covering the spectrum of grammar school skills, more modern agriculture, community development, elementary mechanics, adult literacy—and involving the latest teaching devices, both hardware and software.

It has yet to devise adequate communications and transportation to give whole regions a sense of community spirit and political entity.

It has yet to solve the urbanization problems of Calcutta; the agriculture problems of Central India; the power requirements of the

Mekong Delta; or the security problems of the Philippine archipelago, where Communist insurgency is still taking its toll.

From a corporate planning viewpoint, and by priority, what are the specific tasks of specific areas which could become commercially feasible and profitable?

What technologies can be brought to bear on these tasks?

What are the opportunities for multinational corporate consortia, where the tasks are too large for any single company or country to take on unilaterally?

A State of Mind

The challenge is equally great, if not greater, for the developing nations, particularly as it relates to their state of mind. Nineteenth-century conceptions of "dollar imperialism" will have to be exchanged for the modern realities of international partnerships. Self-help must become the key, as "development" must become a very personal assignment for the individuals involved; it can be encouraged but not imposed from the outside.

In this vein, what are the incentives which developing nations can offer to make outside investments attractive? How can host-national governments and businessmen best identify priorities? Where can this development process be speeded by regional development banks and by the World Bank family?

Optimum success of such a global joint venture can come only when all partners discard outmoded notions of "rights" and "obligations." The gap between rich and poor will never be closed if the developed nations consider it their "obligation" to devote, for example, 1 percent of GNP per year to development, for purely humanitarian reasons—and if the developing world views the receipt of such funds as their legitimate "right." Transactions must be on a businesslike basis; and as Paul Hoffman, administrator of the U.N. Development Program, said recently in the *Saturday Review*, "The economic rewards of development are considerable."*

Mr. Hoffman pointed out that the people of the less developed

173

* Paul G. Hoffman, "The Rich and the Poor: 1966," *Saturday Review*, September 17, 1966, pp. 24–25.

countries comprise the world's largest potential market. They represent the new economic frontier. As income increases, so does purchasing power. Secretary of Agriculture Orville Freeman has estimated that every 10 percent increase in per capita income abroad results in a 16 percent increase in the commercial exports of the United States. Every $1 billion worth of additional exports creates more than 100,000 jobs in this country.

Mr. Hoffman concluded:

> The more developed a country becomes, the better a customer it is. The present biggest export customers of the United States are the most highly developed nations—the countries of Western Europe, Japan, and Canada. With a population of 20 million, Canada buys more from the United States than does all of Latin America, which has a population of almost 250 million. American export sales to Japan have more than quadrupled since U.S. postwar assistance ceased. Mexico, a country which has made substantial development progress, has more than tripled the value of its imports since 1950. If nothing else, development assistance is a sound, long-range business proposition because it builds markets.

174

Next Steps

At Geneva the committee studying these issues proposed as its most important recommendation, "that the Atlantic Institute establish permanent machinery to study the needs, expectations, and capabilities of the developing nations in the years to come." Such a study group, working with the staff of the World Bank, the OECD, and other international groups, could lead to the establishment of an Atlantic action program involving the governments of the Atlantic Community and the developing areas, together with their business sectors.

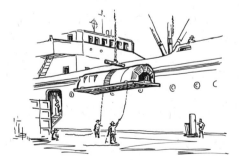

10 *Atlantic Community and the Communist Nations*

PART 1 *Introduction*
by J. Irwin Miller

Board chairman of the Cummins Engine Company, Mr. J. Irwin Miller is an exceptionally distinguished industrialist. He chaired the 1965 Special Committee on U.S. Trade with East European Countries and the Soviet Union, and currently is chairman of the National Advisory Commission on Health Manpower. A trustee of the Ford Foundation and the Committee for Economic Development, he is also a member of the Business Council, the National Industrial Conference Board, and the executive committee of the central committee of the World Council of Churches. In addition to heading the Cummins Engine Company, he is also chairman of the Irwin Union Bank and Trust Company.

It is unwise to write either simply or categorically about East–West trade today. The opportunities and the obstacles in respect to trade with China are one matter, with the Soviet Union quite another matter, with the Eastern European nations a still different matter.

In a short space we cannot consider them all. I choose, therefore, to confine my comments to trade with the Soviet Union, since the obstacles existing here are to some extent present in the other nations, though in differing degrees and forms.

In respect to the Soviet Union, it is good to begin by recognizing that this nation has for a thousand years displayed an intense national desire for self-sufficiency, and has displayed it to a degree that does not characterize the Western nations. This desire is clearly at odds with that country's currently expressed desire to participate in world trade, and it manifests itself in the strong Soviet preference for bilateral barter agreements within limited areas, restricted to selected items, rather than for normal world trading practices.

A second obstacle, which is imbedded in the first, is that the Soviet Union trades as a state, while the Western nations conduct trade mainly through private traders guided by national policy and aided in various ways by state programs. This second obstacle is considerably less formidable than the first, and it is one which the self-styled "free nations" of the West are able to develop skill in handling.

A third obstacle is a very great one indeed. The Soviet Union does not produce, either in raw materials or, most especially, in finished goods, items which the Western nations desire and need in substantial quantities—or even probably in quantities commensurate with the Soviet desire for purchases. There are, of course, exceptions—more in the area of raw materials than in the area of finished goods; but before the volume of East–West trade can be significant in relation to total world

trade, the Soviet Union must decide it wants that trade badly enough to shift its allocation of resources, and to design and sell products and commodities specifically aimed at being competitive and attractive in world markets.

Finally, another obstacle to East–West trade has been found in the attitude of Western governments—especially the United States—toward this trade. In this respect, nearly all Western nations are now changing and seeking ways to increase the trade profitably for themselves. And several organizations in the United States, both business and labor, have expressed the need for a modification of national policy.

Solutions Rest on Soviet Action

If, then, these are the major, or some of the major, obstacles to Soviet trade with the West, what might be done about them? With respect to most of these obstacles, the burden of removal clearly rests on the Soviet Union itself. Does it genuinely wish to be a world trader, and to seek for its whole population the material gains that accrue to successful trading nations? Or does it intend to remain ambivalent, hoping to gain the advantages of world trade and at the same time grow in self-sufficiency? Does it intend to continue to try to sell to other nations not what they want, but what the Soviet Union chooses to make, at the same time restricting its own purchases in good part to areas in which state planning has fallen short, and to one-shot capital equipment or advanced technology?

The price of self-sufficiency in terms of national material prosperity is today a great and most expensive one. I cannot believe but that it is to the long-term advantage of the Soviet nation (whose able people have the ability to do very well indeed those things to which they assign first importance) to trade broadly and aggressively and to buy broadly and aggressively. I believe that it is in the interest of us all to do what we can to conduct this trade along normal multilateral rather than abnormal bilateral lines, with growing use of convertible currencies rather than barter, and to encourage the Soviets to bring their trade practices into line with normal world trade practices.

What Are the Western Obstacles?

Not all the obstacles exist on the side of the Soviet Union, however. The Western nations, and particularly the United States, have erected barriers which require thoughtful examination. All of the larger industrial nations subscribe to the Coordinating Committee on Export Controls (COCOM) list, which proscribes sale to the Soviet Union of goods or products that would contribute to its military effort, and there is neither disposition nor reason to abandon this position in the face of the U.S.S.R.'s announced aims and pattern of postwar actions.

In respect to those articles open to trade there is, however, a tendency—more marked in recent years—to grant increasingly longer terms of credit, in violation of the Berne Convention. This might seem, at first glance, a stimulus to trade. In the long view, however, I am not certain that it is. Under conditions of state trading, as contrasted with private trading, very long-term credits really constitute economic assistance. This has the effect of permitting the country receiving such terms to postpone a serious confrontation with its real problem, which is the shifting of production toward the creation of more foreign exchange. And, if credits should become substantial, it leaves the creditor nation open to possible future difficulties, with the alternatives of granting political concessions or losing an investment.

In respect to the United States, a principal obstacle to the development of this trade lies in our present inclination to link this trade with short-term politics. Because of the language in our Export Control Act banning exports of "contained technology" which may make "a significant contribution to the economic potential" of a Communist country, licenses are difficult to obtain, and when obtained are granted after many uncertainties and long delays.

What Are the Political Values?

The present and future money values of this trade to the West are not great—less than 4 percent of free world trade and less than 0.5 percent of U.S. trade—but the political values may be very great indeed. The Communist peoples very possibly pose their greatest threat to the industrial non-Communist nations when they are impoverished, when the peoples have little to lose. Conversely, individual prosperity and material well-being, even among those who oppose us, may well be a major contribution to the cause of peace in the present time.

In conclusion, it must be clear that this has been no more than the briefest of introductions to the problems and obstacles of East–West trade. The comments on the Soviet Union are not wholly relevant to the Eastern European nations, and even less relevant to trade with China. However, they do call attention to the kinds of problems that must be solved, even though these problems will vary from country to country, and from year to year.

10 PART 2 Atlantic Council Report

Few issues are more explosive, both within the United States and between America and its Atlantic Community allies, than the question of East–West trade.

On the one hand, many highly respected observers are convinced that the world has entered into a "post cold war period," in which trade and most other relations can be greatly expanded for the benefit of all. The one exception to relaxed tensions, they say, is Southeast Asia, notably Vietnam and Red China. But even here, respected world leaders, of the stature of U.N. Secretary General U Thant, believe that the central disagreement is not basically the ideological one—Communism v. democracy—which has characterized cold war contentions to date. Many honest observers believe that world Communism, as an aggressive militant force, is no longer a prime threat to the security and independence of the free world.

On the other hand, other observers—equally intelligent and equally respected—are just as convinced that world Communism in its various forms *is* a prime threat and will continue to be for the indefinite future. They see the Communist countries holding to the long-range objective of world domination. And they believe that any trade to any Communist country will simply "give aid and comfort to the enemy." To substantiate their case, they point to the Soviet's continued high budgets for military-technological aerospace programs. As another example, they refer to the Soviet space program, which is costing approximately the same as that of the United States but is squeezed out of a GNP only about half the size.

Between these diametrically opposite views there are a myriad of shadings and other interpretations. For example, within the United States there is a growing conviction among even some of the most adamant anti-Communists that trade can be deployed as an instrument of national policy to defeat Communist expansionism. Outside the United States, a number of our strongest allies feel that America is suffering from a "paranoid complex" which is frustrating rather than furthering U.S. efforts for the kind of peace exemplified by normal, growing, international commerce among the community of nations.

Background on Miller Statement

J. Irwin Miller's introduction to this chapter lays out cases for and against a more liberalized U.S. trade policy toward the Soviet Union. His remarks should be viewed against the background of the Presidential report bearing his signature, submitted in his role as chairman of the Special Committee on U.S. Trade Relations with East European Countries and the Soviet Union. This White House report is dated April 29, 1965. In addition to Mr. Miller, it was signed by Eugene R. Black, William Blackie, George R. Brown, Charles W. Engelhard, Jr., James B. Fisk, Nathaniel Goldfinger, Crawford H.

Greenewalt, William A. Hewitt, Max F. Millikan, Charles G. Mortimer, and Herman B. Wells. It is significant that the Miller report was endorsed unanimously by the committee members. One member, Mr. Goldfinger, wrote a brief summary statement expressing certain reservations, such as the need to place greater emphasis on the political aspects. But he said that he wished to make it clear, at the outset, "that I am not opposed to the expansion of economic and financial relations with the Soviet bloc under all conditions."

In its introductory passage, the Miller report gave full heed to the hostility of the Soviet government, by words and deeds, to the United States. It recognized that without the preponderant military power of the United States, it would be idle and even dangerous to explore the possibility of expanding peaceful trade or any peaceful relations with the Soviet Union. But it concluded:

> With a secure defense, on the other hand, we can prudently seek practical means of reducing areas of conflict between ourselves and the U.S.S.R. Indeed, we assume the United States has an obligation in today's nuclear world to pursue such possibilities as part of its long-term commitment to strengthen the prospects for peace in the world.

The report then recognized that ties within the European Communist bloc have weakened and that the forces of nationalism have increased. All this is particularly true of the Soviet Union and Communist China. There is also a ferment in the European Communist countries as their people yearn for a better life with increased independence. The report observed:

> There are signs that pressures for greater openness within Soviet society are mounting. The reasons may be pragmatic rather than ideological, but they are nonetheless real.
>
> We desire to encourage the growth of forces in the European Communist countries that will improve the prospects for peace. Within these countries we seek to encourage independence from Soviet domination and a rebuilding of historical ties with the West. In each of these countries, including the U.S.S.R., we seek an opening up of the society and a continuing decentralization of power.

In that broad context, the Miller committee considered trade as a tactical tool to be used with other policy instruments for pursuing U.S. national objectives. It was not considered a panacea in itself, but one of many instruments—including the maintenance of a powerful deterrent defense. It recognized that trade was a form of politics which could be pursued only through careful negotiations, firm bargaining, and constructive competition. There was no wishful thinking that somehow the Communist threat would "go away" if only Americans would "be more friendly." Both sides of the argument are presented:

1. The case against expanding peaceful trade with the European Communist countries comes down to the proposition that these countries are hostile toward us and we should not strengthen them through trade. By selling to them goods and services of any nature, whether wheat or our technologically advanced machinery and equipment, it is argued that we help them to solve some of their pressing internal problems and make it easier for them to use their limited resources for building up their military power and strengthening their potential for subversion abroad. Moreover, this argument states that by expanding trade with these countries we bestow upon them a kind of respectability and prestige which will enhance their position in the developing countries of the world, and which they will use to our ultimate disadvantage. In sum, this argument holds that the risks of expanding trade outweigh the potential gains.

2. The case for expanding peaceful trade comes down to the proposition that trade is the most effective device in the free world arsenal to influence the internal evolution and external behavior of Communist countries. Trade provides us with a policy instrument to encourage the movement toward greater national independence in Eastern Europe, and the trend toward greater concern for consumer needs in all the European Communist countries. By refusing to trade, we deliberately deny ourselves the tools to shape internal developments, as well as the basic leverage needed for our overall strategy toward these countries. Our refusal to trade cannot importantly limit Soviet military power. Refusal does help reinforce the Leninist belief in the need for Soviet self-sufficiency. A willingness to trade, on the other hand, would involve our adversary in dependence and orderly conduct in the very system we espouse and he fears. Underdeveloped countries concurrently would receive evidence that we genuinely believe in the efficacy and ultimate triumph of open societies, far outweighing any

possible enhancement of Soviet legitimacy. In sum, this argument holds that the gains are significant, with the risks relatively negligible.

East–West Trade Relations Act

In proposing the 1966 East–West Trade Relations Act to Congress, Secretary of State Dean Rusk quoted Presidents Eisenhower and Kennedy, who put forward arguments similar to those described above in advancing the case for expanded East–West trade. He also recalled President Lyndon B. Johnson's 1965 State of the Union message:

> In Eastern Europe restless nations are slowly beginning to assert their identity. Your government, assisted by leaders in labor and business, is exploring ways to increase peaceful trade with these countries and with the Soviet Union.
>
> The intimate engagement of peaceful trade, over a period of time, can influence Eastern European societies to develop along paths that are favorable to world peace. After years of careful study, the time has now come for us to act, and act we should and act we must.
>
> With these steps, we can help gradually to create a community of effort. Thus will the tide of human hope rise again.

Secretary Rusk cautioned that there is abundant evidence that without this legislation, the United States will continue to lose significant opportunities to influence the course of events in Eastern Europe. He affirmed that the new legislation would not weaken the U.S. position in any way, nor would it in itself make any grant or concession to a Communist country. The President would be authorized to enter into a commercial agreement with individual Communist countries (not the bloc) only when he determined that the terms would promote the U.S. national interest. In addition, he would have authority immediately to terminate such bilateral agreements if the other party were failing in its obligations or if the U.S. national interest so dictated.

Communist China, North Korea, North Vietnam, Cuba, and the Soviet Zone of Germany were specifically excluded from the authority of the act.

Finally, the proposed legislation contained other safeguards, such as renegotiating such agreements every three years. The bill would in no way change existing laws and regulations prohibiting aid and limiting credit to Communist countries. Under the act, the President would also have authority to give the same tariff treatment to the treaty party as we give all other trading partners—the so-called "most favored nation" treatment.

At this moment, the legislation has not been passed nor even pressed because of congressional and public sensitivities over the war in Vietnam. Stated simply, the argument has been: Why should America strengthen one Communist country while another Communist country is shooting and killing American servicemen?

The administration's viewpoint, voiced by Secretary Rusk, is that expanded trade is a sound policy when—and even because—America may be fighting against Communist weapons in Vietnam. "Indeed, it is when we are resisting force with force that it is most important to hold open every possible avenue to peace." In short, the stick is an absolutely essential device with which to make it clear to Communist nations that their best interests are not served through force. But a complete diplomatic arsenal uses carrots as well as sticks. To foreclose peaceful trade is to deny ourselves the carrot.

185

The Opposite View

Some remain unconvinced. Mose L. Harvey,* writing from the University of Miami's Center for Advanced International Studies, presents the opposite view:

1. There is an unbroken continuity in Soviet aims since the war.
2. These remain as dangerous to the United States today as ever.
3. The Soviet regime is finding it increasingly difficult and costly to achieve its aims and carry out its commitments.
4. It nevertheless is persevering in its efforts and is seeking, at mounting costs, to attain technological superiority over the United States—on the calculation that this will provide a springboard to general superiority, including especially superiority in both economic and strategic power.
5. The regime estimates that because of the "laws that govern capitalism" the United States (a) will be unable to match over the long pull the Soviet drive in the technological field, and (b) can, because of its need for

---

* Mose L. Harvey, "More East–West Trade?" *NAM Reports* (published by the National Association of Manufacturers), November 15, 1965.

foreign markets, be brought to aiding the U.S.S.R. to achieve the very technological superiority that will contribute so much to U.S. doom.

Expanding on his theme, Mr. Harvey states that East–West trade denial is not a policy in itself but part of a strategic design developed over four successive administrations to cope with the Communist threat.

A central aim of the design is to deny to the Communists any fruits from the struggle they wage against the United States, and at the same time to build up the costs to the Communists of the struggle to the end that they will in time abandon the struggle and the hostility that underlies it.

In today's climate, the U.S.S.R. is in a worsening position, vis-à-vis the United States, besieged from within by Soviet bloc nations and people seeking greater autonomy, and battered from the outside by Communist China. Mr. Harvey continues:

The feature about the U.S.S.R., and its current position and prospects, that looms far above all else in importance is the quiet but deep and many-sided crisis that for some years has been increasingly pressing down on the Soviet regime in both its domestic and external affairs. The crisis has brought the Soviet Union to a crossroads point in its struggle against the United States, in its drive for world hegemony for its system. The issue at stake for the regime is whether the Soviet Union can long continue to serve its deeply rooted commitments to world communism and its revolutionary goals without bringing disaster to itself.

The question asked by Mr. Harvey is whether or not the United States wants to bolster the position of the major Communist power, which is still dedicated to the proposition of "burying" America, at the very moment of the Soviet Union's greatest vulnerability. He concludes:

The United States can serve its national purposes through a continuation of trade denial. It can also, and perhaps better, serve its national purposes through a controlled use of trade to achieve certain specific ends with regard to the U.S.S.R. and its policies and conduct. It cannot serve its national purposes by simply relaxing and allowing trade to develop as it will.

It is significant that even this outspoken proponent for caution should state that a controlled use of trade (another way of saying "peaceful trade") can achieve certain national objectives in what has been termed the "protracted conflict." He feels that while the United States should seek maximum cooperation with its allies, it will still need to operate on a bilateral basis. It would need to attach specific conditions to trade with the U.S.S.R. (which the administration also vigorously asserts as a need), and should use trade to promote trends toward greater national assertiveness on the part of Soviet satellites (also a high administration priority). Lastly, Mr. Harvey stresses that, "U.S. leadership would need to take special care to keep a 'new' U.S. policy in perspective."

A Case for Flexibility

Eugene M. Braderman, Deputy Assistant Secretary of State for Commercial Affairs and Business Activities, underlined this precaution. He urged that we

. . . be flexible in applying our trade policy as it relates to three basic objectives:
  a) Preventing the Communists from extending their domain.
  b) Achieving agreements which could reduce war dangers.
  c) Encouraging evolution towards independence, peaceful cooperation and open societies within the Communist world.

From time to time and from country to country the situation will vary. Sometimes the behavior of a Communist country will warrant U.S. denial of any trade whatsoever, as now is the case with the Communist countries of the Far East and virtually so for Castro's Cuba. Other times freer trade should be encouraged, Mr. Braderman said, giving these examples:

1. *Yugoslavia.* As this Communist country broke off from what was then a monolithic Soviet bloc in 1948, the United States encouraged similar actions by other countries by stepping up both economic and military aid to help Yugoslavia maintain its independence. Today about 65 percent of Yugoslavia's trade is with non-Communist countries.

2. *Poland.* Despite ups and downs in relationships, Poland has moved toward greater independence in both internal and external affairs since Stalin's death. It is relatively open to Western influence, with the United States carrying on an extensive information program.

America has responded to changes in Polish policies and attitudes by selling agricultural products through PL 480 programs and credits through the Export-Import Bank. It has eased restrictions, including restoring most-favored-nation status to Polish imports. Trade has grown in both directions and Poland is paying its debts to the U.S. government.

3. *Romania.* With the fastest industrial growth rate among the Eastern European Communist countries, Romania has increasingly demonstrated a desire to expand relations with the West. It boldly and successfully rejected proposals of the Communist Council for Economic Mutual Assistance which would have restricted its industrial expansion and would have subordinated its economic interests to the needs of other Communist countries. In 1964, the United States and Romania concluded negotiations in Washington to increase trade and improve relations between the two countries. Consequently we are now following a more liberal export policy toward Romania also. Romania, in turn, has given assurances that it will not permit the re-export of United States goods or technology, and will protect industrial property rights and processes. As a result of these developments, Romania has expanded its commercial relations not only with the United States, but also with other free world countries.

4. *Czechoslovakia.* There have been growing trends toward expanded relations with the West and some internal liberalization.

5. *Hungary.* A recent interest in change.

6. *Bulgaria.* Same as for Hungary.

7. *Albania.* Change seems nonexistent.

There is no common policy for all Communist countries, and their degree of Communism—liberal or conservative—is not a determining factor. Few would argue, for example, that Romania has moved very far toward an open society. But unlike Albania, for example, its attitude toward the United States has been less hostile.

A philosophical and political point behind all this is that Communism's greatest claim to strength has been its ability to move around the world, thrust, withdraw, and maneuver according to a single plan, and with monolithic force. To the degree that pluralism can supplant centralism, to the extent that decision making can be spun off from Moscow, with the other capitals acting on their own rather than according to a bloc plan—to that same degree and extent is Communism weakened as an aggressive international force.

According to this argument, whether or not societies are becoming more liberal, whether or not individual states are advancing toward or away from capitalism, whether or not countries "like" America—these considerations become of less importance. The strongest advocates of the administration proposal would seem to agree that the key must be flexibility, coupled with tough-minded judgment as to the "art of the practical" in any specific case. Without this as a guiding principle, there are many who would fear that liberalized trade would lead to a weakening U.S. position on the international scene.

U.S. Government's Next Steps

Barring unpredictable developments in East–West relationships, the U.S. government can be expected to follow a course of probing and testing, pointing toward continuing liberalization of commercial policies vis-à-vis the Soviet Union and Eastern European Communist countries. This policy was articulated by President Johnson in New York City on October 7, 1966, when he said, "Our task is to achieve a reconciliation with the East—a shift from the narrow concept of co-existence to the broader vision of peaceful engagement."

As later analyzed by Alexander B. Trowbridge, Secretary of Commerce, the President's announcement was significant because of the tangible government action to follow it, on at least three fronts:

First, the President repeated his intent to work for early congressional approval of the Consular Agreement with the Soviet Union and the East–West Trade Relations Act.

Second, the President authorized the Export-Import Bank to guarantee commercial credits for industrial transactions with Poland, Hungary, Czechoslovakia, and Bulgaria, and to finance American exports for the Soviet-Italian Fiat auto plant.

Third, the President stated in his October 7 speech that the United States would reduce export controls on East–West trade with respect to hundreds of nonstrategic items. Just five days later this action took place, with over 400 items included from the Commerce Department's Commodity Control List—many textile products, certain metal manufactures and machinery, various chemical materials and products, and a considerable number of manufactured articles. These items are now freely exportable by a U.S. manufacturer to any of the Communist destinations of Eastern Europe (except the Soviet Zone of Germany), without the obligation of applying for and awaiting the issuance of U.S. export licenses.

Attitudes of U.S. Businessmen

Corporate thinking over the past few years has seemed to follow generally the trend of U.S. government thinking: namely, that international trade policies should be modified vis-à-vis the Communist nations, as Communist attitudes change toward the United States.

In the Research Institute of America survey of 1963, cited in Chapter 2, Executive Director Leo Cherne said that nearly all respondents to the RIA questionnaire agreed that strategic and semistrategic materials should not be sold to the Soviet Union. In fact, a large minority believed that even nonstrategic materials should not be sold and that the government should prohibit all sales to all Communist countries. They also believed that strong pressure should be brought to bear on America's allies to follow the same line.

It is interesting to contrast this view with that of government leaders. At that time, the near-unanimous government opinion was that America should sell nonstrategic materials to the Soviets and should not put strong pressure on other nations to reduce their own Red-bloc trade. Thus, Mr. Cherne concluded, "The government comes out as the believer in more East–West trade, the business community as opposed—a clear instance of *national* goals placed above *economic* goals by businessmen."

Three years later, in the second RIA survey on this subject (conducted as part of the Atlantic Council study), Mr. Cherne reported on changes in business attitudes.

Corporation executives now suggest a loosening of restrictions on nonstrategic trade with iron curtain countries as a possible way of easing the U.S. balance of payments problem. According to the second survey, however, approval varied sharply depending upon the country of destination. Two out of three companies would still turn thumbs down on exports to

Red China. As for trade with the Soviet Union, 62 percent voted "O.K." Here, company size was an influencing factor. Response was more favorable among the larger companies than among the smaller. Taking all American executives as a group, it is doubtful that a numerical majority would approve.

The report further revealed that over 70 percent of respondents were in favor of trade with the East European Soviet satellites:

Trade with the satellites is, in fact, now permitted on a restricted basis, but some of the hazards of actively engaging in it are illustrated by the recent experience of Firestone, which backed away from a proposed construction contract for an industrial plant in Romania after the matter became controversial.

Mr. Cherne added:

A special problem in this connection, encountered mostly by larger companies, stems from the fact that our controls over trading with the East apply not only to the U. S. parent company but to foreign subsidiaries as well. This is highlighted by the fact that one company in eight, among those familiar with the "Trading With the Enemy Act," has already run into these restrictions and found them a handicap. There is presently a proposal in Congress to ease the regulations of this legislation. It would seem likely, however, that the financial, economic, and political obstacles to East–West trade will remain more important than the legislative ones.

The RIA's last point, above, points to the fact that there are no easy solutions in expanding East–West trade. As a firm "goes international," setting up an operating headquarters on foreign soil, it naturally must observe the desires and economic plans of the host government. If those plans include expanding trade with the Communists, difficulties can follow. This is not an academic situation, but a practical dilemma which both U.S. companies and the U.S. government are facing increasingly. This becomes especially delicate when there is a serious question as to whether or not the product is strategic or nonstrategic. What France or Italy might like to sell to East Europe or even Red China can easily seem "strategic" to the U.S. government and to U.S. companies located in these countries. Granted that Americans can and perhaps must stand for their convictions, that does not ease either corporate or international relationships when the other "team members"—the host government and the local corporate partners—feel equally as strong in the opposite direction and insist upon exercising their national prerogatives.

For the businessman endeavoring to operate in the crossfire of conflicting national policies, such as a situation can be less than pleasant. As one U.S. executive commented:

> Far be it for me to criticize our government in this regard, especially since the host government is stretching our patience a good bit. Nevertheless, the fact of the matter is that we have here an example of what could be termed anti-European practice. Here is a situation where foreign governments may be pardoned for thinking American-owned manufacturers in their own countries are not free agents and are subject to the political whims of Washington. If that should really become the prevalent opinion, then heaven help us in our ideas and thought of doing business on an international basis.

Conclusions from Crotonville and Geneva

American businessmen at the Crotonville conference seemed generally to support U.S. government efforts to liberalize trade in non-strategic items on a selective basis with individual countries in Eastern Europe, along the lines of the Miller committee recommendations. They recognized that the volume of trade would not be significant.

Serious concern was expressed about the growing discrepancy in trade terms offered within the Atlantic Community to Soviet-bloc countries. Support was given for U.S. government policy of limiting this credit to a maximum term of five years.

As could be expected, perhaps the most serious concern registered by U.S. businessmen was that in overseas operations they often find themselves in the middle of a tug of war between the U.S. and host-country governments. As long as the policies of the U.S. government and of the Atlantic area governments are not fully coordinated in this field, it was felt that every effort should be made to avoid making U.S. overseas affiliates the targets of conflicting signals from different governments. Conferees felt that this objective could be advanced by a greater degree of flexibility in administration of U.S. controls and increased intergovernmental collaboration in individual cases.

At the Geneva conference six months later, where Europeans and Americans were present in approximately equal numbers, the dialogue was carried further and resulted in a final statement which reflected considerable consensus:

As elements of the market system are introduced into the Communist countries, and the pressures for higher living standards grow, a new perspective opens for enhanced East–West trade in the 1970's. Growing East–West trade offers not only the prospect of economic benefits, but of better relations between East and West.

Nevertheless, the familiar obstacles to the growth of East–West trade persist. In the East the earning power of Communist countries remains limited and their currencies inconvertible. Policies of self-sufficiency inhibit purchases from the West. In the West, strategic considerations rightly limit sales of certain products. Individual firms must show caution in selling know-how and technology. At the same time, these new and welcome opportunities in East–West trade raise the danger that Western firms and governments will compete with each other in the offer of excessive credit terms, and thereby suffer economic and political division.

To minimize these risks and make the most of the new opportunities, governments in the Atlantic area must seek to extend their cooperation and develop common policies in the following fields:

1. The development of a common policy on credit terms.
2. The exploration of ways of assuring Western exports, long-term markets in Communist countries and a place in their plans in return for Western liberalization. If the full potentialities of East–West trade are to be realized, new, mutually agreed rules are needed to link the two systems and provide protection against abuses such as dumping.
3. Periodical review of COCOM's list of strategic materials.

The political climate between East and West inevitably conditions East–West trade, but concerted and constructive action by Atlantic countries in this field can in turn help to improve the prospect of a more stable world order.

Disagreement on Specifics

Unfortunately, agreement on broad principles does not automatically yield agreement on specific practices. These practical differences, among men of good faith from the several Atlantic Community nations, were reflected in the report by the U.S. nonprofit organization, the Committee for Economic Development. It was entitled, "East–West Trade—A Common Policy for the West." The final policy statement was developed through joint discussions by the CED with French, German, Italian, and Japanese groups—members of other economic committees. Throughout the statement, points of disagreement are stated explicitly. For example, the French, German, Italian, and Japanese groups would apply the same policy guidelines to Red China as to the Eastern European Communist countries of Poland, Czechoslovakia, Bulgaria, Romania, Hungary, and Albania. America's allies pointed out that "consideration must be given to the special characteristics of this country which represents approximately one fifth of the world's population and which is going through a stage of intensive development."

The CED (U.S.) dissented from this position:

Mainland China, with North Korea and North Vietnam, are a special case and require special treatment. There is no sign that the internal economic regime of China is evolving in a way that permits more nearly normal trade relations. Neither is there evidence of any policy by China to enter into more stable political relations with the rest of the world, a policy which if it existed might be encouraged by the development of trade relations.

Any move by the United States to trade with Mainland China would be an event of great political significance and must be considered in that light. In present circumstances such a move would undoubtedly be considered, in Asia and elsewhere, as a step toward recognition of the Chinese regime and acceptance of Chinese ambitions. There is no reason in present conditions for the United States to relax its policy of embargo on trade with China.

The significant point in all these discussions through the CED, the Atlantic Council and the Atlantic Institute, and other groups not mentioned in this discussion, is not that there were basic disagreements but that the representatives from the several nations were willing to examine these differences and strive for a consensus whenever possible. In just a short span of 18 months, observers who have followed the program from both Europe and America have been seeing a "closing of the breach" on issue after issue as the various viewpoints are set forth, documented, and discussed. At the very least, matters are now "discussable," which only a short time ago was not the case.

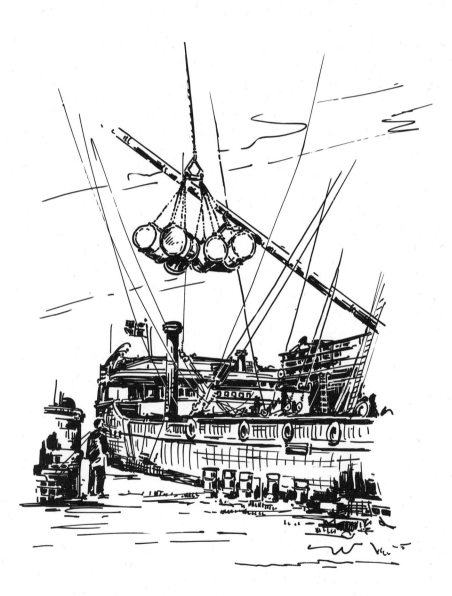

11 Stimulating Worldwide Trade

PART 1 Introduction
by Eric Wyndham White

For nearly 20 years, Eric Wyndham White has played a prominent and influential role in the field of international trade. Before World War II Mr. Wyndham White practiced as a member of the English Bar, and was at that time closely associated with the work of the International Chamber of Commerce. Since the war he has devoted himself exclusively to international affairs. Since 1948, he has been executive secretary, and then (since 1965), director-general of the General Agreement on Tariffs and Trade (GATT), the international commercial treaty organization of some 80 members and associated states aimed at expanding international trade. He played a crucial role in the success of the Kennedy Round negotiations concluded in June 1967 in Geneva. He also chaired the November 1965 Fontainebleau Conference sponsored by the Atlantic Institute and the European Institute of Business Administration (INSEAD).

Photo by UNATIONS

Economic cooperation among the nations of the Atlantic Community should have two main objectives. The first is to seize all the opportunities for expansion and growth which partnership and cooperation can bring for the industrialized countries themselves. The second is to work in unity on the staggering problems of the so-called "third world."

The present advances in technology, coupled with the general expansionist climate of economic activity everywhere, have created enormous opportunities for bringing "the good life" to more people in more countries than ever before.

In this process of stimulating world trade and economic development the attention and efforts of the international trading community over the past few years have been concentrated on the Kennedy

197

Round of trade negotiations in Geneva.

These negotiations have been successfully concluded. Their results are far greater in magnitude and coverage than those attained in any previous operation of this sort. This success is a great achievement of international cooperation. It will have important consequences for world trade and for international trading relationships. Both developed and developing countries will benefit.

The outcome of the Kennedy Round constitutes a positive basis for our future action. There will undoubtedly be many difficulties and complexities ahead; these have been clearly revealed to us in the course of the Kennedy Round. But they can certainly be overcome, given the political will and courage of governments and negotiators that enabled the trade negotiations to be successfully carried through.

It will take many months to digest the results of the Kennedy Round. There will, therefore, be time for us to take stock and to explore the possible direction of further advances. There will be adjustment, as well as technical and administrative problems, for governments and for those who produce and consume the goods that are involved. Much of the task of assimilating and adjusting to the changed conditions will fall on private business. While this is go-

ing on, however, the groundwork must be laid for the consultations that will be necessary in preparation for a further forward movement.

In this task of preparation, it is important for us to bear in mind the central elements in the world trade and economic picture, for these will continue to make up the overall backdrop against which national and international policies will evolve.

First, there is the multilateral cooperative effort represented by the success of the Kennedy Round. This is a positive factor, just as failure to agree would have been decidedly negative in its impact and consequences.

Second, there is the continuing trend toward economic regionalism. Here, as was clearly demonstrated during the Kennedy Round, the member countries of economic groupings have a tremendous stake in trade with non-members, and a fundamental economic interest in participating in a continuing movement toward the liberalization of trade.

Then there are the problems of the developing areas of the world that will continue to be a major, if not the major, politico-economic issue of our time. The Kennedy Round has made a contribution toward the solution of some of these problems.

Finally, there is the question of East-West trade, which has been increasingly engaging our attention in the GATT and which was pointed up in the Kennedy Round through the participation in the negotiations of individual countries of Eastern Europe.

After the Kennedy Round?

In the years ahead we must aspire to ever-broadening areas of free trade. Certain possibilities are already discernible and we might usefully apply our minds to these.

Thought will need to be given to the problems that were thrown up in the Kennedy Round, but not finally resolved. We should decide which of these should be actively pursued now that the main negotiations are out of the way.

Prominent among our unfinished business are the complex problems that arise in trade in agricultural products. In the Kennedy Round, an advance was made in the cereals sector and some significant results were achieved in the meat sector and elsewhere but, generally, the progress made was modest compared with the results in the industrial area. Nevertheless, within the Kennedy Round, the international trading community got to grips for the first time with all the ingredients of the intractable problems that confront us here. There is the prospect, if we are prepared to grasp it, of a continuation of the discussion on national policies and a progressively greater degree of international collaboration in an area which, before the Kennedy Round, had remained by and large outside the compass of international negotiation.

We must likewise press in the GATT for further progress on non-tariff barriers. These, with the reduction in tariff levels, will assume an added importance in international trade.

In the industrial field we should examine the possibilities offered by the "sector approach" which evolved during the trade negotiations. This should be done with a view to bringing about a tariff reduction to zero—in other words free trade—in the case of commodities, or groups of commodities, where such a move might be possible.

I am suggesting here what might be called free trade arrangements, not free trade areas. It appeared to me, in the course of our technical and other studies in the Kennedy Round, that there are sectors where the technological progress and the advantages of specialization are so great, and where demand is projected to increase at such a rate, that a priori the conditions for free trade would seem to exist. In the consideration to be given to this problem, the close cooperation of the private sector would be essential. For example, an important aspect to be taken into account would be the question of future investments.

As an ancillary to this, we should try to get rid of the many minimal tariffs that will remain and which, in fact, have only a "nuisance" value.

Unilateral Trade Liberalization?

Looking ahead, I would stress that individual governments must always be ready to take, whenever possible, unilateral measures of trade liberalization. I permit myself the hope that the detailed examination of national interests that went on as part of the Kennedy Round has prepared the ground for such action. We hope that the position could be reached where a country might not demand reciprocity even from other countries at a comparable stage of economic development. This is clearly an area in which the business community must exercise leadership if progress is to be made.

The Developing Countries

The question of the trade and economic development of the developing countries and their urgent need for a substantial increase in export earnings must continue to engage our fullest attention in the GATT. We must build on what has been done and profit from the special experience and expertise, as well as from the more soundly-based knowledge of the problems, that have emerged from the Kennedy Round. We must press on with the task of easing the trading and competitive position of these countries in the interests of their economic development. Failure to pursue this course energetically would have unfortunate consequences and would profit neither the developed nor the developing countries.

Associated with these problems is the question of market disruption in the industrialized world. This will become an increasingly important issue as modern techniques of production become available, and the desire to industrialize becomes more pressing, in the developing countries. It will present an adjustment challenge to the private sector, but not as great as one might think, given the increasing product diversification in economically advanced countries.

East-West Trade

As for the East-West trade the difficulties inherent in differences in economic and trading systems are well known. But the opportunities, particularly in the light of the evolution of economic policies in Eastern Europe, are great and we should not neglect them through any lack of effort on our part. Here again, the cooperation and advice of business will be much needed.

Building Foundations for Cooperation

In our past efforts we have sometimes seemed to concentrate in a rather incoherent manner on our differences, instead of directing our efforts to laying and reinforcing the basic foundations for confident cooperation among the major countries.

We now have the example of the Kennedy Round and the great cooperative effort which it represented. This should encourage us for the future. For international trade is in a constant state of evolution. Unsolved problems will insist on reappearing and new ones will present themselves. Of great importance will be the frequent exchange of views and frank dialogue of the kind which the series of conferences like those sponsored by the Atlantic Council and the Atlantic Institute bring out. In continuing to discuss and clarify the major problems on the international trade scene we shall all be more likely to recognize where our common interests lie, what the opportunities are, and what courses of action are available.

In my view, this is vitally important, because economic development on the scale which will be needed in the coming decades is not something which will take place smoothly or automatically. It will require conscious measures of cooperation, and the way we approach the task may well determine the economic future of the world. In this process of cooperation and clarification, the private sector has a vital role to play.

---

11 PART 2 *Atlantic Council Report*

Stimulating Worldwide Trade

During the early stages of its industrial development, the United States remained largely detached from world affairs. Its policies of political and economic isolationism were characterized by high tariffs, which remained long after the country had become the world's foremost industrial economy.

In fact, it has been just during the past few decades that U.S. trade policy has reflected the new role of the United States in the world community of nations. A series of reciprocal reductions in trade restrictions opened the path for the nation to assume a new leadership and demonstrate in a concrete way its willingness to work together with all free nations in a wider sphere of economic partnership.

But it was the formation of the European Common Market and the European Free Trade Association, the first mass market outside the United States, that presented America with a whole new dimension in free world cooperation. The result was the late President John F. Kennedy's proposal for a trade expansion bill, which became a legislative reality in 1962. That act authorized the President to reduce tariffs, on a reciprocal basis, by as much as 50 percent over a period of five years. For the first time, the United States was able to strive for bold reductions in trade barriers that would give a major impetus to economic growth and bind the major nations of the industrialized world in a stronger partnership—politically, economically, culturally. President Kennedy described the benefits if the two sides of the Atlantic could reach the necessary agreements at the next round of the General Agreement on Tariffs and Trade in Geneva:

> Growing together, the two great markets astride the Atlantic, containing as they will 90 percent of the free world's industrial strength and half a billion customers, can generate the resources and skills to guarantee the economic progress of free peoples everywhere. We must seize this opportunity. Whatever the adjustments needed, however complicated the negotiations may be, we must develop broader economic horizons here at home and use all our influence to encourage our allies to do the same. For only as we dilute preferential arrangements among free nations and throw off the false protection of trade barriers can we truly form the enduring and open partnership we have sought.

Late last year, as the trade talks approached their critical stage in Geneva, United States Treasury Secretary Henry H. Fowler termed them "the boldest approach to multilateral liberalization of trade barriers ever undertaken. For its part, the United States is firmly committed to the fullest reductions possible of all trade barriers." He affirmed that mutual concessions were the key, and that "Kennedy Round success is a matter of highest importance to the continued economic strength of the free world." He added:

Should the negotiations fall victim to economic nationalism or regionalism, the free world stands in danger of growing economic distortion and inefficiency, perpetuated by an inward-looking illusion that all is well. If there are any who take this as a flight of the imagination, I invite them to take a look at the nations of the Marxist persuasion—each imprisoned within its own central economic plan—where the abolition of competition in all of its creative forms has worked a miserable result. It *can* happen to the free world, and it is not necessary to be Marxist. The immense benefits of market competition can be lost just as easily without doctrine as with it.

The Kennedy Round, completed and signed in June, 1967, was the sixth since GATT was formed in January 1948. The matters with which it dealt were of a delicacy and difficulty without precedent, and had far-reaching economic and political significance. As First National City Bank said, these matters affect the vital, bread-and-butter interests of many countries, including all the principal trading nations other than Russia.

About 50 countries negotiated in the Kennedy Round. All the results will be accorded to all GATT countries, which now number about 80. Success hinged in large measure on how far the industrial nations were willing to go in cutting tariffs with a minimum of exceptions. The bulk of the bargaining was among Western European nations (with the six members of the Common Market negotiating as a single unit), the United States, Canada, and Japan, with Australia, New Zealand, and South Africa also taking part.

In addition, the talks tried to recognize the trade needs of some 30 developing countries. Here, however, full reciprocity was not required. It was acknowledged that the less developed nations should not be forced to make reductions in their trade barriers that might be inconsistent with their development efforts.

The complexity of the total picture is hinted at when one realizes that the most-favored-nation principle is in operation, where a concession for a given product to one nation is necessarily a concession to all.

What Are the Stakes?

Since Western Europe and the other advanced industrial countries account for approximately three fifths of total U.S. purchases abroad, the importance to the United States of the GATT negotiations becomes self-evident. European countries are affected even more deeply since, nation by nation, they are substantially more dependent upon international trade than the United States.

The Trade Expansion Act came into being as part of President Kennedy's "grand strategy," which included forging a stronger Atlantic partnership. It assumed that the United Kingdom would become part of the European Common Market. It provided a formula that would have made possible eliminating industrial tariffs where the enlarged Common Market, coupled with the United States, provided four fifths of world exports (not counting internal trade within the Common Market or with Russia and its Communist bloc).

Throughout four years of tough negotiations, the results were always in doubt. Time and again it looked to the public as if the talks were about to collapse. As the June 30, 1967 deadline approached—when the U.S. President's authority under the Trade Expansion Act would expire—the prospects for success seemed dim. And the U.S team made it clear that they would accept failure of the Kennedy Round rather than accept compromises they believed unfair to the United States. The final hours of negotiation broke the deadlock, and agreements were reached for a broad spectrum of tariff cuts averaging about 33 percent in the industrial fields. No doubt arguments will continue for years as to the real significance of the Kennedy Round, and as to who (if anyone) actually "won." But the fact that these unprecedented agreements were reached at all is, in itself, of historical importance.

While those who supported the Kennedy Round firmly believed that all parties to the agreement should benefit from expanded trade and better use of resources, they also recognized that some adjustment problems would arise. These should not be severe, it was pointed out, in view of the essential strength and resiliency of the GATT countries. The adjustments should be helped through the programs of adjustment assistance that are available and the fact that the tariff reductions would be introduced gradually in five annual stages.

Changing Government and Corporate Attitudes

One of the most remarkable achievements to date can never be measured at a negotiating table: namely, the sweeping change in U.S. government and corporate attitudes brought about by the Trade Expansion Act itself. As the President began to implement the trade expansion program, the President's "Herter committee" (chaired by the late Christian A. Herter) invited scores of business leaders and trade association executives to testify as to how the act would affect them. The result was a depth education for all parties involved. Company after company studied government trade policy as never before, not just from a corporate viewpoint but in terms of the national interest.

Government negotiators, in turn, had the unique opportunity of learning about business firsthand as never before. For months, they lived with business statistics and case examples, wrestling with matters which literally determine the success or failure of whole business operations (and tangibly affect the national economy). The discussions were frank and cordial. There were obvious areas of disagreement, but a substantial start was made toward closing many historic gulfs.

Within companies, there were pressures to oppose the act, a temptation which the majority of top management rejected. This is especially significant when we recall the business climate in 1962, when many companies were facing an onslaught of European and Japanese products rivaling the best in America, from German Volkswagens to Japanese transistor radios, from Italian typewriters to Swiss chocolates.

Within government circles, there were traditional suspicions about American businessmen which still characterized capitalism as being in its less responsible days of the 19th century. The Herter committee rejected such notions and conscientiously itemized and documented the industry message regarding what businessmen believed it would take in Geneva to protect U.S. business interests—including urging other countries to lower the protectionist barriers which were effectively blocking the flow of many U.S. products to Europe.

Instrumental in changing both business and government attitudes —or, rather, in finding common ground—were the business trade associations which came out in favor of the Trade Expansion Act, urging national support for what was obviously a national objective. The U.S. Council of the International Chamber of Commerce was representative of such associations. As its president, Christopher H. Phillips, told the Atlantic Council:

> Both the ICC as a whole and the U.S. Council have pressed continuously for successful completion of the Kennedy Round which would implement the Trade Expansion Act.
>
> To this end practical acceptable solutions are sought to the problems standing in the way of agreement among the major nations—solutions which do not abandon the liberal spirit with which the Kennedy Round was initiated. The ICC is convinced that if this spirit is not realized, the world risks a return to economic nationalism and that regardless of the relative success or failure of the Kennedy Round, much remains to be done to further liberalize tariff and nontariff barriers, both among industrialized nations and as they affect the developing countries.

Parenthetically, the International Chamber of Commerce was created in 1919 to provide a framework within which business leaders from all nations could work out their common problems and bring their combined weight to bear on governmental policies affecting the economic well-being of the world. (More on the ICC and its U.S. Council appears in the chapter on multinational organizations.)

Keeping up the Momentum

Even before the 1967 GATT agreements were reached, a number of business-and-industry associations and financial institutions began the search for initiatives "beyond the Kennedy Round." There was a growing consensus that the momentum toward liberalized trade should be kept up regardless of how the Geneva talks turned out.

Alternative approaches, involving trade liberalization on a regional basis, were advanced as possibilities that might be considered if the Kennedy Round failed. In the judgment of some observers, a number of these possibilities still warrant study even though agreements were reached successfully during the Kennedy Round. Here is one such example as analyzed by First National City Bank in its September, 1966 Economic Letter:

A North Atlantic free trade area might be established, initially linking Canada, the United States, and EFTA, but with an open door to the EEC and other industrially advanced nations, including Japan, Australia, and New Zealand. The new grouping would commit members to lower gradually tariff and nontariff barriers on manufactured products. It might also offer concessions to Latin American and other less developed nations if these countries adopt a clear course toward freeing trade among themselves through reductions in trade barriers that could later become effective also for imports from more developed countries.

The idea of regional groupings beginning with the North Atlantic countries has been approached from various vantage points. For example, the Canadian-American Committee, a group of some 70 influential leaders of industry, finance, labor, and agriculture, has for some years been studying the implications of free trade between the two countries. In June 1966 it expanded this concept with the recommendation:

That as a first step the governments of the United States and Canada initiate discussions with the United Kingdom and its partners in EFTA to explore their interest in establishing, under GATT rules, a broad free trade association of developed nations, recognizing that special consideration must be given to less developed countries.

With regard to developing countries, there is growing sentiment that their pressing need for improved export opportunities would justify temporary tariff preferences for their benefit. President Johnson expressed the U.S. attitude at the Western Hemisphere summit conference at Punta del Este in April 1967 as follows:

We have been exploring with other major industrialized countries what practical steps can be taken to increase the export earnings of all developing countries. We recognize that comparable tariff treatment may not always permit developing countries to advance as rapidly as desired. Temporary tariff advantages for all developing countries by all industrialized countries would be one way to deal with this.

We think this idea is worth pursuing. We will be discussing it further with members of our Congress, with business and labor leaders, and we will seek the cooperation of other governments in the world trading community to see whether a broad consensus can be reached along these lines.

The President's concept expressed at Punta del Este recognizes the need to increase purchasing power in the developing countries in order to raise their standards of living, to enable them to produce more and import more from each other and from the industrialized nations. The temporary preferential arrangements would be "temporary" not in the sense that they would be terminated by return to higher rates but rather that the reduced rates would then be applied to trade between the industrialized nations.

To summarize the point on regional groupings and specialized arrangements, the field is now wide open for fresh approaches. Both the U.S. Council of the ICC and the International Chamber as a whole are presently devoting a major part of their attention to the future of international trade within the context of present regional groupings, the possible creation of other groups, and the whole most-favored-nation policy of the GATT.

The Nontariff Barriers

While there may be a diversity of approaches, there seems to be a growing consensus among most business-oriented associations that the momentum toward more liberalized trade must be kept up. And this time, it is emphasized, there should be a concerted attack on *nontariff* barriers. Almost simultaneously with the signing of the Geneva agreements, the U.S. Council released a statement to this effect. The Chamber of Commerce of the United States began its own program for further trade liberalization where nontariff barriers will be a key.

In corporate circles, a strongly-expressed conviction was that *unless* nontariff barriers were removed, the net result of the Kennedy Round could be a U.S. business loss rather than a gain. The reduced tariff barriers would open up American markets to Europeans even while Americans were excluded from European markets by such restrictive practices as export subsidies, government-backed credit terms, border taxes, and nationalistic purchasing practices. There was major concern that American businessmen would suffer as European governments strive to support their own industries through government policies that discriminate against American imports.

This point came out at the original Herter committee hearings, where company spokesmen said that they would be willing to take their chances in a totally free international market if it were to exist, but that it did not exist at the present time. As one spokesman said, many customers around the world would prefer to buy American-built equipment but are prevented from doing so by nationalistic devices to protect whole industries.

To quote him further:

> You can understand, then, the frustration we American manufacturers of this equipment feel when we read about the success stories and golden opportunities for so many U.S. products in two of the great industrial markets of the world, Western Europe and Japan. We know—even as we digest the figures and are exhorted by our government to export more and more—that we are virtually foreclosed from these markets.

This same spokesman pointed to what he considered to be needed reform in the tax structure to make U.S. products competitive in areas where outright restrictions do not exist. As one example, he noted the "border tax," over and above regular custom duties, for U.S. products going into Germany. This is intended to equalize or adjust for the so-called turnover taxes already levied on competing German products inside the border. But, the spokesman advised:

> The U.S. export has already borne its share of the direct U.S. corporation income tax, but now it has as much as a 15 percent additional tax imposed on it at the German border.
>
> Yet when that same German product is exported to compete with an American product in, say, Latin America, it leaves Germany tax free because the internal German turnover taxes are "remitted" or "rebated."
>
> Competitively speaking, this is having your cake and eating it too. However valid the system may be under prevailing tax theory, and however much it is permitted under the GATT, some pretty ridiculous situations emerge. For example, thanks in large part to the border tax system, French cold-rolled steel, with a mill price of $8.24 per hundredweight, can be laid down in New York for $6.66 (because of the export rebate), while equivalent U.S. steel, with a mill price of $7.36, is laid down in LeHavre for $11.00 (because of tax "adjustments" imposed at the French border). And believe it or not, the U.S. tariff is 3 percent higher than the French tariff.

The feeling is strong that U.S. businessmen have been more than cooperative in supporting the U.S. government throughout the Kennedy Round. They did so even as they realized that in some fields their support could worsen their competitive positions vis-à-vis the Europeans. They did so because they believed that the national interest had to come before the corporate interest. Now they believe that cooperation must be a two-way street, with the government helping them to go "the second mile" toward truly liberalized, non-restrictive world trade.

Cooperative Efforts Needed

Regardless of the framework for trade agreements, one U.S. chief executive suggested that the overriding need is for the U.S. government and U.S. industry to agree on a strategy of international competition. He recognized that "strategy" may be too formal a term, implying closer industry-government commitments and relationships than either might want.

"But the important thing," he added, "is that neither side can go it alone, for international competition (in 'protected' industries) is so intimately related to the economic policy of foreign governments that there must be some coming together in common cause."

Government officials concur in the need for cooperative efforts with industry, even while recognizing the complexity of the next steps. No one seems prepared to define *how* the problems of nontariff political restrictions can best be handled (or even approached). The most likely immediate possibility "beyond the Kennedy Round" is for a breathing spell—to let the dust settle, to assess results, to sound out where, when, and how to move next. But this very breathing spell offers an excellent opportunity for thinking and planning by private business associations and companies. They can: a) assess the impact of the Kennedy tariff cuts on individual businesses; b) determine actions they can take by themselves, *without* U.S. government assistance; c) define precisely where U.S. government assistance *is* needed; and d) prepare proposals accordingly. This is the kind of initiative called for by Eric Wyndham White in his introduction to this chapter when he said: "In this process of cooperation and clarification, the private sector has a vital role to play."

The European Viewpoint

As the Atlantic Council representatives conducted their interviews with European businessmen, they heard complaints that manufacturers in other countries considered that they were not being adequately represented at the Geneva trade negotiation tables. Some expressed a belief that the current U.S. administration is more pro-business than earlier administrations, and that the result could be more protectionism against European exports. It was interesting to note in European offices many of the same complaints which were registered in American business offices:

"We can compete on a price basis under present tariff restrictions, but it's the array of nontariff barriers which is killing us."

One conclusion to be drawn from this conflicting set of attitudes, on who is being restricted most, is to encourage more coordination and more contact between U.S. and foreign manufacturers. For example, the head of one of Europe's larger business associations proposed that a carefully selected group of businessmen, perhaps no more than a dozen, get together at their own private sector conference table to present corporate viewpoints from the United States and from Europe. The agenda would consist of their respective complaints and the purpose would be to find out where there might be a rationale for more common policies. Working completely separately and distinctly from government offices, the conferees would then return to their own government negotiators so that new viewpoints could be set forth officially in the multinational government negotiations.

The Most Essential Task

Thus, despite the problems in reducing the barriers and stimulating worldwide trade, progress continues on several levels.

Knut Hammarskjold, former deputy secretary general of the European Free Trade Association, (the "Outer Seven" of Europe as distinguished from the "Inner Six" of the Common Market), has been well aware of the formidable problems, especially those that lie between the EEC and the EFTA in arriving at common trade and tariff policies. But, nevertheless, he has been optimistic. In his words:

The most essential task now is simply to enlighten the public as to the benefits of free trade and free flow of investments. The man on the street must be made to understand that he is the one whose standard of living will be improved, and he is the one whose opportunities will be broadened by the establishment of the widest possible trading community, including the U.S., EEC, and EFTA. This should lead automatically to a true world trading community.

12 Multinational Companies

PART 1 *Introduction*
by Olivier Giscard d'Estaing   213

Formerly dean of the European Institute of Business Administration (INSEAD), Olivier Giscard d'Estaing is currently vice president of Societe des Verreries Reunies du Loing (SOVIREL). He also serves as chairman of the board of Gibbs and Hill (France), and as a board member of IBM (France), Interpublic, S.A., and several other companies and organizations. A former vice president of the International Junior Chamber of Commerce, he holds a doctor of law degree from the University of Paris, and a master's in business administration from Harvard University.

In recent years it has become apparent that the most constructive tools for building up the sense of common interest and partnership among nations lie in the economic arena. The more we become interdependent economically, the closer we shall come to intergovernment cooperation in other fields.

The efforts at economic cooperation today between Europe and America parallel to some extent the relations between the six countries of the Common Market in 1954–55. In 1954, we had failed in what had been foreseen as the European Defense Community. The true Europeans were dismayed, and we asked ourselves if the first timid efforts at cooperation—notably the European Coal and Steel Community—were solid enough to withstand attack.

In the midst of the searching questions being asked, it was at Messina, Italy, in 1955, that the Belgian statesman, Paul-Henri Spaak, put the issue in sharp perspective. He said, "Now then, forget for a moment the problems of defense. The field in which we can and should collaborate, which will be the most solid base for subsequent political cooperation, will be the economic field."

Since then, it has indeed been the economic field where the will has existed to create a Common Market, aimed at a free movement of men, goods, and capital—with first, an extremely well-defined intermediate stage, spreading over 15 years, to permit the separate national structures to adapt themselves to a new whole; and second, the institutions to permit the achievement of genuine competition among the vastly different industries of our six nations.

The Next Phase of Economic Activity

Returning to the present, I do not know whether it is because our differences in the defense field have accumulated that the economic difficulties have become less serious—some say this is so. But at any rate, we can now discuss European and American economic cooperation with less passion and more serenity than in, say, 1963 or 1964. It appears that it is high time to try to preview the legal and institutional structures which will facilitate the transition between our present economic and political situation, and the next phase of international economic activity. It seems somewhat abnormal to me that we do not have international agreements which would cover antitrust situations, for example, or other cases of everyday international business practice. As Ambassador Cattani clearly states in an earlier chapter, some sort of structure is needed, within which men can collaborate and compete without discrimination or excessive national predominance, for the enrichment and well-being of humanity.

The real action to build the Atlantic Community into a true common market, with the progressive liberalization of the movement of men, capital, and trade, must come from governments. But the multinational company can be a strong "pressure force" to help achieve this goal. In addition, the development of the truly multinational corporation would strengthen transatlantic business ties further, and would diminish some of the European concerns about foreign participation in their economies.

Multinational Companies Defined

A few years ago, I would have described a multinational firm as a company which is producing and doing research in several countries. Today, I would say it is a company which is producing, doing research, and whose ownership is distributed among several countries. In the year 2000, I will probably define it as a company whose board chairman is of a different nationality than the country of the home office. In effect, a totally multinational company results much more from a specific attitude of the management, which conceives its business as an economic tool for service to multinational economies and as an international pool of human and financial resources to fulfill its objectives.

Any company, until it achieves a truly multinational structure and attitude, is essentially an alien in all countries where it operates except one—its home base. For old established firms in foreign countries, the alien image is practically ignored and unharmful. For newcomers to foreign soil, however, specific action has to be taken to give a familiar concept to the product, the branch, and the company name. Differences of behavior according to nationalities are obvious and will remain. Languages, too, pose a problem. There are specific problems of management in the various fields of personnel practices, employee communications, and in communicating the overall company performance to the public. It is true that after years of experience, most companies can easily overcome these and other difficulties. But it does require specific action from management— especially for the newly arrived company—to create a climate of better understanding.

Education Can Help

The role of the educational community in spreading the understanding of the contributions of multinational companies cannot be stressed too much. At INSEAD (European Institute of Business Administration) we require that our students—who come from all over Europe—speak at least two languages and have a working familiarity with one other. The principles of operation for multinational companies which we stress are very much like those followed by many companies today, including good corporate citizenship, long-term planning to become a permanent part of the host country economy, regular relations with manufacturing associations and public administrations, and respect for local traditions.

To our students we teach eight principles of organization for the multinational company:

1. *Product Policy.* Sell what the local market needs and wants, not necessarily what is sold at home.

2. *Production Facilities.* Insure production facilities in different countries. This is step one of a multinational firm, and can be accomplished through licensing arrangements, joint ventures, or direct investment. The joint venture may consist of sharing skill and technical information, taking advantage of local human resources, and production and marketing facilities. Although many, if not most, American firms have preferred the wholly owned subsidiary to the joint venture, the second would seem to be preferable, in my view.

3. *Research and Development.* Take advantage of local resources, and conduct research in different countries, thus stimulating the local branch's laboratory and helping to meet the local need to use and hold its brainpower. Some Europeans fear a "brain drain," noting that over 30,000 engineers and 9,000 researchers have gone from Europe to the United States in recent years.

4. *Financing Policies.* Use and attract local financial resources, where possible, to develop a feeling of a common stake in the firm's success.

5. *Use of Human Resources.* Train personnel to become true internationalists, with emphasis on qualifications rather than nationality. Organize communications and meetings systematically to create the right corporate *esprit de corps.* Try to rotate personnel among different countries, at least at the management level.

6. *Decision Making.* Concentrate policy decisions at headquarters level, leaving as much decentralized responsibility and initiative at the local level as possible.

7. *Management.* Give opportunities to foreigners to manage not only operations in their country of origin, but also to reach management positions at the corporate level, including board of directors.

8. *Ownership.* Make available either the stock of the local subsidiary or of the parent company in all countries where it operates and where legislation and economic situations permit. It is this final step which makes a company truly multinational. That is the way to reach a genuine feeling of participation in the success of multinational firms.

Twofold Ambassadors

We also try to impart the feeling that the multinational manager—

hopefully, the future role our students will fulfill—must be a two-fold ambassador. On the one hand, he must follow the parent firm's total multinational strategy, and thus satisfy his superiors. On the other, he must adapt that strategy to local conditions to further his company's interests in the country where he is located.

Thus, the manager of the multinational corporation plays a fundamental role in today's evolution, because his corporation prefigures our international society of tomorrow. By his attitudes and decisions, he sets up new patterns.

Not only does he serve an economic function, which is important and difficult enough, but he also exerts a key influence on our democratic society. He can be, as U.S. Treasury Secretary Henry H. Fowler has said, "our best assurance of peace with freedom and a healthy, dynamic, economic society."

---

12 PART 2 *Atlantic Council Report*   217

The purpose of this chapter is not to restate the philosophy presented by Olivier Giscard d'Estaing in his guest introduction, but to see the impact of various philosophies in action. The intent is not to re-cover the ground in Chapter 5 on management attitudes and practices, but to see the results of these attitudes and practices as applied across Europe.

The starting point is to define the end result which most international managers hope to achieve. One graphic description of internationalization was given by Gabriel Hauge, president of Manufacturers Hanover Trust Company:

The internationalization of business makes clear the point that capital has no citizenship. Corporations are not really citizens of the nation where they were first established, nor of the country of birth of major stockholders or of management. Corporations are citizens of all the markets they serve, and of all the places where they undertake production. In a real sense international business holds multiple passports.

Arriving at that end result is the problem of the multinational corporation, which raises a myriad of operational questions, whose answers will obviously vary from company to company.

The Tough Questions

1. In terms of *organization*—wholly-owned subsidiaries, joint ventures, licensing agreements, and various other arrangements—which among the many patterns of corporations are most attractive?

2. In terms of *ownership*, what are the relative merits of complete ownership, majority or minority ownership, and availability of stock across national borders?

3. In terms of *control*, where and how should it be centralized, delegated, shared?

—In the subsidiary?

—Representation on the parent company board?

—Division of management responsibility between host-national management and representation from the parent organization?

4. In terms of *operations*, what are the basic criteria?

—For labor, management, and production methods—so as to increase efficiency with minimum dislocations?

—For research and development—so as to build host-national or multinational resources?

Various attempts have been made to set guideline answers on how a multinational corporation should operate. At the Crotonville conference, executives concurred that there are no set rules and that it would be totally impractical to force corporations into preconceived molds that could only block progress. At the Geneva conference, an international executive confessed that he could not honestly define a "multinational corporation" even though he had lived most of his corporate life in one. Others came more bluntly to the point when they questioned, "What difference does it make as to the form as long as host-national interests are observed?" At the Paris conference, Jacques Maisonrouge, the French-born head of IBM Europe, summarized his criteria for multinational companies:

1. The new company should contribute something new and needed by the host country. (Objection is to straight take-overs of existing companies without bringing in anything new.)

2. Management should have authority to act at the point of operations. (Not management by "remote control." The essential point here is that the European subsidiary must fully consider the constraints of the environment. It means that managers must know it thoroughly.)
3. Management should accept and respect the basic interests of the host country. (Avoid a "conflict of interest"—e.g., resisting national economic policies and practices.)
4. Build up technological resources and capabilities locally. (Do not contribute to "the brain drain" in which all or most of the R&D work is done in the United States.
5. Manufacture in several countries, and have in these countries a full industrial operation.
6. Stabilize and strengthen the economy. (That is, avoid the inflation which results from entering an area where there is already full employment and perhaps a materials shortage; avoid bidding up labor costs; and appreciate the differences in labor relations concepts and practices.)
7. Whenever possible, evolve management and ownership on a multinational basis. (Through multinational representation on the operating staffs and boards of directors; and through joint ownership of the capital—either through joint ventures, etc., or through stock participation and availability on the local market.)

Note that IBM is not a joint venture. It is a wholly-owned American company just as Unilever is Dutch and Olivetti is Italian. It is a powerful force by any measurement—sales volume, employment, impact on the economy. And it is widely welcomed and accepted. IBM's record in Europe would seem to bear out M. Maisonrouge's managerial-operational philosophy: as long as the corporation contributes to the host-national interest as a host-national organization, the other questions become of lesser significance.

Company Philosophy Is What Counts

The same principle applies for each country: it is not so much form as philosophy which determines whether or not a company is truly multinational. This point was expanded in Germany by U.S. Ambassador George C. McGhee in a June 30, 1966 address to the Rhein-Ruhr Club at Düsseldorf:

American business in Germany is German business. It operates under German laws; pays German taxes; provides work for thousands of Germans; purchases goods and services giving work to other German business and industry; and—last but not least—makes a major contribution to

Germany's overall exports. Indeed, we must consider American business in Germany within a scope which includes all business operations. Germany as a sovereign country knows full well that all businesses within its borders are its businesses, foreign connections notwithstanding.

The current trend in big business, Ambassador McGhee continued, is for operations to become increasingly international both in scope and character, no matter where the head company is domiciled.

This is particularly true in the petroleum, automotive, and electronics industries. These comprise large firms which have originated in many countries—and are now owned by investors all over the world. Their executives, chosen with little regard to nationality, are equally at home in Europe, or America, or Asia. They carry with them no political design— only the desire to make their business efficient and profitable. In doing so they make the maximum possible contribution to the economies of the countries in which they are operating.

Ambassador McGhee questioned "the conventional wisdom" that a serious and unbridgeable technological gap exists between the United States and Europe:

There are, indeed, other competitive factors which I believe are of possibly greater importance, such as: organization of the capital market to mobilize funds for industrial investment, maximum use of automation, sales and service-oriented management, the cultivation of a mass domestic market, and product-improving development. These, as well as the state of technology, are all of prime importance as factors influencing the success of business enterprises.

But let us look at the technological problem itself in more detail. America's annual research and development budget—both government and private—is some $22 billion; the Federal Republic, on the other hand, spends only some $2 billion—a ratio of 11 to 1, or almost twice the ratio between our respective national products. Naturally this creates something of a technological disparity between the two countries—and one which is beyond the resources of American firms in Germany to bridge through their own efforts.

The obvious conclusion was that the results of research done by the parent company in the United States are fully available to its manufacturing subsidiaries abroad. Through this link, he said, access is provided to the required technology for the manufacture in Germany of the latest computers and other business machines, which would not otherwise be available. Moreover, there is an increasing tendency on the part of American firms operating abroad to decentralize their research and development activities, to the end that an increasing percentage of their total research will be done in Europe. Ambassador McGhee referred to one large American subsidiary in Germany which is initiating such a decentralization, which will bring Europeans—including Germans—more directly into participation in pure research. In some cases, this is being done on a Europewide basis. One such example is Esso's new European research laboratory now being built in Brussels.

In this context, a growing number of observers believe that it is not just useless but actually destructive to heat up and prolong the argument which would pit Americans against Europeans in a seeming struggle for technological superiority. Even the question, "How soon can the technological gap be closed?" would seem inappropriate, as companies increasingly lose their national identity in favor of world citizenship. Such corporate transnationalism could mean that the technological race would no longer be between two competing and clashing continents but between companies spanning those continents.

The technological gap may well cease to exist as an issue as it becomes impossible to define which country is "ahead" in a race being run among internationalized companies. As one example, which country should be considered "in the lead" in the NATO Hawk program, involving a five-nation consortium of industrial partners? Again, which nation is "winning" in an electronics joint venture involving companies headquartered in the United States, France, and Italy? Finally, and to use a much older illustration, which country is "out front" in the SAS Airline venture, involving three national efforts from Norway, Denmark, and Sweden?

Many Americans are quietly yearning and openly striving for the day when the companies they represent will no longer be singled out as "American." That would immeasurably improve relationships among the businessmen and their respective countries. Speaking for this viewpoint was retired General Electric executive William C. Wichman, now of Rochester University, after participating in both the Crotonville and Geneva conferences:

Somehow Americans find themselves maneuvered into a position where U.S. companies are on trial for being a special case of an international phenomenon—the multinational company. We just have more of them; but you can think of European firms like Unilever, Nestlé, and Philips, and many more who would like to be. The unique feature of *any* multinational company is that it tries to operate in such a way as to offset the effect of nationalism. Our U.S. companies simply now happen to be at the crest of a wave, which together with the emergence of a market economy in Europe—plus our alleged technological superiority and economies of scale—cause resentment in Europe.

A final few words on form: The Atlantic Council survey indicates that if a poll were taken of Europeans, most government and business representatives would probably vote for joint ventures in contrast to other organizational arrangements. In Holland, where response was more or less typical for the continent, Dutch representatives stressed the advantage of this form as a means for combining U.S. efficiency and know-how with Dutch understanding of local conditions. Approximately 100 joint ventures are in operation in Holland as compared with 200 wholly-owned U.S. subsidiaries. Dutch ownership definitely is preferred.

But the consensus among the larger companies of all nationalities, should they be polled, might easily run counter to the majority viewpoint. There is strong feeling among such executives that each company must evolve its own unique rationale. While there is great merit in including foreign nationals on boards of directors, and this is becoming the pattern for most international companies, that does not automatically assure that joint control means good management. Exactly the opposite can be the result.

Degree of ownership is another issue which cannot be solved automatically through the easy solution of "50–50." Some companies operate with great success on a basis of 100 percent U.S. ownership and 100 percent host-national management. Others consider majority ownership satisfactory, and still others do very well with a minority interest. Some Europeans insist on a partnership, some on ownership. Others feel that it is adequate to have stock available on the local market. Still others are satisfied with no ownership, provided that management is national. Finally, the degree of ownership between Europeans and Americans may vary from year to year, to the satisfaction of the several participants, and certainly with no ill effects for the host government, the consuming public, or the employees.

Corporate Examples

The secret to management success, as viewed by one rather caustic writer, is to be "so deft at imparting an international flavor to American methods that their national origin remains concealed."

There is no question that a new breed of international manager is coming into its own, combining the best of both worlds. Whether he is an Americanized European or a Europeanized American is incidental. The point is that differences between American and European management methods are disappearing as a distinctly Euro-American style evolves into its own. How this has evolved and is being practiced will constitute the balance of this chapter, through a series of corporate vignettes of international business in action.

1. *Ford.* Perhaps under the adage that no news is good news, Ford Motor Company seems rather proud of its unheralded entry into Europe over half a century ago, when Henry Ford established a company in Great Britain in 1909. Except for the official ribbon-cutting ceremony, the beginning went almost unnoticed. Nor was a great deal of attention paid to Ford during the next 25 years, as the company opened affiliates in every country, which today includes the EFTA and EEC trading blocs. Ford looks on its "dull" story as a demonstration of good corporate citizenship. Settling in, joining the community, taking on local coloration, losing the "taint" of American ownership— all this was done in most countries before many of the U.S. companies now investing in Europe were even founded.

Company officials comment that anyone looking for the dramatic or the spectacular will not find it in Ford. They believe that a combination of sound national management over the years, coupled with generous reinvestment in the future of individual companies and their employees and dealers, has made Ford an acceptable "local" (as opposed to "American") operation in the great majority of the European countries in which Ford does business. In Belgium, it was Henry Ford himself who selected the site of a plant to build his model T's, back in 1922, before any other automotive company had established Belgian facilities. By World War II it was the largest in the nation, with additional growth coming after the war.

First there was a sizable investment in new machinery and equip-

223

ment. Then came a huge parts depot to supply all of Europe with parts for American Ford products. Later, in 1958, Brussels was chosen as the site for the company's European staff headquarters, and a Belgian Ford executive was appointed to head the organization—which serves as a link between the parent corporation in Dearborn, Michigan, and its subsidiaries in Austria, Belgium, Denmark, Egypt, Finland, France, Italy, The Netherlands, Norway, Portugal, Sweden, and Switzerland. Only the English and German companies continue to have direct reporting lines to Dearborn.

Rumors that Ford was pulling out of Belgium began in 1963, precipitating what company officials termed the only serious corporate citizenship problem the company had faced in 40 years of community relations.

The cause was a management decision to convert the Antwerp plant from the assembly of automobiles to the manufacture of tractors. Plans called for the closing down of the facilities for a period of about six months. During this period the plant was to be expanded and modernized to permit it to produce all of the Ford tractors sold in Europe. At the time, Ford had only two major manufacturing locations for tractors: one in Detroit, the other in Basildon, England. Antwerp was slated to be the third—an honor that was lost on the some 1,400 assembly line workers who worried about being dismissed after an average of 16 years of service with the company.

As it turned out, an arrangement was worked out between the Belgian government and Ford insuring that all of the workers were paid at least 80 percent of their salary during the plant conversion period. Special schools were set up by the company to teach the men the new skills required to build tractors and manufacture component parts. And eventually, according to company officials, all of them returned to positions equal to or better-paying than those they formerly had.

One of the most critical phases of Ford's recent history came at a time when Americans and Europeans were equally concerned about the impact of launching new operations in the hypersensitive climate which characterized the early 1960's. That was when Ford opened a huge $140 million automotive assembly plant near Genk, in a North Belgian province—in the words of one spokesman, "creating hardly a ripple." One Ford executive later said that in a sense it was unfortunate that the "good news" could not be used to improve the company's image in the nation.

This operation, in 1964, was a sizable one. The plant covered 3.2 million square feet; the work force included 8,000 people; the assembly operations ran to 1,000 cars a day. All this was started with so little fanfare that press attention was not drawn to the project until after the plans were announced and the cornerstone laid.

As a result of what the company terms "modest corporate citizen" policy, the average Belgian may not be aware of the role which Ford has played and continues to play in his nation's economy. The Belgian Ford Company which started out 44 years ago, and as recently as 1963 employed only about 1,500 people, today makes the following contributions:

a) Employs over 10,000 Belgians.

b) Pays out more than $29 million in wages and benefits.

c) Contributes almost $14 million in taxes and duties.

d) Purchases about $90 million of materials from local suppliers.

2. *Upjohn.* In the manufacture of medical products which the company considers important in medical care, Upjohn believes that it is making a contribution to the public and medical profession in each country on a local basis by building factories in Europe. Between 1952 and 1965, Upjohn formed national limited companies in the United Kingdom, the Benelux countries, France, Italy, Spain, West Germany, and Sweden. In France and Spain, Upjohn is in partnership with national companies.

In each of these countries, with the sole exception of one non-national manager, the day-to-day management is the entire responsibility of host nationals. The entire labor force in each company is also host national. Virtually all production equipment used in the European division is manufactured in Europe. In the United Kingdom, Upjohn is taking its first step toward internationalizing R&D through a new product research laboratory being built at Crawley, Sussex.

The same approach applies to outside services and projects, such as the new plant being erected near Milan, Italy, where the company has contracted with an Italian architect and is using local labor and materials.

As for employee practices, a corporate official stated that each Upjohn company in Europe "endeavors to maintain salaries and benefits on a par with the most progressive national industries in its particular country." A single overall benefit plan in each country—e.g., pension, life insurance, holidays, sickness benefits—applies to all Upjohn personnel, irrespective of status or rank. All staff members share equal facilities. Such employment practices, the company feels, have resulted in the long-term retention of employees as compared with neighboring industries. To upgrade their skills and prepare them for greater responsibilities, Upjohn conducts intensive training programs on both a national and international level. The company feels that international training often makes up for shortcomings on the local scene and improves the skills of local managers.

Just as American companies within the United States have felt a social responsibility to contribute to outside research organizations, so Upjohn is making substantial contributions to national medical research within Belgium. Promising young university medical lecturers, selected by professors of medicine in Belgian universities, are helped to pursue study in the United States. In the United Kingdom, there are 15 to 18 Upjohn traveling fellowships, administered by the U.K. College of General Practitioners, which make it possible for British general practitioners to do postgraduate work in the British Isles.

3. *J. Walter Thompson Company.* The explosive growth of American marketing and advertising methods in Europe is one of the more obvious phenomena of "the new Europe," which makes this case history especially interesting. J. Walter Thompson Company established a Dutch company in Amsterdam in 1958. This company has grown, in eight years, from a staff of only a few, with under $138,000 billing, to 100 personnel with a billing of $5 million, thus ranking it among the top five advertising agencies in Holland.

The company credits its growth and rising profits, on a year by year basis, to the combination of servicing a growing list of international clients and at the same time attracting major local clients in the market. The initial management team was a blend of American and Dutch management. But moves were quickly needed to train and retrain strong Dutch personnel in important positions so that Dutch management would be dominant in the office, always supported by American counterparts.

Strong internal pressures were exerted to underline the international character of the organization and impress upon employees the importance of international commitments. The office was placed on an independent profit center basis, providing management incentives to improve performance each year. "From the beginning," one staff member recalls, "all members of management understood that occasional problems would arise when international commitments were at odds with profitable local operations, and positive resolutions were always sought. Therefore, rather than being a problem area, it became an area to apply creative thinking to find the best and most balanced solution."

As for the image of a large company working in a relatively small community, the management took the position that it must be conservative and very careful in dealing with all personnel. "Therefore, we did not try to raid other agencies of good people, but aimed at attracting them through our name and good work, as well as training enthusiastic, talented young people."

Consistent with the account mix in the local office, management incentive takes two forms: a management bonus based on the performance of the local company, and ownership by the top management of stock of the parent company.

5. *Eastman Kodak Company.* The British, French, and German subsidiaries of this American firm have all been in business for decades, and have the advantage of a highly respected brand name for their products. They are wholly owned by the American parent, and managed entirely by Europeans. Not since World War II has an executive of the British subsidiary been an American. The parent firm has only a minority of membership on the subsidiary boards of directors. With the exception of three areas—dividends, capital expenditures, and markets in third countries—the subsidiaries have very considerable autonomy. Their senior executives meet regularly with those of the parent company.

In matters of labor relations, the subsidiaries follow substantially the policies of the parent, except where local traditions or legislation dictate modifications. Their wage scales and benefits rank high in each of the three countries. The wage scale of the French company is said to be among the top 10 in France, and its combined wages and benefits are said to be among the highest in the country.

Although the parent firm is looked to for the great bulk of R&D considerable research is carried out by the French and British subsidiaries. A number of processes which have been designed and developed in Europe have been adopted by the parent firm. There is also considerable short-term exchange of technical personnel. A number of the overseas staff, for example, regularly work for limited periods in the United States, learning new techniques, and a number of Americans are working overseas for short periods.

There is a high degree of communication, cooperation, and complementation among the various subsidiaries and between each of them and the parent company. Importantly, the executives of the subsidiaries feel that they are a full part of the total corporate team.

6. *Esso Standard Italiana S.p.A.* This subsidiary of Standard Oil Company (New Jersey) has been in business in Italy since 1891, and today employs some 2,500 people—almost all of whom are Italian, including the management. It uses about 20 percent of the capacity of Italian tankers, and 17 of its ships have been built in Italian shipyards—of obvious benefit to the shipping and shipbuilding industries. In 1965, more than 40 percent of Esso's capital investment was in the depressed area of Southern Italy. In Avigliano, the company has instituted a test project for the training and rehabilitation of unskilled labor.

Its extensive activities in recreation, sports, and cultural events are primarily conducted through its 15 Esso Clubs. The company also sponsors such noted events as the national ski championships, international tennis competitions, and soccer and bridge tournaments. It also distributes educational films to about 1000 high schools, and sponsors a high school physics competition.

7. *Subsidiary of Medium–Sized Process Control Company.* The Dutch subsidiary of this U.S. medium-sized company was established in 1958, in a residential area of a smaller community. At the outset, the firm tackled its community relations head on. One of the two American executives sent to set up the subsidiary visited each of the prospective plant neighbors for mid-morning coffee—a tradition in Dutch

homes. Explaining the nature of the plant's production, and displaying architects' plans, he allayed any developing fears that the plant would bring an industrial look to the community. The approach was welcomed, and the opening, in June 1959, was regarded as a happy event by the entire area.

Today the plant employs some 300 personnel, including a number of technical student trainees, and employee loyalty runs high. Except for one British executive and the two Americans who established the plant, the management is entirely Dutch. At a recent employee meeting, the firm's employees were delighted to hear their American deputy managing director present his entire address in their language.

8. *Compagnia Generale di Elettricità S.p.A.* One of the larger U.S. subsidiaries in Italy, CGE is 80 percent owned by the General Electric Company, and is one of the primary Italian firms in the electromechanical field. The vast majority of the 16,000 CGE system employees, including management, is Italian. CGE is sourcing for export from Italy for General Electric such diverse products as refrigerators and numerical positioning controls—the former from a factory employing over 700 people located in the depressed Southern Italy region. The company recently entered into an important joint venture with Finmeccanica, through Ansaldo San Giorgio, in the heavy electrical equipment field, which will be supported by substantial infusion of General Electric technology from the United States.

In another area, General Electric's joint venture with Olivetti for the development of computers and data control processing is expected to enhance Italy's ability to develop this important field internally, as well as to be a significant exporter of this type of equipment.

9. *Remington Rand Italia S.p.A.* All of the management of this subsidiary of Remington Rand and Sperry Rand is Italian, including the general manager. Two of its plants are located in the depressed South. It has created many scholarships, and also has seaside and mountain resorts for the benefit of its 1,600 employees. In 1964 the company was awarded the "Mercurio d'Oro" by the Italian government for special merit in industry.

10. *IBM Italia S.p.A.* This subsidiary of IBM has been in Italy since 1928, and has more than 3,700 employees. It has made a unique

contribution to the Italian university system by giving special favored treatment for the purchase or rental of electronic data processing equipment. Recently, it installed an important EDP system at the University of Pisa, which has been placed freely at the disposal of other Italian universities. The company has complete Italian management.

11. *Medium–Sized Electrical Manufacturer.* One of the first decisions of this medium-sized electrical equipment firm when it began to set up a fully owned Dutch subsidiary in 1958, was that the entire employment—from managing director on down—should be "nationals of the country of settlement." Executives of the parent firm have acted mainly in an advisory capacity, principally aiding in the transfer of necessary manufacturing know-how. As far as practical, U.S. designs are translated into European components and manufacturing methods, and the Dutch subsidiary is left the greatest possible freedom in this respect.

Dutch rules and customs have also been followed closely, if at all possible. Employee fringe benefits, for example, were set up along the Dutch pattern.

So far, R&D is done only on a very limited scale by the subsidiary, but an increasing amount is planned for the future.

Despite the excellent two-way cooperation across the Atlantic, both the Dutch and Americans are quick to point out that their differences in approach to various situations are undeniable and real. In such areas as social patterns and thinking, and business and managerial ways of operating, both sides have had to give ground. But in the process, the operation has achieved a successful business position, with excellent employee morale and community relations.

12. *3M Minnesota Italia S.p.A.* A recent arrival in Italy is this subsidiary of 3M Company, which was established in 1959, and now has some 500 employees. It built one of the first plants in the depressed Southern Italy area, and was the first to bring dry copy reproduction to Italy. Recently, it donated a number of luminous blackboards to the center charged with eliminating illiteracy in Italy. The management is entirely Italian.

13. *Medium–Sized Service Company.* Out of a total office force of some 400, the subsidiary of this service industry firm employs 15 Americans in management and technical positions. Although it is

striving to replace the Americans with Dutch managers and engineers, the firm feels it will be several years before they can be replaced completely. Some of the U.S. executives are there to supply skills which the company feels are not available in Holland, but most are there because the firm cannot find enough local skilled people to keep its labor force in proper balance.

Well over 90 percent of the management decisions are made locally, and decision making is being increasingly delegated to lower levels of management.

In labor relations, the company tries to marry the best features of normal Dutch practices with those common in the American parent. For example, a profit sharing bonus plan was set up recently in the subsidiary as an extra incentive toward improved efficiency.

14. *Merck, Sharp & Dohme, Nederland N.V.* Merck, Sharp & Dohme established a manufacturing and distributing operation in Holland in 1954. Incorporating under local law, the company quickly recognized the importance of complying with local legislative requirements, local languages and schools of thought, and the use of local talents.

By early 1957, the company was firmly established and was operating a small chemical and pharmaceutical plant with office facilities in Haarlem. In the less than 10 years since its original plant opening, facilities have been expanded twice, and several new projects are on the drawing board for the coming five-year period. Substantial future growth is expected.

Merck's choice of The Netherlands as the base of its European operations, company officials report, was based partly on the objective of The Netherlands government to attract foreign business operations which could serve to broaden the country's economic base. Especially attractive to Merck was the government's policy of having one single office deal with all the major problems confronting foreign businesses, even though some problems might be the responsibility of several ministries and departments. "In those days of restrictions and permit-ridden economies, this approach was invaluable," Merck executives recall.

From its experience, Merck has set forth six basic elements for a successful business venture in The Netherlands:

1. A clear policy statement by the parent company, expressing the business philosophy under which the subsidiary should operate.
2. A set of business objectives and a blueprint for meeting them.
3. Recognition of the need to develop a subsidiary to earliest possible maturity by a willingness to delegate authority to local management, commensurate with responsibility for meeting objectives.
4. Special attention to the development of good communications between parent and subsidiary, based on clear delineation of authority.
5. A sincere policy of good citizenship, good neighborliness, and active community membership.
6. A proper and justified use of the company's international position and a willingness to share its broader knowledge and experience freely when compatible with the company's interest.

Any company which is prepared to show a sincere desire to practice these points, Merck believes, will succeed in attracting the cream of local talent, and in stimulating and motivating this talent to perform at a very satisfactory level, even in a period of inflation and overemployment. With reference to the host country, The Netherlands, Merck is convinced that from many viewpoints this country forms a most preferable corner of the Common Market, both in its present configuration as well as that of the future.

Joint Ventures Increasingly Attractive

Despite the success of many multinational firms in setting up wholly owned subsidiaries, as shown by the examples above, many companies have turned to the joint venture as an effective way of entering the European market. There are many examples of successful joint ventures. Here are two:

1. *Siemens–RCA*. These two electronic giants—one German, the other American—have signed an agreement to pool R&D efforts to develop new computers in Germany. This is one of the most sensitive fields in Europe, with respect to American investments, and is often cited as a yardstick of the level of technical development of an economy. By one recent estimate IBM had about 72 percent of the German computer market, with other U.S. companies holding most of the rest. Thus, the Siemens–RCA joint venture has had considerable goodwill effect.

2. *Dow–Badische.* This is an example of reverse investment, in that a German and an American chemical company have founded a joint venture in the United States. Leaders of the German chemical industry have generally been reluctant to invest in America because of the disposition of the I. G. Farben holdings in this country after the war. Thus, this venture is an important bridge. It is of great importance that the seat of this operation is in the United States.

What most of the businessmen are saying in these remarks has been summarized by George D. Bryson in his book *Profits from Abroad.** He writes:

The sooner we can arrive at the point where there is completely free intercourse of free enterprise and free competition, the sooner the standard of living throughout the world will be brought to an acceptable level, and the safer mankind will be from wars. While . . . this day is a very long way off for the whole world, I believe it is attainable for the Western world in the reasonably near future, and within a very few years for Western Europe, the United States, Canada, and possibly Japan.

-----

* George D. Bryson, *Profits from Abroad: A Reveille for American Business* (New York: McGraw-Hill Book Co., 1964). Used by permission of McGraw-Hill Book Company.

233

13 *Multinational Organizations*

PART 1 *Introduction by Daniel Parker*

Daniel Parker, chairman of The Parker Pen Company, is one of the "new breed" of dynamic young American business leaders committed to international affairs. Currently the vice chairman of the National Association of Manufacturers, he will become chairman later this year; and it is in this capacity that he has prepared this analysis of transatlantic industry associations. He is a director of the Atlantic Council of the United States, trustee of the U.S. Council of the International Chamber of Commerce, trustee of the Committee for Economic Development, and his memberships include the International Committee of the Chamber of Commerce of the United States, the USA Business and Industry Advisory Committee to the OECD, and the National Export Expansion Council. Corporate directorships include Corn Products Company; **Asia Magazine;** Rex Chainbelt, Inc.; Merchants and Savings Bank of Janesville, Wisconsin; P. W. Minor & Son; and Omniflight Helicopters, Inc.

Photo by Karsh, Ottawa

Multinational organizations—both government and private—can and should be trailblazers in planning for the 1970's. In this introduction to Chapter 13, I shall single out industry organizations because of my personal familiarity with their great and virtually untapped opportunities for progress on a transatlantic basis.

In preceding chapters, the Atlantic Community has been viewed from many angles, and suggestions have been made about directions which it should take. All these statements and suggestions admit of one fact—the Atlantic Community does exist, unique in its endowment, and possessing an opportunity and a duty to develop its potential for world good.

The uniqueness of the Community is undenied. The nations bounding on the North Atlantic encompass the bulk of the free world's man-created assets. These nations are the primary source of

235

social progress, scientific break-throughs, and industrial production. And as such, they share not only a common culture, history, and progress, but also a common responsibility to the other countries of the world, who could and must benefit from the forward strides which these Atlantic nations make. Therefore, the term "Atlantic Community" has a two-fold meaning: first, in terms of what *has been done;* and second, in terms of what *must be done.*

The latter is the challenge which the members of the Community must meet. Its scope—to be ready for the future, as outlined by Dr. Aurelio Peccei in the introduction to Chapter I—is so vast that only concerted effort can hope to meet it. Internally, the members of the Community must search for a key to group participation, an organized coordinated effort to become a true community. Only then can the Community turn outward to meet its responsibilities to the balance of the world and the present challenge to freedom.

The search, then, has a dual purpose with an ultimate common objective: seeking to know and to overcome the divisive disparities, and at the same time seeking to identify the similarities in existing institutions.

Many of the disparities have been identified in preceding chap-

ters. They are popularized and dramatized in the press as "gaps" and as "nationalism." What must be realized, and, more importantly, admitted, is that nationalism has two faces. The dangerous aspect of nationalism is the inward-looking, self-defeating nationalism that thinks of "self" not first, but *only.* The beneficial, and less publicized, face of nationalism lies in the inherent strengths of national character, achievement, and pride which each member has to offer to the whole. When the former is finally eliminated, both the Community and those countries looking to it will have entered into a new era of progress and cooperation.

Industry's Role as "Common Ground"

While the Atlantic Community may truly become "a highway that unites" for the seventies, the road to and through the seventies will be largely influenced by one segment of the Community—industry. In its products and contributions to scientific knowledge, in its systems and its modes of thought and planning, industry has the means to close, or at least narrow, many of the various gaps—technology, empathy, communications, and understanding, among others.

The industrial sector is one of the most stable, continuous institutions in all the Atlantic Community nations. Each advanced nation of the free world, and especially those in the Atlantic Community, possesses an established, viable, industrial sector, with common goals and similar methods and philosophies. This industrial sector can serve importantly as a "common ground" on which to build true Community effort.

This is a world of people, and free governments exist only to serve them. No nation, developed or undeveloped, can achieve its potential economic growth except in response to the practical needs of private business. Governments can and must provide the environment, and some can help others, but real economic growth and rising standards of living depend upon private enterprise.

It is appropriate here to look more specifically at the uniqueness of the industrial sector, since it does have distinct characteristics which enable it to fulfill additional roles in the overriding mission of the Atlantic Community.

One of the most elemental similarities among all industrial efforts is the ultimate direction of their activity. The industrial entity produces in order to sell. This serves as an intuitive guide through the entire industrial process. Reflection upon this rather platitudinous statement reveals some pertinent characteristics for international development.

First, this means that industry must use all of its capabilities to serve its market, lest a better equipped competitor might satisfy its customers. Thus, in private enterprise environments, industry involves a self-initiated, self-stimulated, dynamic effort toward excellence and toward the attainment of progress for the benefit of all.

Second—again seemingly a truism but having particular international significance—industry must "go where the action is." It must be where its market is. And where it goes it brings and bestows a part of itself into its new environment in a lasting way. Because of their consumer-dependence and their need for local raw materials and labor to produce with their capital investment, manufacturing activities have a large stake in the stability and orderly progress of the political body in which they live. Manufacturing thus becomes ingrained into the economic processes of its political body differently than trade and commerce-type activities. This stability becomes particularly apparent in business among nations, where successful manufacturing entities put roots into the local soil, and, as has been suggested earlier, become "part of the landscape."

Putting Roots into the Local Soil. This point brings us to a par-

237

ticular uniqueness of industry, for in crossing national borders industry has recently been demonstrating a forward-looking adjustability in the trend to multinationalism. It is more than just an "inter" relationship, as in international commerce, for example. Industry not only *does*, but of necessity, *must* put its roots into the local soil. It goes a step beyond internationalism, to *multi*nationalism. It must orient itself to its immediate environment, its market, its reason for being in that specific place, and even its general *raison d'être*. In international economic terms it becomes in many ways tantamount to a basically local, national, industrial entity.

But fundamentally, in terms of the economic activity it stimulates, a multinational, industrial activity is an on-going contributor to the host country. This is in contrast to trade which, in a sense, is comprised of a series of individual transactions of mutual benefit between international buyers and sellers. While the host country may reap some rewards from such commerce, the gain happens once only to each transaction in the form of tariff or tax revenues and, of course, some citizen gratification. Contrast to this the benefits which accrue when a manufacturing entity locates in the same host country, with its continuing property tax revenues, employment

opportunities, local raw material demands, export potential, and probable buildup of the industrial infrastructure to support and supply its manufacturing efforts.

A further unifying and desirable characteristic of manufacturing activity is its dynamic momentum. Because continuity is essential to its operations, industry emphasizes orderly, planned progress internally. And it encourages similar predictability in its surrounding environment. However, while industry has a vested interest in orderly government, it is less susceptible to environmental change and to the effects of inward-looking nationalism than more transient business efforts. In this way industry encourages stability and provides a steadying influence within its environment.

To this point we can see both the unifying characteristics of industry and its uniqueness within each country. The strengths of a nation's industrial uniqueness should, of course, be preserved and enhanced to augment each nation's role in international commerce. But where areas for improvement appear, efforts must be made to improve, in order to have intranationally a balanced strong economy capable of existing effectively in the world. The pressures upon us—the needs of the world—are greater than can be served by permitting industry to progress in its own way, leaving mankind's benefit largely to chance or to by-products of that progress.

Extra Dimension in Common Goals. More can be done if we will find the extra dimension of industry. Even though industry is in a sense divided, competitively, in pursuit of its markets, it does find both a need for, and a compatibility in, attaining certain common goals. These generally concern the environment in which all industry operates.

Within each of our advanced private enterprise economies there exists a large and strong association of industries. It may be the Patronat in France, the BDI in Germany, or the NAM in the United States. While each of these is different in its mode and construction, each shares with all the others the same unifying characteristics of relating industry to its environment. This is a two-way street, too, in that the industrial association not only represents its own overall interests, but also serves to interpret environmental factors to its members. No longer preoccupied with one-sided self-servingness, these associations are leaders in, and harbingers of, an ever-changing environment. That each is different presents great international potential in that each thus can serve to represent the "good face" of nationalism in international affairs. For example, the associa-tions help newcomers in adjusting to their new environment. Conversely, they can assist their members in adjusting to new influences brought from outside.

Dealing with the Technology Gap. Let's look at one change which industry itself through its associations might be able to deal with by particularly unique private enterprise means—the so-called technology gap.

The first aspect of this problem which needs consideration is the question of quantity. Does the United States have too much technology? The answer to this must be no, because it is generally agreed that the world needs all the technological progress possible. Since the solution, therefore, is not to take technology from the United States, the answer must lie in increasing the technological competence of the other Community members. To do this, however, a closer examination of the real meaning of technology is necessary.

Thoughtful questioning, in fact, reveals that the technology gap is not a single gap, but rather a two-faceted problem. First, America possesses vast quantities of the raw material—new and raw technology. This new technology stems largely from the preeminence of the United States in space research and space-connected applications. The vast dimensions of the U.S.

space effort, competitively stimulated by the parallel efforts of the Soviet Union, produce immense spin-off potential in knowledge as well as products.

A high proportion of this technology is nonmilitary, nonsecret, and broadly available for licensing. The sheer size of the effort makes it doubtful that the world should invest in a possibly redundant third such effort. However, careful selection of other major technology programs could yield leadership and resulting economic advantages.

The other facet of the technology gap is the problem of converting the raw technology into commercial industrial products. The American industrialist, by his own intuition and through his association contacts, organizes to take advantage of this technological raw material. An ingrained industrial reaction takes place, from sales to research, from finance to factory, to seek out and create new products to gain, hold, or increase the share of market.

This is possible because of the unique sharing aspect of U.S. research efforts. Industry has learned how to participate in the great public sector technology programs as private contractors in research and development as well as in production. Industry has also learned that the benefits of this research lie not in the immediate profits from the research contract, but in the extension of knowledge gained toward commercial application. While the economic significance, per se, of a Saturn V–Apollo moon rocket is slight, the American industrialist—research- and consumer-oriented—can translate bits and pieces of the Saturn's pioneering technology into mass-produced new products and make the new technical advances a viable factor in the U.S. economy.

Industrial managements throughout the world can benefit both themselves and their markets by learning how to emulate this American industrial example of research and market orientation. The exercise of the entrepreneurial spirit by European management, seeking applications which are economically sound and commercially viable, will go a long way toward closing the closable part of the technology gap.

It is, of course, unlikely that individual industrial enterprises would be willing to share their own specific know-how with their foreign competitors. However, it is very likely that through their industrial associations much information about techniques and administrative attitudes could be developed for international sharing, just as these and other national associations now do in order to advance management science within their own countries.

A Council of Atlantic Industrial Associations

Importantly, the tools now exist for like-minded associations to begin examining the potential for such communication and cooperation. There is no need for them to await the bringing together of our Community nations by government action.

The uniqueness of multinational industry—that each nation's industrial sector manifests a strong, functional, modern association of industry—suggests that a more international viewpoint might well be taken by such industrial associations. Unlike other facets of business, the industrial associations are not internationally united as is the International Chamber of Commerce—nor as the very effective AmChams of the U.S. Chamber of Commerce.

Bilateral steps in the direction of internationalism can be taken—and this might be the ultimate extent. A bolder concept, though, may be envisioned as an expanded opportunity toward which we might direct our initial steps. The opportunity exists to form a Council of Atlantic Industrial Associations, based on all the common interests and goals already mentioned. In such a forum the "understanding gap" could be met head-on by men already possessing not only common interests and goals, but common experience and problems. Such a Council, essentially nonpolitical and multinational in outlook, could address problems from a common ground of industrial understanding, and serve as a base from which to approach gradually the more fundamental problems facing the Community.

Such a Council might initially be constituted as a council of leaders of the various national associations of industry which exist in every country of the Atlantic Community. In bringing these association leaders together, contacts would be made among the Community nations for discussion and mutual effort somewhat independent of the current political scene. Here in such a Council, for example, the first steps toward closing the technology gap could be taken by those most intimately concerned with technology.

If it is true that government is not an end in itself, but rather a tool to serve its people, then let us proceed to find new ways to enhance the truth and logic of this wonderful premise. Let the people take the first steps along the highway, and then seek government help with those things which they cannot do alone. Let us perceive that international harmonies, obviously needed more than ever before—quantitatively because of our increasing complexity and togetherness, and qualitatively be-

cause of the trauma of separate-
ness—are harmonies amongst peoples, and are formalized by the governments of peoples.

Thus, let us develop every possible means for the peoples themselves to find the harmonies of
their not so disparate ways. Let industry with its unique international capability for unity help lead
by the example of self-initiated ac-
cords. Let industry and its associations exercise the virtues of private
enlightened enterprise toward
closing the gaps in a natural
empathy.

---

13 PART 2 *Atlantic Council Report*

The Atlantic Council invited Daniel Parker to introduce this chapter
on multinational organizations in order to underline the magnitude
of the challenge facing private corporations and their business-and-
industry associations. But multinational opportunities and responsibilities are by no means confined to the private sector. Governmental
action is vitally important and often must come first.

Our purpose in this chapter is to indicate the nature of that action
to date and the respective roles of government and industry organizations. Such a review necessarily begins with a review of the chaotic
state of European affairs following World War II and the early action
of government leaders.

The Role of Government Organizations

During the two decades since World War II, we have witnessed
tremendous forward movement in both the concept and the achievements in the Atlantic Community, thanks in large measure to the great
visions of leaders such as Schuman and Marshall and many others.
These visions were given substance in great action—primarily in three
fields: in security, in monetary affairs, and in the field of trade.

1. *Security:* The first task of governmental action during the
European recovery phase was to build a firm foundation on which

citizen enterprise could be built. At the start of the period military security was lacking. The question of the day was not whether Russia would attack, but when. It took the organization of NATO to subdue that fear and provide the confidence in the future essential for investment and economic growth.

2. *Monetary Affairs:* The second task related to governmental action needed in monetary affairs. For some years after the war there was lack of confidence in the value of the money by which business and trade could be conducted. To correct this was a job for governments. Under exceptional leadership the Atlantic countries did this. By extraordinary efforts they set their own budget and monetary houses in order. In addition they used such mechanisms for joint cooperation as the Bank for International Settlements (BIS), the International Bank for Reconstruction and Development (World Bank), and the International Monetary Fund (IMF). The result was that by 1958 most of the Atlantic currencies were freely convertible one with the other, a truly brilliant achievement and a great encouragement to private enterprise.

The World Bank and the IMF are widely acclaimed to be the most successful of the functional agencies affiliated with the United Nations. They may well set the pattern for other international organizations of the future. Although they possess large and heterogeneous memberships, they have been blessed by the absence of Soviet or Satellite participation. While the national interests and situations of members vary widely, they all have a strong common interest in national and collective solvency and in monetary stability.

These two organizations have unique advantages. One advantage is realistic weighted voting on a finely graduated scale. Voting power is roughly proportionate to the amounts of capital subscribed, adjusted slightly to favor the smallest subscribers. Each country has 250 votes plus one additional vote for each million dollars of capital subscribed. The present range is from the United States, with 25.50 percent of the total voting power, down to one country with .11 percent. The relative voting power is not without interest:

United Kingdom—10.50 percent of the total;

France and Germany—4.30 percent each;

India—3.30 percent;

Japan—3.19 percent;
Canada and China—3.10 percent each;
Italy—2.76 percent;
The Netherlands—2.30 percent;
Australia—2.23 percent;
Belgium—1.90 percent;
Argentina and Brazil—1.59 percent each.

Here are brought together lenders and potential borrowers, the developed and the less developed nations, on a businesslike basis. Further, these organizations pay their own way, are financially independent of governments and annual appropriations. This provides not only a high degree of independence of thought and action, but also has enabled them to develop an especially competent career service.

The World Bank and IMF have developed integrated teams of experts of various nationalities to advise governments all over the free world. These teams represent technical assistance at its best. Through them and through integrated headquarters operations, the World Bank and IMF have come to have major influence over monetary and fiscal policies and exchange rates in most free countries. They have done so by persuasion and establishing confidence, with no legal powers or sanctions other than that of a credit rating and authority to give or withhold loans. But these have proved powerful and in fact have conferred considerable authority.

3. *The Field of Trade:* If the first task of governments was to provide a foundation of political-military security and the second was to strengthen the monetary base, then the third task was to stimulate expanded world trade. The war had left a heritage of trade barriers of many sorts, and governments went to work to beat them down—laboriously, painfully, but effectively. Again they used international organizations: the Office of European Economic Cooperation (OEEC), Organization for Economic Cooperation and Development (OECD), General Agreement on Tariffs and Trade (GATT), the European Economic Community (EEC), and the European Free Trade Association (EFTA). Again, it has been a brilliant achievement, well on its way but far from finished.

Long negotiations in GATT have whittled down tariffs to a significant extent but far more remains to be done. EEC and EFTA have succeeded in abolishing internal tariffs between their members, but only between their members. The EEC has done valiant pioneering in seeking to harmonize the economic policies of its members and to grow the roots of unity necessary to serve the common, rather than their divergent, interests. But it has very far to go, even among six nations.

The OECD has done valuable technical studies but, suffering from lack of governmental interest in contrast to the more glamorous EEC, it has not even begun to realize its potential for the economic integration of the Atlantic Community.

Special mention should be given to the OECD. If it did not now exist, it would have to be invented. In the economic sphere, it represents the 15 NATO countries plus Austria, Ireland, Japan, Spain, Sweden, and Switzerland. And through its Business and Industry Advisory Council (BIAC), it represents private corporate enterprise in those same countries. Finally, it illustrates the basic truth of this era that the public and private sectors will become more, rather than less, interdependent. Increasingly there will be "gray areas" where these sectors must cooperate in the common interest. As just one example, let us look at the so-called technological gap confronting both countries and companies to see the kinds of initiatives being assumed by the OECD.

OECD and the Question of Technology. During the exact same time frame when private companies began exploring the technological gap through the series of business conferences sponsored by the Atlantic Council and the Atlantic Institute, the OECD created a Science Policy Committee with a working group to try to answer such questions as:

1. What are the differences between member countries in their scientific and technological potentials?
2. What effects do these differences have on the attainment of economic and other objectives?
3. What action is appropriate to ensure that member countries' scientific and technological potentials will be increased and effectively utilized in the future?

To this end, the working group is now committed to:

a) Analyzing the most recent research-and-development statistics on expenditures and manpower, and their economic effects within the OECD countries.

b) Appraising the migration of scientists and engineers—that is, the so-called brain drain.

c) Studying research, technological innovation, and economic performance in specific industries.

d) Assessing technical trends during the next decade and their implications for industrial development.

e) Examining how to strengthen international cooperation in science and technology.

Both OECD and U.S. government officials are inviting industrial counsel and involvement in this fresh appraisal of technology. For it is self-evident that governmental statistical research would be largely academic and even meaningless unless geared to the hard-core planning and capabilities of private corporations. And it is equally obvious that private companies could not begin to realize their technological growth potential without the array of facts and perceptive insights which governmental and multigovernmental research can provide.

All of these things Atlantic governments have done to remove the underbrush, to lay down a paved road on which individual citizens and private business can travel, seeking a higher standard of life for all. But there is still another encouragement to private enterprise in relation with government which deserves acclaim; namely, a growing recognition in country after country that private enterprise is the motive power of business progress.

The Role of Business–Industry Organizations

The Atlantic Council program on transatlantic business development began with an assessment of U.S. business associations working in the international field: who was doing what, how effectively, and what more needed to be done. The most recent activity has been a similar appraisal of industry associations in Europe, conducted by Daniel Parker and this writer. Our objective in Europe was to explore ways to establish industry association alliances across the Atlantic.

There is obviously a major gap in working relationships between industry representatives from America and those in Europe. From the

British Isles to the Iron Curtain, European industry associations are drawing together, harmonizing industrial-corporate policies and developing joint opportunities for their memberships, while American industry associations stand somewhat alone on the other side of the Atlantic.

Americans have long prided themselves on the rapport that exists between America and Great Britain. Hence it came as somewhat of a surprise to see that, today, British industry associations—*outside* the Common Market—are becoming linked far more closely to their counterparts *inside* the Common Market than to similar associations in America.

Indeed, the growing isolation of American business-industry associations vis-à-vis those in Europe is not confined just to those associations in the United Kingdom and the Common Market. America has, as phrased by Jay H. Cerf, International Manager of the Chamber of Commerce of the United States, an "ostrich policy" for all of Europe. Mr. Cerf observed to us that American business "bridge-building" with its counterpart organizations abroad is remaining comparatively static even while European organizations are looking out in all directions. As one example, Mr. Cerf referred to such phenomena as occurred this past winter when, for instance, Soviet Premier Alexei Kosygin was the featured guest speaker of the Confederation of British Industries, where the purpose of that program was to explore new commercial linkages between Britain and the U.S.S.R.

As further indication of a "relations gap" between American and European industry, while on the continent we were told by one industry association chief executive that even though he had visited American organizations for 18 years, this was the first time that American industry association representatives had come across the Atlantic specifically to pay him a similar visit on his home ground.

The encouraging point is, of course, that this is an error of omission, not a deliberate act on anyone's part. Everywhere the welcome was warm, honest, and pragmatic. Without a single exception, each meeting ended with the commitment on both sides that we should think and plan on how we could enhance our ability to gain mutual benefits through collaboration. Enthusiasm for closer corporate ties through counterpart organizations was voiced not just at the industrial level but by political leaders as well. There may be stalemates on the European political front, but the business-economic front is fluid and moving forward.

Case Example: UNICE

As one example, take UNICE (Union des Industries de la Communaute Europeenne). It proves the principle of multinational industrial cooperation, and suggests one pattern for progress. UNICE is a permanent, working secretariat of the six industry associations representing the Common Market countries. It is a multinational group created and designed to harmonize industrial policies across the EEC for the benefit of all countries and companies. Further, UNICE has extended its area of effectiveness through inviting industry associations outside the Common Market to attend specific meetings. It seems logical that this broader form of collaboration should increase rather than decrease. Indeed, UNICE's successful experiment could well set the example for participation across the Atlantic Community including the United States and Canada.

American Business Associations

In these few pages we can do little more than offer a swift and perhaps superficial review of some of the business-oriented organizations concerned with multinational business development. A well-documented bibliography is needed to do justice to these many fine groups. Recognizing, then, these shortcomings, here are several association profiles.

National Association of Manufacturers: The National Association of Manufacturers is a voluntary organization of industrial and business firms, large and small, located in every state; it vigorously supports principles that encourage individual freedom and through which the association develops and engages in programs for the advancement of the economic well-being and social progress of its member companies. It also supports the National Industrial Council, which includes some 350 trade associations representing the many types of individual industries in the United States.

Chamber of Commerce of the United States: With a basic membership of over four million, the "National Chamber" is the largest voluntary business association in the world. It includes in its programs the spectrum of free-world and less-developed-country trade, aid, and investment programs and policies affecting its vast membership network. In addition to its more than 3,700 organization members, local, state and regional Chambers of Commerce and trade and professional associations within the United States, it includes 43 American Chambers of Commerce (AmChams) abroad in 25 countries. The purpose of the AmChams is to create international good will, to foster and uphold the highest standards of commercial practices, and to promote the mutual interests of businessmen from both the United States and within the host country. Without the full partnership of the National Chamber and the subsequent cooperation of its European AmChams, the Atlantic Council survey and follow-on program would have been difficult if not impossible.

U.S. Council of the International Chamber of Commerce: This group consists of U.S. companies with international interests and represents these interests within the worldwide framework of the International Chamber of Commerce. The ICC, in turn, is headquartered in Paris and has national committees in 41 countries and members in 35 more countries, giving it representation in 76 countries in all. It is today a valued advisor to individual governments and intergovernmental bodies on all matters affecting the movement of goods, capital, and people across international boundaries. It is well placed to coordinate the efforts of private industry throughout the world.

National Foreign Trade Council: Since 1914 the NFTC has brought together executives of U.S. business organizations to examine important issues in foreign economic policy. The NFTC is exclusively concerned with the promotion and protection of U.S. foreign trade and investments. The Council issues policy declarations on current economic problems, and has published semiannual studies on the outlook for U.S. exports and the U.S. balance of payments as an aid to management and export planning. In addition, it sponsors the National Foreign Trade Convention (widely known as "the annual meeting" of the U.S. international business community), and has worked to negotiate mutually beneficial commercial treaties with other nations.

The list of American organizations is long, and should include the Business Council for International Understanding, the Business Council (formerly the Business Advisory Council), the Committee for Economic Development, and the Council for Latin America, to name a few. The four organizations singled out for special comment above were selected because they represent the four groups comprising the USA Business and Industry Advisory Committee to the OECD.

European Business Associations

Here again the list is long, and we can cover only highlights. The following examples are merely representative:

Federation des Industries Belge. (The Federation of Belgian Industries, [F.I.B.]): The representative organ of Belgian industry at the national level, it covers a large number of professional associations representing all sectors of industrial activity in Belgium. The purpose of the F.I.B. is to publicize and defend the views of industrial circles on all major economic and social problems and to represent industry at the national level. Some 35,000 industrial enterprises, associated in F.I.B.'s member federations, are represented by the F.I.B.

Conseil National du Patronat Francais (C.N.P.F.): Generally known as the Patronat, this powerful organization groups most of the French trade associations representing a wide majority of individual businesses in the fields of manufacturing and commerce, as well as banking and other services. It represents the interests of its members vis-à-vis labor and the government. The Patronat favors a free market economy and endeavors to exercise a liberalizing influence on French economic policies and relevant legislation.

Bundesverband der Deutschen Industrie: This association of the top-level organizations of 39 branches of German industry embraces over 90,000 enterprises. The emphasis of its operations lies on committees covering all important fields of economic policy. As the representative body of German industry, BDI makes its voice heard on all matters of government policy affecting its members' interests.

Confederazione Generale della Industria Italiana ("Confindustria"— the General Confederation of Italian Industry): Confindustria is roughly the equivalent of the NAM. It is the organization of regional industry associations and national trade associations. In 1965 the Confindustria included 78,060 establishments employing 2.4 million. It represents industry in dealing with government authorities and labor unions and actively studies industrial development and the national economy. It supports bodies of professional instruction and of assistance with the aim of improving production.

Confederation of British Industry: The CBI is the central body which represents British industry nationally. Membership consists of approximately 13,000 individual firms and 280 trade associations, plus more than 50 employers' organizations. The CBI is recognized by the government as a channel for consultation between government departments and representatives of private employers as a whole. It acts as a representative to the government for its members on a nationwide basis. CBI representatives sit on a number of government advisory committees, and other statutory and voluntary bodies concerned with industrial matters.

The above examples obviously cover neither all of Europe nor the other groups within the countries identified. For example, the extremely effective Chambers of Commerce are not listed. But the above descriptions are useful because they bring to light the impressive array of responsibilities which in many cases exceed those of U.S. associations. Note, for example, that the role of the F.I.B. in Belgium is to represent industry as a whole to the Belgian government; that the Patronat is involved in French economic planning; that the BDI in Germany can speak with one voice for German industry; that the Confindustria is responsible for actual labor negotiations in behalf of Italian companies; and that the CBI is recognized by the British government as a channel to private employers as a whole. No such parallel exists for any organization within the United States.

Learning the Other Fellow's Viewpoint

Closer ties among business and industry associations provide one of the quickest and most effective means for erasing narrow nationalistic impressions and prejudices. These associations provide listening posts for learning the other fellow's viewpoint.

For example, association representatives in Paris told us that two phrases which irritate Americans—"state planning" and "socialism" —have quite different meanings in France. And the situation in practice is far less inimical to private enterprise than the words suggest to Americans. In the first place, many Frenchmen, in fact, object as strenuously as do Americans to what would be considered too much government control. In the second place, it is pointed out, in France the French system of government-industry cooperation *is* effective. And so they ask, "Why should one fight a system when it works?" A two-way dialogue often wipes out what seem to be differences and roadblocks to cooperation.

Similarly, in Germany, the intent American listener would learn that he is welcome, despite headlines to the contrary. But he would also be cautioned that the political climate is now very sensitive, as evidenced by signs of a reemergence of nationalistic sentiment. He would be told that a corporate miscalculation which might go unnoticed during calmer periods could ignite a small political explosion today.

In Italy, the American observer of Italian association practices would gain indispensable insights into the tough, touchy labor situation. He could learn to separate facts from fables about Communist influences in labor ranks so that he could plan his own labor policies more intelligently.

In Belgium, would-be U.S. entrepreneurs would find the industry association well out in front in *anticipating* problems before they actually happen. He would find his presence particularly welcomed if he could make some contribution to the business community in management education and development.

In the United Kingdom, this same American would discover a "new look" in industry relations, thanks to the merger of several national groups into a single, aggressive entity. He would find that the government is turning to this new organization on questions regarding pricing policy and other items of immediate concern to all businessmen, American and British included.

The very diversity of these several groups is the source of their strength. They provide channels for developing a wide variety of private-sector alliances with a minimum of friction and a maximum of returns. Daniel Parker's proposal for a Council of Atlantic Industrial Associations, in his introduction to this chapter, suggests a positive approach in this direction.

From the U.S. side, such a Council should build on present programs and relationships already in being, such as those established through the American Chambers of Commerce in Europe. It should seek to avoid dilution of efforts; hence the proposal for establishing a more or less single Council that speaks for all American business interests abroad. Properly staffed and supported, the Council's role could be twofold, with vast benefits for the entire community: it could become a meaningful voice for American business in Europe; and it could provide a window for European companies seeking business-expansion possibilities in America.

Summary

Looking ahead, we can see several hopeful lines for the meshing of public and private effort across national lines in this ever more complex and interdependent world.

One is the meshing of industrial associations just discussed.

Another is the invigoration of intergovernmental organizations such as the OECD, and coordination of private effort with theirs, by Business and Industry Advisory Committees. A BIAC to the World Bank, for example, might do much to coordinate public and private investment in developing areas.

A third lies in the adoption or adaptation of those elements of corporate organization and procedure so successful in the cases of the World Bank and the IMF, for intergovernmental activities in other fields.

A fourth approach to public-private cooperative efforts is to set up new organizations geared to specific tasks. An early space age example is the Communications Satellite Corporation (COMSAT), an unprecedented mixture of government, private industry, and individual stockholders. COMSAT serves as manager and 61 percent owner of the global consortium established by the 1964 "Agreement Establishing Interim Arrangements for Global Commercial Communications Satellite System." Here is how the consortium works:

55 countries were represented as of March 1, 1967.

Membership in the consortium is by the governments themselves, except for the United States, where COMSAT is the representative.

Share of ownership is based on the contribution of each country to the cost of the space segment of the system.

Arrangements for the construction, ownership, financing, and operation of the "earth" stations are left to each country and may be public or private, national or multinational.

Regardless of the specific approach, the field is wide open for creative solutions which bring together multinational organizations and institutions to meet common challenges.

14

Planning for the 1970's

PART 1 Introduction
by Samuel C. Waugh

For eight years, from 1953 to 1961, Mr. Samuel C. Waugh was active in the global work of the U.S. government's Export-Import Bank of Washington, for three years as a director representing the Department of State and five years as its president and board chairman. Other appointments included Deputy Under Secretary of State, Assistant Secretary of State for Economic Affairs, Deputy Governor of the International Bank and International Monetary Fund, and U.S. representative at many foreign economic and financial conferences. Still active in international banking after a career that spans more than 50 years, he currently is a consultant to The Bank of New York and to the Blaw-Knox Company of Pittsburgh. With the Atlantic Council of the United States, he is chairman of the Committee on Trade, Monetary, and Corporate Policy, and served as a chairman of the Crotonville Conference referred to in this book.

Photo by J. S. Wright

"We do not say a man who takes no interest in politics minds his own business. We say he has no business to mind."

This statement of Pericles, the Athenian politician, was made 2,400 years ago and was quoted by Edmund F. Martin, chairman of Bethlehem Steel Corporation, in addressing the American Iron and Steel Institute on May 25, 1966.

The subject of the increased role of private business and its relationship with governments has been the basis of studies made by the Atlantic Council during the past two years.

"Would the Atlantic Council of the United States be interested in looking to the issues being raised by the rapid growth of U.S. investment in Europe? They are considerable, yet I believe they can be resolved to the great advantage of the corporate, the national, and the

255

public interest of all concerned."

Those words, expressed by Gene Bradley during a visit to the Council's offices in November 1964, sparked the program which prompted this book. They fell on the receptive ears of a man who, when serving as ambassador in a Latin-American country a few years ago, received a letter from the Secretary of State asking his views on how the image of the "American presence" in that country might be improved.

The American presence in that country, as in many others, was predominantly a business one. The Ambassador invited the local managers of the principal U.S. companies for a luncheon discussion, which became a weekly affair and still continues as such.

Initially the general attitude was: "We pay higher salaries, have better medical facilities, more enlightened policies than anyone else; it is just a public relations problem to get the story across." One businessman, whose company was threatened with nationalization, was the lone dissenter: "Like hell it is. There are lots of things we ought to be doing better. Let's look at them seriously and see what we can do better." Within a few weeks the group had agreed upon many things they felt could and should be done better in the interest both of their companies and of the American presence.

Then came trouble with the head offices: "Forget this altruistic stuff; remember the stockholders." It took a little time to convince the top management that some practical altruism was definitely in the stockholders' interest, but it has proved to be so. A great deal has happened since, there and elsewhere, that has brought greater profits and warmer official and public acceptance to the companies directly concerned, and has benefited American business in general and the national interest of the United States, as well as that of the country concerned.

The Atlantic Council picked up with enthusiasm Gene Bradley's suggestion of starting programs on the problems and opportunities of U.S. investment and business operations in Europe. It borrowed him from General Electric for a month to undertake a survey of who was already doing what, how well, and what else needed to be done. He has been spark-plugging the program ever since.

Need for Clearing House

The initial survey, conducted first in this country and then, with the cooperation of the Chamber of Commerce of the United States in Europe, revealed that many organizations were working in the vineyard, and working well. But each was working in its own way, usually with little knowledge of what others were doing. Thus there seemed to be clear opportunity for the Council to act as a clearinghouse for the experience of companies and industrial organizations, and to try to stimulate the development of both governmental and corporate policy along constructive and mutually beneficial lines. Throughout, the Council has been determined not to duplicate anything anyone else was doing but to stimulate what others could do.

In the Spring of 1965 General Norstad asked me to chair a committee on Trade, Monetary, and Corporate Policy, of directors and sponsors of the Council specially qualified in business and finance. The Committee of 17 comprised a cross-section of professional men, many of whom had served in various executive branches of the United States government.

The Committee's first report, on "Monetary Modernization," was prepared after extensive conversations with representatives of the executive branch of our government—notably, the Office of the President (Special Representative for Trade Negotiations); the Departments of Treasury, Commerce, and State; as well as the Federal Reserve Board. After full discussion the report was approved by the Council, transmitted to government agencies, and disseminated to key bankers and businessmen. A brief press notice brought orders for 4,500 copies.

Emphasis on Private Sector Role

The substance of that report is a story in itself, but the cooperation in its development between the representatives of the executive branches of our government and those of private business was most welcome. In fact, it was this development which in part inspired the private business sponsors of the Atlantic Council of the United States and of the Atlantic Institute in Paris to emphasize—in their basic program of developing Atlantic unity—the all-important role to be played by the private sector.

Others are writing on the preliminary meetings at Fontainebleau and Paris, in the fall of 1965 under the sponsorship of the Atlantic Institute. However, special mention should be made of the conference at Crotonville, New York, December 12–15, 1965, called to discuss the subject "The Atlantic Community and Economic Growth." The magnitude of the challenge, presented at the outset of the meeting, was made apparent in the estimate that in the coming decade the new capital requirements of the Atlantic Community

257

would total a trillion dollars for the private sector.

The conferees at the Crotonville Conference, an outstanding group of business executives and government officials, agreed that closer transatlantic relationships in business and finance had contributed toward a greater degree of unity beneficial to the national, corporate, and public interest in both North America and Europe. There was a complete meeting of minds that the business executives of the private sector and the government officials of all countries could best accomplish the desired results by working together. The discussions sought to develop ideas leading to closer and stronger relationships among businessmen and governments on both sides of the Atlantic.

The conferees voted unanimously to request the Council and the Institute to convene a similar meeting in Europe with roughly equal participation by Europeans and Americans. It was held in Geneva at the beginning of June 1966.

Ambassador Dowling will tell that story, but when General Norstad sent President Johnson the Action Program approved there, the President replied:

It comes to us at a good time. As I have made clear both within and outside the government, I intend that the reorganization of NATO required because of General de Gaulle's deci-

sions, be accompanied by the maximum number of creative initiatives we can launch with our allies within the Atlantic, as well as East–West relations.

We are also looking ahead in many fields to the 1970's to see what we ought to begin to think about and do now which would help solve those problems we can foresee in the decade ahead.

For these reasons I can assure you the paper you forwarded will be carefully staffed out in the government.

I wish to commend you and your colleagues in the Atlantic Council for the important constructive effort you are carrying forward.

Within weeks of this letter an informal Cabinet committee was formed to work with the Atlantic Council and to explore how the government could back up but not dominate its private sector program. The Chairman, Secretary Fowler of the Treasury, described the results of the series of business conferences conducted by the Council and the Institute as "one of the few bright spots on the horizon at a time when the Atlantic is wider than it used to be."

The work of planning for economic growth in the 1970's, by governments and by companies, has barely begun. Yet, as the various contributors to this book indicate, a great deal of thought is being given to it by topflight minds on both sides of the Atlantic. The Atlantic Council intends to do everything in its power to stimulate and encourage these and other minds in their thinking *together* on how the enormous mental, technological, and material resources of the Atlantic Community can best be integrated to develop our unlimited common potential.

---

14 PART 2 *Introduction by Ambassador Walter Dowling*

Ambassador Walter Dowling has been director general of the Atlantic Institute in Paris since shortly after his retirement from the U.S. Foreign Service in 1963. His last post was Ambassador to the Federal Republic of Germany. He had previously served as the Assistant Secretary of State for European Affairs, as Ambassador to Korea, and Deputy High Commissioner in both Austria and Germany during the postwar occupation period.

Photo by Blackstone-Shelburne, N.Y.

To insist on Atlantic cooperation today may seem a paradox, for the governments of the Atlantic Community are in disagreement on many things.

Yet in at least one area there is a remarkable measure of coherence and a mutual desire to move on toward greater coordination of efforts and resources, as well as a closer harmony of policies. The Atlantic business community has recently demonstrated again an appreciation of the need for cooperation in the economic and financial fields.

This awareness of interdependence is evidenced by the Atlantic Institute's conference on Atlantic Cooperation and Economic Growth—Planning for the 1970's, held at Geneva on May 29–June 1, 1966. The conference was, as outlined elsewhere in this book, the outgrowth of the series of meetings initiated in October 1965 by the Atlantic Institute for the discussion of economic and related problems common to the member states of the Atlantic Community.

A major purpose of the previous conferences had been to make explicit both points of common interest and points of conflict in contemporary Atlantic economic relations. With this background, the aim of the Geneva Conference was to identify and examine the

259

salient issues which unite or divide the Atlantic peoples on the economic plane.

The views of the European and American participants disclosed—not surprisingly—a number of unresolved divergences. But at the same time they evidenced an extraordinary degree of understanding and agreement on significant issues.

In fact, a number of specific agreements resulted, and the several areas of accord became the recommendations of the conference for implementation by public authorities and the private sector in the countries concerned. To the end that the recommendations and the goals of the conference might be put into effect, the conference urged that a continuing action program be launched under the auspices of the Atlantic Institute.

Of the problems which presently confront the Atlantic countries in the economic field, some may be expected to be of an immediate or temporary character (e.g., balance of payments difficulties and the effects of programs to cope with them). Others, on the contrary, are decisive for the future.

Guidelines for Atlantic Economic Relations

The Geneva Conference attempted to focus attention on those future problems, the solu-

tion of which will continue to have long-term consequences for Atlantic relations. At the same time, the conference took into account specific key guidelines and boundaries within which Atlantic economic relationships will have to develop.

One guideline is the *idée forcée* which has guided European development in the 1960's and which will continue to work late into the 1970's. Embodied in a broad sense in the Treaty of Rome, it includes trade liberalization and expansion, not only among the original signatory nations but eventually in other areas as well.

The Treaty of Rome also laid the groundwork for economic and political integration. On the latter score, the Europeans at the Geneva Conference felt they must "be somewhat patient." Both inside the EEC, and among those nations which the Community hopes to encompass, there are governments presently wary of political integration. But with respect to economic integration, it was agreed that concerted efforts should be exerted immediately, covering as wide a field as possible.

Beyond the declarations of any treaty, however, there exist important economic realities which will have a preponderant influence in the next decade. The role of science and technology in expanding economic growth is one of the most important. There are now more scientists alive than those that humanity has produced in the whole of its past history, and it follows that discoveries and inventions will be even more significant in the future than they have been since the end of World War II.

Thus, one of the important tasks for the 1970's will be the integration and cooperative use of science and technology for the benefit of all. The Conference therefore urged that the Atlantic Institute initiate a study of this problem and endeavor to develop recommendations for its solution. This the Institute intends to do.

Population growth now poses new challenges as well as new opportunities. From now to the end of the next decade, world population is expected to increase by about one billion people, which was the *total* world population in the middle of the last century. At the same time, the combined GNP of the Western nations by the end of the next decade will probably be above $2,000 billion.

New Action and Thinking Needed

In short, conventional action and thinking will be no match for the problems the next decade will bring. New instruments, new institutions, new philosophies, bolder in concept than those which have so far characterized the postwar period, must be developed. Continuous joint surveillance, thought, and action by the analytical researchers of the Western world will have to be enlisted to meet these unprecedented demands.

The bulk of the new population (and hence of these problems) will be outside the Atlantic world while the bulk of the new wealth will rest within. Hence it will be necessary to understand and know how to deal with the social organization of communities different from those of the Atlantic countries. It will also be necessary to recognize the geometrically growing needs of the world for food, investment capital, and other instruments of orderly development. And it will be necessary to minimize latent conflicts among the various parts of the world. In short, the perspective of the 1970's is one of awesome challenge.

Geneva Conference Perspective

To explore ways of meeting this challenge, the Geneva Conference provided a platform for a confrontation between European and American businessmen. Each group had met earlier in Paris, Fontainebleau, or Crotonville meetings, and so the conclusions of the Geneva meeting were cumulative. The conference perspective was a longer one: it focused on those actions needed now to provide a proper base to cope with the great challenge foreseen for the 1970's.

Current concerns which are self-equilibrating in nature were not the prime concern of the conferees. In the opening remarks, the co-chairmen of the meeting, General Lauris Norstad and M. Paul-Henri Spaak, had emphasized the continuing concrete contributions which economic growth, and with it expanded trade and investment, can make to the sense of community among the Atlantic nations, and to the developing nations as well.

In the main, the Geneva Conference corroborated the need and desire for expanded economic relations across the two continents. The conferees developed goals for future joint action in two major areas of economic life: (1) trade (within the Atlantic Community, with the developing nations, and with the East); and (2) investments, mainly between Europe and North America but with the developing nations as well. To summarize the major recommendations within these subheads:

1. *Trade:* A sine qua non for the continued expansion of world trade was deemed to be reasonable, in the Kennedy Round.

Beyond this lie new needs which successful conclusion of the Kennedy Round, per se, cannot solve but which will be exacerbated with-

out this step. These include the problems of nontariff barriers, agriculture, price stability of primary commodities, and, particularly, the reduction of barriers between the regional free trade areas.

The expansion of trade and investment in the developing nations on an equitable basis deserves the active support of Atlantic corporations and governments. In addition, East–West trade should be expanded, but to do so requires further liberalization of Eastern techniques and practices and concerted action to establish appropriate criteria on the West's part.

2. *Investment:* The continued flow of investment from the United States to Europe is necessary and desirable. The major problem in U.S.-European relations was said to be a growing "technological lag" resulting from the faster utilization of scientific discovery in American industry. To define and analyze this lag and its economic consequences, a special study group under the aegis of the Atlantic Institute was recommended.

European direct investment in the United States should be encouraged and steps taken on both sides of the Atlantic to reduce the barriers to it.

Since the Geneva Conference, Congress passed the Foreign Investors Tax Act of 1966 which provides additional tax incentives for foreign investment in the United States. The Department of Commerce has also established in Paris a European office to seek such investments, headed by Johnson Garrett, formerly vice president of the First National City Bank of New York.

The basic problems with respect to investment in developing areas were recognized to be: (1) the need for the governments of those areas to provide a climate which would attract private investment; and (2) the need to coordinate, multinationally, public and private investment with a view to developing self-sufficiency.

Not Too Early to Mobilize

The Conference concluded its proceedings with the widely held conviction that, important as is the solution of the economic problems with which the Atlantic Community is currently grappling, there loom on the horizon problems of a magnitude which challenge and promise to strain to the limit the combined talents, imagination, and capability for cooperative action of all our countries. It is not too early to mobilize our common resources to meet this challenge.

The conferees urged that a continuing action program be launched under the auspices of the Atlantic Institute. The Conference statement was as follows:

An Action Program for Economic Growth

In order to achieve the enormous potential for economic growth made possible by the vast resources and technological progress now available to the West, concerted action, both in the public and the private sector, is essential. This cooperation and the goals toward which it is directed are of vital concern to all countries, including the less developed countries.

However, the countries of the Atlantic area, which share a common historical, cultural and economic heritage can—and because of their wealth and influence should—take the lead in elaborating a purposeful program for the attainment of common objectives. The Conference requests the Atlantic Institute to stimulate action through continuous contact with governments and the business community.

The Institute is now carrying out this recommendation.

The Action Committee

The Action Committee will not duplicate the work now being done by others already operational in this field—government, industry, trade, or associations—but rather should serve as catalyst to these existing groups, providing an overview and perspective not now attainable from any single source.

It will not report to (or be responsible to) any other one group, public or private, national or mul-

263

tinational, or attempt to replace, rival, or expand any existing group. It will be composed of respected private businessmen and financiers who, in the end, hold active responsibility for achieving economic growth through business expansion.

Its members include Douglas Dillon, former Secretary of the Treasury; Neil McElroy, chairman, Procter & Gamble; W. S. Lambert, president of the Private Planning Association of Canada and the president of Alcan International; Aurelio Peccei of Olivetti; Dr. G. van der Wal, president of K.L.M.; Wilfried Guth, director of the Credit Anstalt fur Wiederaufbau; Lord Sherfield of the banking firm of Hill, Samuels (who, as Sir Roger Makins, was British Ambassador in Washington, Under Secretary of State for Economic Affairs, Permanent Under Secretary of the Treasury, and Chairman of the British Atomic Energy Commission); and others of similar caliber.

14 PART 3 *Atlantic Council Report*

In 1947 when Europe was prostrate from the war and the West had hurriedly disarmed, Ernest Bevin, the tough, fiery little ex-dock worker who was then His Britannic Majesty's Principal Secretary for Foreign Affairs, expressed privately to Secretary of State Marshall his conviction that "the survival of the West depends upon the formation of some form of union, formal or informal in Europe, backed by the United States and the Dominions, such a mobilization of moral and material force as will inspire confidence and energy within and respect elsewhere."

During the next few years, representations by various American ambassadors on the importance of Britain's integrating with Europe were invariably met by Bevin's blunt question: "When are *you* going to integrate?"

Bevin was once asked in the House of Commons what his foreign policy was. He replied simply: "I want to be able to go to Victoria

Station, without passport or visa, go anywhere I want to go, do what I have to do and come back."

Secretary of State Acheson once defined the goal of U.S. foreign policy as "the kind of world in which freedom can endure and prosper." Since the days of Ernest Bevin much progress has been made toward the objective he and Dean Acheson visualized, but the distance to go before reaching our goals was forcefully stated by the Atlantic Convention of representatives named by the parliaments of the NATO nations which met in Paris in 1962 under the chairmanship of the late Christian A. Herter, former secretary of state. The "Declaration of Paris" adopted by the Convention began by expressing the conviction that "our survival as free men, and the possibility of progress for all men, demand the creation of a true Atlantic Community within the next decade."

The Declaration contained a number of specific recommendations of which the key one was that: "The NATO governments promptly establish a Special Governmental Commission to draw up plans within two years for the creation of a true Atlantic Community, suitably organized to meet the political, military, and economic challenges of this era."

In his speech to the Convention, Secretary Herter had declared:

Our vision should not be bounded alone by anticommunism. Our nations should not rest on mere alarm as to security developments. We are going with the grain of history. The destiny of the Atlantic nations lies in a greater unity. We should fulfill this destiny regardless of whether Soviet hostility waxes or wanes.

What concrete results do I as an individual hope for this convention?

1. A deep commitment by each member to the goal of a close-knit Atlantic Community during his or her lifetime.
2. An agreement on principles to guide our steps to this goal. Among others, I would like to see considered:
   a) Strengthened ties on all levels—political, military, economic, and cultural. Too great reliance on one or even several channels of cooperation should be avoided.
   b) The Community should be conceived as "open ended" so that any qualified nation could associate with it.
   c) Measures to achieve Atlantic unity should be taken in a manner designed to avoid prejudice to developing unity between any smaller group of states in the Community.

d) While the ultimate political framework of the North Atlantic Community cannot now be foreseen, our respective nations should not rule out of consideration any approach, no matter how ambitious.

The Special Governmental Commission has not yet been appointed. Official inertia has been strong. Governments have consistently felt that the time was not "auspicious." They were right, but the time has gotten steadily less auspicious.

But while official inertia and perverse policies have held back government progress toward these goals, in another area vast progress has been made. Private business has been developing the Atlantic Business Community by leaps and bounds.

Two Diverse Forces at Work

Aurelio Peccei has described the state of the world toward the end of the 1960's as the "explosive phase of human society." Never before in human history, he notes, have the possibilities for progress been so bright, so breathtaking, so fast-moving. He stresses the need for an all-out effort of research and planning so that "the march toward the future will take an intelligently charted course, rather than be guided by chance and gamble."

Two powerful forces—which are at work at one and the same time today—will play a central role in the type of planning effort envisioned by Mr. Peccei. One set of forces is pushing countries and continents apart in new forms of nationalism; other forces are pulling them together in closer bonds of regional and intracontinental unity.

In the United States, these conflicting forces are competing for national attention as Americans weigh their domestic responsibilities against their international commitments for the security and progress of all men.

Within the EEC, member nations are pressing forward with an integrated Common Market at the same time that opportunities for political integration are fading.

African nations are striving for continental cohesion even while nationalistic explosions are rending relationships between countries and even within nations.

In Asia the fires of nationalism are burning brightly in country after country during the same period that their leaders are seeking common approaches to "nation-building" and to preserving their regions from aggressive world communism.

South American political leaders are supporting hemispheric solutions through the Alliance for Progress and regional trading communities as they make clear, simultaneously, the need for each country to be treated and respected as a national entity.

Hence the phenomenon of the second half of the 20th century is that the two basic trends of mankind are nationalism and internationalism—the former towards fragmentation, the latter, towards unity.

Nationalism, most obvious in those parts of the world formerly under colonial rule and now in a hurry to catch up with the 20th century, springs from the basic human desires for freedom, dignity, and equality of opportunity.

Internationalism, most evident in the highly developed nations, arises from the need to find ways of fulfilling those same desires in the crowded, jet-propelled, nuclear-powered, transistorized, and computerized world of today and tomorrow.

Are nationalism and internationalism incompatible? Surely not, since both spring from the same basic desires of human nature. Yet these desires must be recognized as strong, and a peaceful and prosperous future depends on finding ways to fulfill them. President Eisenhower expressed this thought in his farewell message to NATO:

Together we must build a community which will best safeguard the individual liberty and national values of our respective peoples and at the same time enable us to deal effectively with those problems with which no nation, alone, can deal adequately today.

These basic human desires for freedom, dignity, and equality of opportunity are manifest not only in the developing areas but in the industrialized world as well. "Equality of opportunity" motivates the proponents of protectionism and its opponents alike. (Or do both want something more than equality?)

Such desires are inherent in European attitudes toward both the U.S. government and American business, regardless of the degree of validity of the attitudes in any one specific case. Witness de Gaulle's desire to be free of "American domination under the guise of integration." Witness the talk of an "equal pillar" in Europe able to speak to the United States with an "equal voice"; European allegations of American economic domination of industry; the pressure for European corporations to merge, the better to compete with the American "giants" (and, for business reasons, the preference of European firms to merge with American rather than other European firms); the "brain drain"; and many other evidences of desire for freedom, dignity, and equality of opportunity.

Power, science, technology, and capital formulation are cumulative in today's world. America's lead in all of them is more apt to increase than to decrease. U.S. relations with other countries will pose major problems for many, many years.

The paramount position of the United States in the Atlantic Community imposes the obligations of leadership and humility, of vision and practical wisdom in government and business alike. Future growth requires the exercise of our political, financial, and industrial power in ways which give others a share and a genuine sense of participation in common progress.

What Kind of World?

What kind of world economic, financial, and trading community could best serve the needs of the world's people a decade from now? And what are we prepared to do now to take concrete steps toward the economic horizons of the 1970's and 1980's?

Agreement on broad goals is relatively easy; difficulty arises in agreeing on the specific policies and actions necessary to attain them.

The goals of Bevin, Acheson, Eisenhower, and Herter might be combined as: a world of peace, freedom, and opportunity for economic growth, with minimum hindrance from national restrictions.

These are the goals which far-sighted businessmen are today adopting as their own objectives. To achieve them they need a climate influenced by constructive government action.

Let us list a few requirements for this "optimum" climate of 1975. If some of these requirements seem far-reaching to those who matured before World War II, they may well seem unduly limited to those now maturing in the early years of the space age. They cannot all be realized at once. But all are attainable goals, and steps toward realizing them by 1975 *can* be taken at once.

1. *National treatment.* This means freedom for business of whatever national ownership to operate in any country under no greater restrictions than business owned in that country. It means the removal of national restrictions on the movement of goods (free trade), capital (freedom to invest and repatriate), services (transportation, communications, and insurance), people (labor, skilled, if not unskilled), and ideas (science, technology, and know-how brought in and out by whatever means).

2. *Positive incentives for growth.* This means sound fiscal and monetary policies and positive encouragement for investment and technological development. In the developing countries it also means reasonable expectation of political and economic stability and assurance against nationalization or expropriation. There it also means the productive investment of national capital, increased earning and purchasing power, and rising standards of education and living.

These two requirements call primarily for separate national action by individual governments. Others call for international (or preferably "multinational") action.

3. *Stable monetary expansion.* This means an international monetary system with sufficient discipline to ensure exchange stability and adequate to finance a rapidly rising volume of trade.

4. *Common or harmonized policies.* No target date can be set for this on matters of common concern; it is a never-ending process. There will always be new situations requiring harmonization of policies—local, national, and international. Each must be dealt with in practical terms as it arises. But harmonization of legislation—for example, corporate law—can be sought.

What Business Can Do

Like it or not, what the private businessman does, or fails to do, tangibly affects the economic growth and technological progress of his own country, the Atlantic Community, and the world in general.

Speaking to the Chamber of Commerce of the United States on February 1, 1967, Leo Cherne, executive director of the Research Institute of America, told the members of his business audience that "management may be properly described as the skill that makes the doable possible" and their real choice was "not *whether* you will participate in 'the public interest' but *how*." He continued:

Precisely because ancient passions have subsided and realities have changed and a new generation with profoundly different outlooks now exists, there is, in part, an opportunity larger than any which previously existed to participate in the determination of the national interest.

During recent years businessmen have been chief engineers and managers of change. The changes which they will help to introduce during the balance of this century will dwarf the sum total of change experienced by mankind to date.

Change can be ruthless; it is the businessman's responsibility to see that it is not so. It can be humanitarian, for the free economic system has proved itself superior to any other system in the world in meeting social responsibilities to human beings. Through this system the wage-earners in America have earned for themselves incomes and living standards—including educational and cultural attainments —exceeding those of the managerial class of much of the rest of the world. Corporation profits in America have helped to make the arts flourish, the professions thrive, and educational institutions expand to degrees far surpassing those of the socialist nations of the world professing to be "people-oriented."

In this decade, the revolution in management thinking regarding its role—and potential—in society at least equals the revolution in technology. As General Electric Vice President Laurence I. Wood notes, the basic *functions* of business have not changed; but the sense of *responsibility* has changed dramatically. The business functions are still to create jobs, produce better products at fair prices, provide a sound economy, and return a profit for the investors. Mr. Wood adds:

But the climate in which business is to perform these basic functions has changed so much that just the carrying out of these traditional tasks means almost revolutionary new responsibilities. The businessman has long since passed the point where he thinks of filling his obligations to society just in terms of producing goods for willing buyers. He has learned that in order for business to grow and to meet the growing demands of people, business must involve itself more completely—it must be more concerned—in all the problems of society.

If businessmen are becoming increasingly idealistic over the kind of society which they can help to create, they cannot afford to become any less pragmatic. They can stay in business only as long as that business runs at a profit. International business planning for the 1970's must not be visionary but as down-to-earth and market-disciplined as any other form of market development. This in turn places demands.

The first task in this advance planning, in the judgment of Eric Wyndham White, is to foster "confident cooperation" among nations so that they face up to the problems that are common problems. What is needed is "a frank dialogue and expression of views. Simply in the process of discussing and clarifying issues, people will clear their own minds as to where their common interests lie."

A second task—and admittedly a tough one—is for business leaders to back off from daily operations far enough for creative ten-year planning; but in truth there is nothing revolutionary about this concept. The Rand Corporation, the Institute for Defense Analysis, and a host of other "think laboratories" have already performed this vital function in the aerospace and defense world. If they can determine with a high degree of accuracy the kinds of products, services, and systems needed to meet probable military contingencies ten years or more in the future, it would seem pessimistic to believe that similar planning could not advance the world's interests on the peaceful fronts of trade and investment. But just as the several nations are finding that no single country has the resources alone to meet international security requirements, so will these same nations find that synthesized action is required in the nondefense sphere. This means making the most of our combined resources. As stated by Walter Ward, General Electric's vice president and area division general manager for Europe:

> The real challenge, in addition to the obvious one of competing over existing markets and investments, is how we can increase the value of resources. This must be done to meet the expanding needs not only of the developed countries but also the developing countries. And this, in turn, requires that we find means to integrate our resources—labor, capital, technology—among all nations on a global basis.

The challenge is no less than "programming" the business-social world that is desirable and economically attainable, and then devising the machinery for getting from the world of today to the world of a decade hence.

The Potential

Based upon all this, the achievements of the seventies can be either extraordinary or practically nothing, depending upon how well the many official and private partners among the Atlantic nations set their goals, seize the initiative, and "program" for success. Steadiness and patience in pursuing such goals and programs will be critical to success.

This process of short- and long-range planning and implementation is equally essential for business and for governments. If these two forces on both sides of the Atlantic can plan together for their common interests, and work together to carry out those plans, our future is unlimited.

The potential is great. In the words of General Lauris Norstad:

Nowhere else has Western civilization flowered as fully as on the two shores of the North Atlantic. Here are the deepest roots of faith in the dignity and worth of the individual, the rule of law, and the successful practice of democratic government. Here lies the great reservoir of moral and material resources, of intellect, science, and of the political, economic, social, industrial, and cultural development necessary to accelerate the progress of the less developed nations. To be effective, such a community must contain and unify the resources of both sides of the Atlantic.